Brave New Causes

Women in British Postwar Fictions

DATE DUE

DEBORAH PHILIPS and IAN HAYWOOD

Leicester University Press
London and Washington

Leicester University Press
A Cassell Imprint
Wellington House, 125 Strand, London WC2R 0BB, England
PO Box 605, Herndon, Virginia 20172, USA

First published 1998

British Library Cataloguing in Publication Data
A catalogue record for this book is available from the British Library.
ISBN 0 7185 0058 X Hardback
      0 7185 0059 8 Paperback

Library of Congress Cataloging-in-Publication Data
Philips, Deborah, 1954–
     Brave new causes : women in British postwar fictions / Deborah
     Philips and Ian Haywood.
          p.   cm.
     Includes bibliographical references and index.
     ISBN 0-7185-0058-X. — ISBN 0-7185-0059-8 (pbk.)
     1. English fiction—20th century—History and criticism.
     2. Feminism and literature—Great Britain—History—20th century.
     3. Women and literature—Great Britain—History—20th century.
     4. English fiction—Women authors—History and criticism.
     5. Working class women in literature. 6. World War, 1939–1945—
     Influence. 7. Women employees in literature. 8. Women in literature.
     I. Haywood, Ian, 1958–   . II. Title.
     PR888.F45P47   1997
     823'.91409352042—dc21   97-16934
                                                                              CIP

Typeset by York House Typographic Ltd, London
Printed and bound in Great Britain by Biddles Ltd, Guildford and King's Lynn

Contents

Acknowledgements

The authors would like to thank Brunel University and Roehampton Institute, London, for providing periods of study leave. Thanks to the staff of the British Museum and the staff at Mills & Boon. Thanks to Steve Wagg, Professor Ann Thompson, Kimberley Reynolds, Jane Pringle, the History Workshop Popular Literature Group and the Leisure Studies Association, and to all family members, friends and colleagues who supplied comics, annuals and popular novels of the 1950s. Particular thanks are due to Theresa Leaning and Garry Whannel.

Grateful acknowledgement is given to John Osborne and Faber and Faber Ltd for permission to include extracts from *Look Back in Anger*. Every effort has been made to trace the copyright holders of material included in this book. If any material has been included without permission, we offer our apologies to all concerned and will happily include acknowledgement in any future edition.

To Ursula Philips and Margery Haywood

1. Rereading the fifties

How many women thus waste life away the prey of discontent, who might have practised as physicians, regulated a farm, managed a shop, and stood erect, supported by their own industry, instead of hanging their heads surcharged with the dew of sensibility, that consumes the beauty to which it at first gave lustre. (Mary Wollstonecraft, *A Vindication of the Rights of Women*, 1792)[1]

Love and a career, ambition and security, often pull in different directions, and it is not easy for the young to sort out their claims. (Front-paper of a Mills & Boon hospital romance, 1955)[2]

The prevailing popular idea of British society in the 1950s is of a period of social stability; whenever there is a media debate about the decline of the family, this myth of the 1950s is mobilized as a touchstone of traditional moral virtues and 'family' values. In the reactionary political climate of the 1980s and 1990s, the 1950s have been adduced by politicians and the Tory press as a golden age of conservative values before the catastrophic Fall into the promiscuous freedoms of the 1960s. Margaret Thatcher, British Prime Minister from 1979 to 1992, described the 1950s as 'an old-fashioned Britain, structured and courteous'.[3] Her successor John Major also mobilized the nostalgic, nationalistic appeal of the myth in the Conservative Party's 'back-to-basics' campaign of 1993–4, when he suggested that the nation needed a good dose of the 1950s' essentially English, homespun qualities. Major quoted George Orwell's famous wartime evocation of the English way of life as typified by 'old maids biking to Holy Communion through the mists of the autumn morning' – an emblem of 'old-fashioned' pastoral and religious values.[4] In a 1994 feature entitled 'The Fifties: was this Britain's Golden Age?', the *Daily Mail* argued that:

> This inconceivably innocent and law-abiding world was under-pinned
> by a rock-solid authority structure in which parents, teachers and police
> were merely the principal players ... the Sixties saw the beginning of a
> truly cataclysmic change in the structure of our society, the death of an
> older Britain.[5]

Crucial to the success and appeal of this myth is the construction put on the
perceived role of women. As a feature in the *Guardian* in 1996 put it:
'"Traditional family values" is now shorthand for a period in the fifties when
Dad worked, Mum stayed at home and nurtured, and divorce and "illegitimacy" brought shame.'[6] Family values of the 1950s are idealized, through
the production of a historical narrative in which women returned to the
home after their war labours and set about replenishing the nation. The
redomestication of women, their absorption into the traditional social roles of
wife and mother, has long been a truism of postwar social history. This idea
can readily be adduced as evidence that a woman's 'natural' place is in the
home, but a surprising aspect of the durability of this myth is that it has been
largely unchallenged by historians and intellectuals of all persuasions.[7]
While there were women who did give up their wartime jobs to become full-
time wives and mothers, this experience was by no means universal. Many
women continued to work: almost all single women worked, and there was
an increasing proportion of working wives who combined the 'dual role' of
paid work and motherhood. Once this fact is acknowledged, the familiar,
glamorized image of the happy wife and mother, a postwar Angel in the
House, surrounded by labour-saving gadgets,[8] can be seen for what it was
and still is: an ideologically conceived distortion of real social experience, the
product of advertisers and consumer capitalism.

In the early postwar years women's work was widely accepted as a social
asset. Both official publications and popular writing for women actively
celebrated the fact as an achievement of the new, egalitarian Britain. Far from
being a decade of reconstituted conventional gender roles within the family
(and by extension, in society as a whole), the first postwar decade actively
promoted women's aspirations to participate in public life and the productive economy. The 1950s were not the restoration of patriarchal
dominance which only 'Angry Young Men' could challenge. We need to
restore to its historical, literary and ideological prominence the figure of the
professional New Woman in postwar Britain. In the light of continuing moral
panics about the irresponsibility of working mothers and their under-
achieving 'latchkey' children (itself a reworking of a 1950s' debate), this
new perspective on a period of women's cultural history that has been so
consistently misrepresented, and has suffered so heavily from cultural

suppression and amnesia, is particularly important.

Popular writing for women in the first postwar decade shows a marked continuity with women's experiences and aspirations during the war years. Moreover, the forgotten fictions discussed in this book use the resources of popular narrative forms to negotiate and imaginatively resolve many of the contradictions within this new model of femininity. It is of course necessary not to invoke a counter-nostalgia and remythologize the 1950s as a lost golden age of 'practical' feminism. The aim of this book is less to attempt a remapping of the decade, than to restore a map that already existed, re-acquainting the era with its own landmarks and re-equipping it with its own achievements.

Paradise ret(r)ained?

Not until Elizabeth Wilson's pioneering sociological study, *Only Halfway to Paradise. Women in Postwar Britain 1945–1968* (1980),[9] was there any serious attempt by contemporary feminist scholars to recover their own immediate pre-history. Wilson wrote the book because she was convinced that 'feminism did not die in the years after the war':

> I had originally set out to discover why there was no feminism between 1945 and 1968 – had believed the myth, in fact – it always seemed improbable that a powerful social movement and political crusade, an expression of the aspirations of (potentially) half the population, should suddenly have withered away, only to reappear as suddenly, and – as it seemed – as if out of nowhere, around 1970. Yet so pervasive was this myth that it has become the 'facts' for the women's movement too. (p. 186)

Almost twenty years on, Wilson's research remains the most substantial recovery of women's experience in the period.[10] *Only Halfway to Paradise* suggested that the 'women's movement' of the 1960s and 1970s had colluded in suppressing the history of its mothers' generation to glorify its own emergence. In fact, there was no sudden radical disjuncture in women's aspirations in 1945, which is not so surprising considering the emancipatory power of women's contribution to the war effort. While women had been required to take on many kinds of work in the First World War, during the Second World War they were even more fully involved in the domestic war effort. They also had more reason to be optimistic about the socially progressive outcomes of the war. After all, there was general acceptance that the war was being fought not only to defeat Fascism but to install a New

Jerusalem of social reconstruction. The 'road to 1945' was paved with egalitarian promises of a Welfare State and the rights of citizenship for all, including women.

The war years had seen women conscripted into forms of work that had previously been exclusively male domains. Women were trained as pilots, mechanics, drivers, farmers, railway workers, electricians, plumbers and fitters. Even in more traditionally 'feminine' occupations, the war brought about huge shifts in the class and gender relations of Britain. In 1931, one-and-a-quarter million women were employed in domestic service; by the war's end more women were employed in offices than in the home. Part of the strategy for recruiting women into war work was the promise of a career path that would continue after the war: as a wartime poster announced, 'You can make a vocation of this war work ... now and in the future'.[11] The war had also provided an infrastructure that made it possible for women with children to work. In 1942 a Mass Observation Report was entitled 'The Demand for Day Nurseries' and by 1944 local authorities had put 1500 nurseries into place.[12] There were also state-run dining-halls, which liberated many women from the need to provide cooked meals at home.

When the war ended, despite the gradual loss of the nurseries which would have helped many women to 'pursue a career', and the slow pace of many promised reforms such as equal pay,[13] the gains made during the war could not be entirely eroded. Not only were there now more women in the working population than ever before, but the kinds of work they could engage in were of a greater range. With high expectations of social ameliora-tion for women, women's organizations campaigned for a better deal across a range of social issues: equal pay, welfare benefits, child allowance and maternity rights. Elizabeth Wilson debunks the myth of 'a concerted effort at the level of government policy to get women back into the home' (p. 188).[14] In 1947 the Labour government launched a recruitment campaign to bring more women into the workplace to fill acute labour shortages both in industry and the service sector. As Wilson notes, official policy was fraught with contra-diction, as if the British state did not want to risk upsetting recently demobbed male workers. The official line was that the 'reserve army' of female labour was only needed temporarily and not for 'jobs usually done by men' (p. 44). Yet employment statistics and census returns from the time show a steady increase in the numbers of working women and the types of work they were undertaking. The numbers grew from six million working women in 1931 to seven-and-a-half million in 1951. Moreover, the proportion of married working women was also increasing: 10 per cent in 1931, 21 per cent in 1951, 32 per cent in 1961. This consolidation of women's function outside the home had a major impact on prevailing notions of bourgeois femininity. There was much discussion of the 'dual role': could a woman cope successfully with the responsibilities of motherhood and work? There was both official and feminist support for the view that, despite the tensions between the two roles, a harmonization could be achieved.

Career girls, dual roles

British feminists of the 1940s and 1950s firmly believed that the apparent contradictions of the 'dual role' could be surmounted within the new consensus of postwar reconstruction. An important, upbeat assessment of women's career prospects was proposed by Caroline Haslett in her book *Problems Have No Sex* (1949).[15] Haslett was a pioneer of women's engineering in the interwar years; she founded the Women's Engineering Society and became the only woman member of the Central Electricity Board after the war. Haslett's career was a model of professional progress, public achievement and democratic participation in society – a paradigm of the aspirations and ideals of the modern bourgeois woman. Indeed, Haslett featured in the government's wartime propaganda films, encouraging women to volunteer for work. In her book she confidently states:

Now it is the accepted thing that when a girl leaves school she will take up some form of gainful occupation at least until she marries. The last remaining barriers of Victorian prejudice against working women outside the home vanished with the war-time mobilization of women. (p. 82)

Haslett positions the new career girl as the closure of the Suffragette narrative. This appeal to a longer tradition of women's emancipation ensures that the war cannot be seen as an aberration in women's historical development, but as a catalyst which helped to speed up the process and allow women full access to modernity. Haslett is also keenly aware that if the career girl is to prosper, as many obstacles as possible must be removed from her path, including the perceived difficulties of the 'dual role':

It is a mistake to state the issue always as a choice between marriage and a career. There is indeed a regrettable tendency in some quarters to think of the 'career woman' as the antithesis of the housewife. There is no valid reason to suppose that a woman who has learnt the necessity of holding down a job, who has been trained to think logically or to use her hands and experience in some special skill, is less likely to be attractive in a feminine way or to be less desirous of having a happy marriage and children. (p. 47)

The message is reassuring and, more impressively, exciting; the career girl need not sacrifice the traditional 'feminine' virtues of beauty and domestic bliss, but can also look forward to acquiring the new, civilizing virtues of rationality and 'logic' and planning her own life. Haslett invokes a feminist discourse of Enlightenment values that stretches back to Mary Wollstonecraft in the 1790s.[16] According to Wollstonecraft, society's failure to educate women to 'think logically' led to their emotional and psychological infantilization, and excluded them from becoming fully human. For Haslett, a profession is the apotheosis of such training in logic and a true measure of social progress. Moreover, Haslett believed the definition of femininity to be expanded and enriched by a career, not compromised or contaminated by it. Elizabeth Wilson may be right to see the aspiration to succeed as a member of the professional classes as ultimately underwriting bourgeois individualism (p. 205), but it is difficult to deny the empowering tone of Haslett's language. Her optimistic assessment of women's postwar prospects can be compared to the more cautious assessment in Simone de Beauvoir's celebrated study *The Second Sex*, which was published in France in the same year as *Problems Have No Sex* and first translated into English in 1953.[17] According to de Beauvoir, the modern woman is trapped inside a contradictory paradigm of femininity; the 'dual role' of work and home is a major hindrance to progress: 'we open the factories, the offices, the faculties to women' but society still insists that 'marriage is a most honourable career' (p. 167). Professional women 'are not tranquilly installed in their new realm: as yet they are only halfway there' and remain in a state of disequilibrium (p. 691). De Beauvoir does not deny that an improvement in women's social position has taken place, but she is exasperated and puzzled by the impeded pace of change.

Nevertheless, by the mid-1950s it seems that women's work had gained wide approval, including the backing of the United Nations.[18] If Haslett's book and other official studies have been largely forgotten, the same cannot be said of Alva Myrdal and Viola Klein's *Women's Two Roles. Home and Work* (1956), which has received some attention from feminist scholars.[19] The book was a major piece of contemporary sociology which traced the problem of women's dual role back to industrialization's separation of work and home. The authors, like Simone de Beauvoir, were less sanguine than Haslett about the ease with which the 'antithesis' of conflicting demands on the modern middle-class woman could be circumnavigated, but their observations illuminate many tensions within the idea of the career woman. Some doubt is cast on the national recognition of married women's contribution to the economy, not because these women have retreated into the home, but because official ideology seems to be resisting a public endorsement of women's work: 'though the fact has impressed itself surprisingly little on the consciousness of the public, every fourth married woman in Britain has a job outside the home' (p. 54). The gap between reality and representation seems as large as that between work and home: 'we are, in fact, the unobservant participants of a social revolution' (p. 183). On the ground, in the reality of many women's lives, steps towards emancipation and equality continue to be taken, and a new consciousness is emerging: 'Children and home may be an emotionally satisfying milieu but they are hardly mentally stimulating . . . Bread winning is no longer a monopoly of men, and home-making should no longer be the monopoly of women' (pp. 147, 162).[20]

According to Myrdal and Klein, it was no longer possible to explain the expansion in women's work as motivated solely by an obligation to the national economy (reminiscent of the war years and the labour shortages of the late 1940s), or a middle-class need to maintain high living standards (that is, higher than the affluent working class); work outside the home is also more 'stimulating' and a positive attraction. Myrdal and Klein believed, however, that while 'feminine occupations' had been professionalized, itself a vital improvement, men had retained a 'monopoly' of traditionally 'masculine' spheres of work: 'a revised version of the traditional division of labour between the sexes still exists' (pp. 75–6). While this reservation about the pace of change is important, there is still a strong evocation of a social landscape of ambitious women seeking personal fulfilment through professional training. The spectre of the discontented middle-class housewife was beginning to emerge in studies such as Judith Hubback's *Wives Who Went to College* (1957).[21] Richard Titmuss had noted in 1952 that women had 'the right to an emotionally satisfying and independent life' beyond childrearing.[22]

Another innovation of *Women's Two Roles* was its recommendation that middle-class women should embark on a new, three-phase life cycle: training for a career; a break for childrearing; a return to full-time or part-time work. This reconfigured career pattern held out the hope that women need not abandon their professional ambitions once they married. Rather than seeing work as a temporary phase between the 'natural' stages of maturation and motherhood, the new pattern places motherhood as an interregnum in a developing career. The three-phase cycle has become a reality for many women to the present day. The expectation and wish that marriage should not be the end of a woman's career development is a recurrent theme in popular women's fiction of the 1950s.

Despite their anxiety that the 'masculine' professions were still effectively barred from women's participation, Myrdal and Klein were clear that a 'social revolution' was being unobtrusively enacted in the 1950s. In the same year that their book was published, two feminist organizations, the Six Point Group and the Married Women's Association, held a joint conference to debate the topic of 'Married Women Out at Work'. In remapping the 1950s, it is crucial to note that the idea of a 'revolution' in women's relation to professional work challenges the myth of the happy postwar housewife. The forgotten literature of the young career woman can also be seen to offer an alternative definition of the period to the more familiar image of the 1950s as a period dominated by a masculine postwar rebel: the Angry Young Man.

The angry decade

The Angry Young Man of the 1950s was a British variant on the American Rebel Without A Cause (the American film of this title, starring James Dean, was released in 1955), and was very much a construction of the time, celebrated by critics and the media as a new kind of contemporary anti-hero and an expression of the younger generation's disenchantment with the complacency, blandness and dishonesty of 'consensus' postwar British society.[23] The Angry Young Man's first appearance on the British cultural scene is usually identified as 1956 (the same year as Myrdal and Klein's book), with the Royal Court Theatre's production of John Osborne's *Look Back in Anger*.[24] The play's hero, Jimmy Porter, spends most of his time railing against the soullessness of a Britain emerging into affluence: 'Nobody thinks, nobody cares. No beliefs, no convictions, and no enthusiasm' (p. 17). His authority to make such pronouncements comes from his bitter personal experience of social mobility. Having risen into the ranks of the middle class by marrying the daughter of a colonel, Porter discovers that he is in a social and cultural limbo. As Richard Hoggart put it in *The Uses of Literacy* (1957),[25] this is the dilemma of the scholarship boy at the 'friction point of two cultures' (p. 242). Porter's 'anger' is an expression of contempt for the ideology of meritocracy in the Cold War, which he sees in Orwellian terms as a gigantic confidence trick, deluding people into thinking that the prewar social battles are redundant:

> There aren't any good, brave causes left. If the big bang does come, and we all get killed off, it won't be in aid of the old-fashioned, grand design. It'll just be for the Brave New-nothing-very-much-thank-you. About as pointless and inglorious as stepping in front of a bus. (pp. 84–5)

This speech encapsulates the play's cultural reverberations. A few months after *Look Back in Anger* achieved theatrical success, Britain embarked on the fiasco of the Suez Canal invasion, which resulted in an ignominious withdrawal and over a thousand Egyptian casualties. In the context of this post-imperial humiliation, Porter's tirades against the sterility of the British establishment seemed to capture a spirit of protest against a national regime of drift, disempowerment and spiritual malaise, in which the Welfare State masked a largely unreformed class system. Jimmy Porter heralded a new generation of stridently discontented working-class heroes voicing an objection to the shiny veneer of social modernization and the illusion of social equality. By the time Kenneth Allsop's book *The Angry Decade* appeared in 1958,[26] he could add the Joe Lampton of John Braine's *Room at the Top* (1957) and the Arthur Seaton of Alan Sillitoe's *Saturday Night and Sunday Morning* (1958) to British culture's burgeoning phalanx of alienated, depoliticized class warriors. In Allsop's opinion, the Angry Young Man sees society as a 'corpse pumped full of a formaldehyde of welfarism' in which 'the old points of reference have been lost' (pp. 215–16). In Robert Hewison's words, the dominant cultural mood before the 'angry' revolution was a feeling of national decline: 'a vitality had gone out of English life as the post-war consensus had entered in'.[27]

One of the reasons for the sway of the Angry Young Man over the image of the 1950s is that the myth offers a radical critique of the postwar settlement: it debunks many of the supposed triumphs of postwar society, highlights the absence of a traditional political agenda for the Left and helps prepare the ground for the upheavals of the sixties. It is a force of disequilibrium within consensus, opening up old wounds, demanding new solutions. It can be slotted into that vital, dissenting British cultural tradition which Raymond Williams mapped out in *Culture and Society* (1958). With the benefit of historical hindsight, there seems to be a neat progression from 'angry' protests at national purposelessness to the emergence at the end of the 1950s of the New Left as a cultural force for effecting a radical intellectual analysis of the failure of postwar reforms. An early *New Left Review* article by Perry Anderson describes the 'causes' of the 1950s in terms reminiscent of 'angry' discourse:

> As material deprivation to a certain degree receded, cultural loss and devastation became more and more evident and important. The chaos and desolation of the urban environment, the sterility and formalism of education, the saturation of space and matter with advertising, the atomization of local life, the concentration of control of the means of communication and the degradation of their content, these became the distinctive preoccupations of the New Left.[28]

While the vital influence of the New Left on subsequent British intellectual development is unquestionable, a glaringly absent 'distinctive preoccupation' from that list of contemporary social evils is any mention of the importance of gender. The initial failure of the New Left to embrace sexual politics or women's experience in the decade of the 1950s was also consistent with the inheritance of an 'angry' agenda. Not only is Jimmy Porter rabidly sexist; much of the power of his harangues depends on the idea that society has become emasculated, effeminized by the 'nanny' state. His own experience of social displacement and loss of self-identity is blamed on middle-class women (and his wife Alison in particular), who represent the false promises of social mobility and the loss of his vigorous working-class masculinity.[29] His Swiftian diatribes against the 'eternal flaming racket of the female' (p. 25) litter the play. His renowned speech which announces that there are no 'brave causes left' ends misogynistically: 'No, there's nothing left for it, me boy, but to let yourself be butchered by the women' (p. 85). In his own little fiefdom, he can at least dominate his wife. The opening scene of the play has Jimmy's wife Alison ironing his shirts and wearing his shirt, a device that signifies his ownership of her.

A similar reliance on what Lynne Segal calls 'new forms of sexual hostility' characterizes the macho appeal of the heroes of other 'angry' narratives.[30] Given the cultural authority that 'angry' texts have exerted over the literary and cultural history of the decade, it is not surprising that so little attention has been paid by critics to the place of women writers in the 1950s, and no attention at all to popular women's writing.

Notes

1. Mary Wollstonecraft, *A Vindication of the Rights of Women* (Harmondsworth: Penguin, 1975; first published in 1792), p. 262.
2. Anne Lorraine, *Emergency Nurse* (London: Mills & Boon, 1955).
3. *Daily Mail*, 29 April 1988; cited in Alan Sinfield, *Literature, Politics and Culture in Postwar Britain* (Oxford: Basil Blackwell, 1989), p. 4.
4. The use of Orwell to bolster a conservative mythology of 'Englishness' was, predictably, deeply disingenuous. Orwell's oft-quoted description appears in 'The Lion and the Unicorn' (1941), a wartime essay in which Orwell argued that 'we cannot win the war without introducing Socialism' and 'laissez-faire capitalism is dead'. See Sonia Orwell and Ian Angus, eds, *The Collected Essays, Journalism and Letters of George Orwell*, 4 vols (Harmondsworth: Penguin, 1970; first published in 1968), vol. 2, pp. 74–134 (pp. 75, 117).
5. 'The Fifties: was this Britain's Golden Age?', *Daily Mail* special feature, 29 January 1994, pp. 24–5.

6. Yvonne Roberts, 'Once upon another time', *Guardian*, 4 November 1996, pp. 4–5.

7. For an early left-wing condemnation of the perceived postwar return to 'traditional values', see Anthony Howard, 'We are the Masters Now', in Michael Sissons and Peter French, eds, *Age of Austerity 1945–51* (Harmondsworth: Penguin, 1964; first published in 1963), pp. 9–15. Apart from the recent feminist studies of the period cited below, most histories of the 1950s have reinforced the idea that the only valuable role offered to women at this time was inside the home. Though the fact that increasing numbers of women in the 1950s participated in paid work is usually acknowledged by historians, the theme is normally given scant treatment, and there is no suggestion of any official or cultural endorsement of this role. See Peter Lewis, *The Fifties* (London: Cupid Press, 1989; first published in 1978), ch. 2; Arthur Marwick, *British Society Since 1945* (Harmondsworth: Penguin, 1982), ch. 4; Liz Heron, ed., *Truth, Dare or Promise. Girls Growing Up in the Fifties* (London: Virago, 1985); Kenneth O. Morgan, *The People's Peace. British History 1945–1990* (Milton Keynes: Open University Press, 1992), pp. 206–7; Mary Evans, *A Good School. Life in a Girls' Grammar School in the 1950s* (London: Women's Press, 1991), pp. 110–11. School textbooks also reinforce the idea that a working life for women in the 1950s was a temporary activity that ended with marriage. A typical history of the period aimed at primary school children has a section called 'Work' which shows a photograph of a secretary; the text beneath reads: 'Many girls left school at 15 or 16 to get a job. This girl got a job in an office. She went to college to learn to type and take notes. She could type 100 words in one minute. She stopped working when she got married.' See Rosemary Rees and Judith Maguire, *Living in the 1950s* (London: Heinemann, 1993), p. 17. For another example of a school textbook which ignores women's work altogether, see Pat Hodgson, *Britain in the 1950s* (London: Batsford, 1989).

8. See Marjorie Ferguson, *Forever Feminine. Women's Magazines and the Cult of Femininity* (London: Heinemann, 1983), ch. 3; Harry Hopkins, *The New Look. A Social History of the Forties and Fifties in Britain* (London: Secker and Warburg, 1963), ch. 26.

9. Elizabeth Wilson, *Only Halfway to Paradise. Women in Postwar Britain 1945–1968* (London: Tavistock Publications, 1980).

10. See Mary Ingham, *Now We Are Thirty. Women of the Breakthrough Generation* (London: Methuen, 1981); Lynne Segal, *Slow Motion. Changing Masculinities, Changing Men* (London: Virago, 1990), ch. 1; Martin Pugh, 'Domesticity and the decline of feminism, 1930–1950' in Harold. S. Smith, ed., *British Feminism in the Twentieth Century* (Aldershot: Edward Elgar, 1990), pp. 124–43; Pat Thane, 'Towards Equal Opportunities? Women in Britain since 1945' in Tony Gourvish and Alan O'Day, eds, *Britain Since 1945* (London: Macmillan, 1991), pp. 183–208; Deborah Philips and Alan Tomlinson, 'Homeward Bound: Leisure, popular culture and consumer capitalism' in Dominic Strinati and Stephen Wagg, eds, *Come on Down? Popular Media Culture in Post-War Britain* (London: Routledge,

1992), pp. 9–46. For an overview of the marginalization of women's history, see Sheila Rowbotham, *Hidden from History* (London: Pluto Press, 1973).

11.   Quoted in Deborah Philips and Alan Tomlinson, 'Homeward Bound', p. 31.

12.   Martin Pugh, *The Women's Movement in Britain 1914–1959* (Basingstoke: Macmillan Education, 1992), p. 284; see also Gail Braybon and Penny Summerfield, *Out of the Cage. Women's Experiences in Two World Wars* (London: Pandora, 1987).

13.   See Pat Thane, 'Towards Equal Opportunities?' In 1944 Parliament agreed an amendment to the Butler Education Act which granted women teachers rights of equal pay. The Prime Minister Winston Churchill was so opposed to the principle of equal pay that he threatened to bring down the government over the issue and jeopardize the war effort. The amendment was withdrawn and Churchill established a Royal Commission to look at the issue. The Commission accepted the case for equal pay but recommended a gradual implementation. Nothing further happened until 1954, when the Tory government agreed to phase in equal pay in the Civil Service over a period of five years.

14.   See also Denise Riley, *War in the Nursery. Theories of the Child and Mother* (London: Virago, 1983).

15.   Caroline Haslett, *Problems Have No Sex* (London: Hodder and Stoughton, 1949).

16.   Mary Wollstonecraft, *A Vindication of the Rights of Women*.

17.   Simone de Beauvoir, *The Second Sex* (Harmondsworth: Penguin, 1976; first published in French in 1949; first translated into English in 1953).

18.   Marjorie Tait, 'The Education of Women for Citizenship: some practical suggestions' *Problems in Education*, vol. VIII (Paris: Unesco, 1954).

19.   Alva Myrdal and Viola Klein, *Women's Two Roles. Home and Work* (London: Routledge and Kegan Paul, 1956). The book has received attention in a number of feminist studies: Elizabeth Wilson, *Only Halfway to Paradise*; Pat Thane, 'Towards Equal Opportunities?'; Jane Lewis, 'Myrdal, Klein, *Women's Two Roles* and postwar feminism 1945–1960' in Harold S. Smith, ed., *British Feminism in the Twentieth Century*, pp. 167–88. Interestingly, Wilson and Lewis expose the limitations of the book's sexual politics for contrasting reasons: Wilson believes it could have been more socialist, while Lewis attacks its reliance on economic arguments for women's work, and a naïve faith in a 'benevolent state and rational planning' (p. 170). Lewis's critique highlights the fact that the 1950s' image of the career woman emerged from within postwar construction, though some of the implications of the new situation demanded changes in social attitudes and social policy which ran against the grain of the postwar settlement. Lewis also shows that the ambiguous status of women's work within postwar definitions of femininity is reflected in one of the discarded titles for *Women's Two Roles*: 'Motherhood and Career – Conflicting Roles or Double Opportunity?' (p. 177).

20.   See also Viola Klein's comments in *The Feminine Character. History of an Ideology* (London: Routledge and Kegan Paul, 1989; first published in 1946), that modern

women are 'almost, if not quite, equal' to men, and that 'a democratisation of the family has taken place' in Britain (pp. 27, 32).

21. Judith Hubback, *Wives Who Went to College* (London: Heinemann, 1957).
22. Richard Titmuss, *Essays on the 'Welfare State'* (London: George Allen and Unwin, 1958), p. 102. The quotation comes from the text of a lecture on 'The Position of Women' first delivered in 1952. See also Viola Klein, *Working Wives* (London: Institute of Personnel Management, 1960).
23. Harry Ritchie, *Success Stories. Literature and the Media in England, 1950–1959* (London: Faber and Faber, 1988).
24. John Osborne, *Look Back in Anger* (London: Faber and Faber, 1976; first published in 1957).
25. Richard Hoggart, *The Uses of Literacy* (Harmondsworth: Penguin, 1958; first published in 1957).
26. Kenneth Allsop, *The Angry Decade* (London: Faber and Faber, 1963; first published in 1958).
27. Robert Hewison, *In Anger. Culture in the Cold War 1945–1960* (London: Methuen, 1988; first published in 1981), p. 86.
28. Perry Anderson, 'The Left in the Fifties', *New Left Review* 29, Jan–Feb 1965, pp. 1–18, (p. 15).
29. This theme is pursued in some detail in chapter 2.
30. See Lynne Segal, *Slow Motion*, p. 15. See also Michelene Wandor, *Look Back in Gender* (London: Methuen, 1987), for a feminist perspective on postwar drama.

2. Women writers, working heroines

The neglect of women's experience in the 1950s is matched by the cursory and unrepresentative treatment of women's writing in literary histories of the period. Those critics who have broadened and deepened the period's range of writers and cultural contexts have given scant regard to women writers, including only a few canonical authors. Alan Sinfield's *Literature, Politics and Culture in Postwar Britain* (1989), for instance, is the most substantial literary study of the early postwar years. Despite embracing a diversity of political and cultural topics such as decolonization, gay sexuality, and youth subcultures, Sinfield's coverage of women writers is limited to a detailed section on Sylvia Plath.[1] Other mainstream women writers who commonly feature in studies of the period include Elizabeth Taylor, Elizabeth Bowen, Barbara Pym, Doris Lessing, Olivia Manning and Iris Murdoch.[2] There is little evidence in their novels of the 'social revolution' being effected by the phenomenon of working women. Taylor and Pym write about some of the frustrations and limitations of middle-class women's lives, but if work is mentioned at all it is only at the outer margins of the narratives, and is not a mode of escape. In Pym's *Jane and Prudence* (1953),[3] for example, the heroine Prudence is technically a 'career girl': she is 29, unmarried, and an ex-student. But there is little focus on her work or her professional motivation, and she is clearly treading water until marriage. Her perception of the 'vague cultural organization' she works for is that 'it would really be so difficult to say what any of them actually did', including herself (pp. 35–6). The comic tone of the novel undermines the pompous inactivity of her boss but leaves no space for a positive image of women in the workplace. The implied readership of such a novel would seem to have few career aspirations. Lessing's autobiographical novels of the 1950s are set in Africa, and it was not until *The Golden Notebook* (1962)[4] that she confronted directly women's experience in 1950s' Britain. While the novel has been justly celebrated for its innovations in both form and content,[5] its two heroines are more representative of the disenchanted radical generation of the 1930s than the New Woman of the 1950s. The issue of work (unlike the themes of art, sexuality, self-identity, psychology and patriarchal power) features very tangentially. Both women lead semi-leisured lives: Anna Wulf survives on the royalties of her best-selling novel about Africa, and Molly Jacobs is a Bohemian actress. At the end of the novel, Anna's intention to teach 'delinquent kids' is presented as a measure of her retreat from her artistic aspirations and ideals.

Olivia Manning's reputation rests mainly on her famous Balkan War trilogy. In the one novel set in contemporary Britain which does have a working heroine, *The Doves of Venus* (1955),[6] the liberating potential of a career is presented only as a form of false consciousness, as Ellie Parsons has no real ability or training; her destiny and true fulfilment lie in marriage. Although Ellie values her job of mocking-up antique furniture (as in Pym's *Jane and Prudence*, the phoney nature of her job is another comic deflation of the image of the working heroine) and regards it as a vital force in helping her break away from her 'suffocating' provincial roots (p. 26), she only obtained the job through the influence of her lover. Once he abandons her, she is sacked, lapses into depression, and finds the solution to her problems in marriage to an artist and a 'transformed life' (p. 313).

Iris Murdoch's early fiction does explore the theme of contemporary women's sexual emancipation in the postwar world, though the issue of work again only figures marginally. Murdoch is more interested in placing female subjectivity within mock-romance and mythic contexts. However, it is worth looking at some of her fiction more closely, to help clarify some of the differences between her vision of the contemporary woman's social role and the forms of popular writing studied in this book.

There is little evidence in Murdoch's novels of this period that she saw work as a potential force for any degree of women's emancipation. Her heroines usually have private means (by marriage or inheritance) and do not need to work, or if they do have a career, it is either invisible, irrelevant or takes place after the narrative ends. At the end of *The Bell* (1958), the heroine Dora is thinking of a career in primary teaching; similarly in *The Sandcastle* (1957) the hero's daughter is about to enter higher education. In *A Severed Head* (1961), one of the mistresses of the male narrator is a junior lecturer at the London School of Economics, but the novel focuses only on her sexual experience. Marian, the heroine of *The Unicorn* (1963), gives up her job as a teacher to embark on a journey to the enchanted castle where a variety of strange adventures occur. In these narratives, therefore, the world of work signifies one of the norms of a social conformity which brackets the location of the main action in eccentric, Bohemian, lubricious, closed communities.

The only Murdoch novel of the 1950s which integrates women's work into the main plot is her second novel, *The Flight from the Enchanter* (1955).[7] The theme is given a satirical and ironic treatment which is characteristic of Murdoch's narrative technique. The young upper-middle-class heroine Annette Cockayne runs away from her Kensington finishing school to seek an education in the 'School of Life'. There has never been an expectation that she should work, and 'Life' becomes a succession of failed affairs and sexual encounters, an incompetent suicide attempt, and a reunion with her parents in Europe. The other heroine, Rosa, has much more impressive feminist credentials (she was supposedly named after Rosa Luxemburg). Her Fabian mother left her in charge of a women's magazine, *Artemis*, whose shareholders are ancient, dotty suffragettes. But after trying careers in teaching and journalism, Annette now works in a factory as a machinist. This implausible career move is explained psychologically:

> She had come to the factory in a mood of self-conscious asceticism. Work had become for her something nauseating and contaminated, stained by surreptitious ambitions, frustrated wishes, and the competition and opinions of other people. She wanted at last to make of it something simple, hygienic, stream-lined, unpretentious, and dull. She had succeeded to the point of almost boring herself to death. Rosa did not imagine that the factory represented anything more than an interlude in her life. (p. 43)

Little wonder that she is regarded by other workers in the factory as an eccentric. While Rosa's voluntary *déclassé* labour has a whiff of rebellion about it (as does Jimmy Porter's job on a sweet-stall in a market), she is indeed an interloper, and the factory soon disappears from the narrative. Its main plot function is to put Rosa under the sexual sway of two unscrupulous Polish engineers and social adventurers. Her enslavement to their sexual rule seems to be a flagrant male fantasy, though one possible interpretation is that Rosa's disempowering factory job made her vulnerable to this predicament. When she recovers some self-confidence, she rejects the Poles, and the factory is not heard of again.

Rosa's strange descent down the career ladder is counterpointed by the character of 'Miss' Casement, the novel's satirical version of a career woman. She achieves a spectacular rise from being a typist to becoming head of a government department dealing with European immigrant labour. We see her only through the male gaze of her fearful, fascinated and ultimately captivated boss, Rainborough. The language he uses to describe her oscillates between a respect for her 'lust for advancement' and 'extraordinary industry', and a traditional masculine loathing of her 'harpy' emasculatory power (p. 86). She also appears stylishly beautiful, and the narrative follows their battle of wills until she acquires a red sports car, completing her usurpation of dominant male behaviour. Rainborough agrees to marry her, though 'what had really happened in that moment was that he had become engaged to Miss Casement's red M.G.' (p. 244). This could be an example of Murdoch's ironic use of the male point of view, so that it is Rainborough who is being ridiculed for his shallowness and indecision. If it is the case that Rainborough is comically debunked for his dyed-in-the-wool views of women, there is one important scene where his image of Miss Casement as a social freak is narratively confirmed. Having agreed to collect her to take her to a party, he deliberately arrives at her flat early to catch her off guard. As hoped for, he discovers that her mask has indeed fallen. The description of her room echoes the debunking of cosmetics in Belinda's toilet scene in Pope's *The Rape of the Lock*: 'The dressing-table was stacked with creams, powders, rouges, lipsticks, tonics, fresheners, varnishers, removers, cleaners and other kinds of cosmetics.' Moreover, she 'looked paler and older' (p. 178). She also swears at him. He is fascinated as the 'transformation' into her public image takes place in a 'cloud of powder' (p. 179). For all her success, she is presented in this scene as just another painted Lamia, and Rainborough finally escapes her clutches at the end of the novel. Miss Casement's aspirations are too fierce, and if her career success is relentless, at least her femininity can be negated.

Murdoch's narrative method does not usually place women's contemporary experience in a realist social setting. Murdoch has been praised as one of the founders (with John Fowles and Angela Carter – both of whom are in her wake) of the 'modern British Gothic'.[8] Like its Romantic and nineteenth-century predecessor, the 'modern' Gothic deals with the sensational themes of domination, incarceration, loss of identity, repressed sexuality and patriarchal power, but places these themes in more realistically described settings, stripped of exotic and supernatural trappings. Indeed, one of the main sources of readerly *frisson* in such fiction comes from plots which reveal 'that the everyday and the "normal" may be sources of horror and terror quite as potent as anything conceived of by earlier Gothic'.[9] Given that modern Gothic has a keen interest in gender, this defamiliarization of the social landscape provides the opportunity to denaturalize the nature of women's oppression, to inject Gothic excesses of power, desire and domination into the experience of a 'normal' heroine. In Murdoch's novels the theme of female emancipation is foregrounded, as most of her heroines embark on strange quests for a richer and fuller life which usually involve transgressing many sexual boundaries, and moving on to the fringes of society. While *The*

Unicorn (1963) is usually cited as the quintessential modern Gothic novel, many of its narrative features can be found in *The Bell* (1958), a story set in a cranky lay community on the edge of a nunnery.[10] The novel opens with the heroine Dora Greenfield (an ex-art student who married an art historian lecturer) bored with marriage. When she lights upon the weird, isolated band of metaphysicians camped in the medieval grounds, she enters into a realm of legend, myth and fantasy that liberates her sexual and spiritual potential. The reader's willing suspension of disbelief is aided not by naturalism but by comic plotting and an ironic narrative tone that constantly reveals the ludicrous, mock-literary nature of the action. This technique makes for entertaining reading but always runs the risk of trivializing the very themes of emancipation it foregrounds. Dora Greenfield, for instance, becomes less and less in control of her actions and more and more subjected to the will of her male lovers and the lure of local legends – eventually she tries to drown herself as a re-enactment of the fate of her legendary precursor. Her quest for liberation has only led to a higher plane of domination and stereotyping, a Lawrentian destiny for numerous Murdoch heroines.

This makes the sexual politics of her novels difficult finally to pin down. As Moore-Gilbert concludes, it cannot always be assumed that Murdoch adopts the male gaze (showing women enslaved by male sexual power, for example) 'in order to deconstruct it'.[11] Some of the experiences of her heroines, in other words, seem to answer the requirements of male fantasy rather than contradict them. Liberated female sexuality remains an ambiguous cultural signifier, both feared and desired.

In the fiction of middle-brow women writers who have received little if any critical attention, the working heroine begins to emerge with greater clarity. In both Monica Dickens's bitter-sweet, semi-autobiographical comic novels, *My Turn to Make the Tea* (1951) and *The Angel in the Corner* (1956), the heroine is a downwardly mobile journalist.[12] The novels show the struggle to survive in an insecure, sexist workplace, and both heroines believe they have a right to work, even if they do not always want to exercise that right. The tone of the novels is sceptical and downbeat, in marked contrast to the optimistic tenor of women's romance fiction of this period. What training Dickens's heroines have received (and the novels do not show this) only fits them for disappointment or stoical disenchantment. At the end of *My Turn to Make the Tea*, the heroine-narrator is sacked and replaced by 'a promising young lad of sixteen, fresh from school' (p. 222). Yet the extent of the narrator's anger or resentment is difficult to judge. The tone of the ending is evasively cynical; as she is given her notice by her editor, 'we agreed that women were a nuisance in an office, anyway'. If these novels are taken to represent the aspirations of a new generation of working women, one can well understand the more alluring attractions for the woman reader of Murdoch's archetypal fantasies.

The most substantial and positive treatment of the career heroine is to be found in popular writing by and for women: romances, stories for schoolgirls and adolescents, Sunday School Reward Books, and magazine journalism. The working heroine was a popular subject for fiction. As Ken Worpole has remarked, the fact that popular literature is 'formed in the marketplace' makes it 'highly responsive to popular interests'.[13] Worpole is drawing here on an important strand of Gramscian Marxist cultural theory which does not see popular culture as a mere tool of dominant ideology.[14] As early as 1960, Stuart Hall noted in the first issue of *New Left Review* that popular culture (both of the more traditional, 'folk' variety, and the 'newer mass art', as Hoggart termed it) must not be dismissed, as it had been by Adorno and the Frankfurt School, as pacifying leisure fodder for mass consumers. On the contrary, maintains Hall, popular culture can be the site of 'imaginative resistances of people who have to live within capitalism, the growing points of social discontent'.[15] If popular women's writing of the 1950s is not overtly politically radical, it does respond, as will be shown in the following chapters, to what Ken Worpole terms 'the involvement of radical aesthetics' (p. 13). Alison Light also sees popular writing as a 'wedge' that can be used to open up dominant ideology's 'imaginary relation to the dissonant and different existences it inscribes', notably women's subjectivity.[16] Romance fiction has been reclaimed by feminist literary critics as a form which, though generically conservative, constructs a Utopian version of everyday reality in which the tensions within dominant notions of femininity can be recognized and healed.[17] In 1950s' romances, a major source of this tension arises from the heroine's experience of working outside the home, and the living out of an emergent paradigm of femininity which reconciles the demands of the 'dual role'. The ideological task of the fiction is to naturalize the resolution of new and old definitions of femininity, but in so doing the narrative must also draw attention to these tensions. Although the heroine's destiny still lies in marriage, the restoration of patriarchal values cannot take place without a recognition that modern femininity now includes a degree of independent participation in the productive and professional life of the nation.

An illustration of the extent to which popular literature acted as a mediator and disseminator of the official endorsement of the working woman can be seen in a story which appeared in the first issue of *Woman's Realm* in February 1958.[18] Entitled 'Something to talk about', it is about a woman embarking on her first pregnancy who has just given up her job as a teacher. At first she is euphoric, as 'the day stretched before her in long, blissful emptiness'. But soon the routine of cooking, shopping and keeping the home spotless becomes boring. She loses her appetite for reading and conversation. Her husband grumbles about their reduced income (they are still paying for those emblems of affluence and domestic bliss, a car, fridge and washing machine). She feels trapped in a spiritually downward spiral, becomes depressed and loses her self-confidence. She begins to hanker after her career again; she 'caught herself planning to go back to school once the baby was old enough to be left; there were crêches these days, or maybe she could find herself a reliable woman'. At this point, the story responds to a 'radical aesthetic' which brings out the contradictions in the heroine's situation. Her thoughts show that she has not fully internalized the dominant ideology of the cult of domesticity, which operates like a false consciousness, attempting to control her. The story also illuminates a contradiction within that ideology, as the same labour-saving domestic gadgets which glamorize domesticity also remove the need for time-consuming drudgery. What is really at stake in her dilemma is not domesticity but the heroine's identity, which is being torn apart by the conflicting appeals of the 'dual role'. Just as it seems that the new life cycle of the professional working woman will triumph, and this period of anxiety will be transformed into maternity leave,[19] she is 'cured' of her ambivalence and loss of self-esteem by the chirpy intervention of a pregnant neighbour, who assures her that these feelings are quite 'natural' and she will soon feel better. After a narrative hiatus of several weeks, we see the heroine embracing her new servitude, revitalized and cleansed of all self-doubt, confident that she has done the right thing. Nonetheless, the narrative has to resort to the clumsy device of a chronological caesura to effect a resolution. Although the heroine's situation has been 'naturalized', the narrative cannot but draw attention to the dividing line between her old and new self.

The presence of this story in the first issue of a popular women's weekly magazine indicates that the attempt to return women to the home was still seen as urgent 13 years after the end of the war, but also attests to the strength of resistance to that expectation. The story demonstrates the ways in which popular fiction of the period could mediate the concerns of official discourses about working women, transforming these discourses into narrative patterns of realism (everyday experience) and romantic resolution (the happy marriage). But in articulating these public themes, the narrative is indelibly marked by them. The contradictory ideological function of women's magazines is to speak to women about their aspirations beyond the home, but within a form which is predicated upon and dominated by stereotypical notions of femininity (primarily, beauty and domesticity). Ken Worpole notes that in the late 1940s, *Woman* magazine 'played a very important part in explaining new Labour legislation to its readers' (p. 40).[20]

The 1950s was a propitious moment for popular romance to embrace the social agenda of women's aspirations outside the home. The paperback revolution allowed for an unprecedented expansion in the geographical and social range of the consumption of romances. As one popular romance author said at the time:

> Every kind of woman reads romantic novels. I know that the addresses in Mills and Boon's mailing file range from S.W.1. through county towns, industrial cities, North, South, East, West, to the Falkland Isles and back again.[21]

The postwar Mills & Boon romance was less formulaic than it was to become in the 1960s after the publishers were taken over by a multinational company. The popular romance of the 1950s could be more open to historical influences and major shifts in social sensibilities, as it had been during the Second World War when women's lives were transformed by new responsibilities and expectations.[22]

While the popular fictions looked at in this book do not abandon the narrative and ideological resources of the marriage plot, they provide a large degree of relative autonomy for the development of the working heroine and her problems and achievements. In the career girl novel (chapter 5), written for the adolescent reader, marriage can be deferred as a distant prospect. In popular romances (chapter 6), the correct marriage has to conform to the new expectations of the working heroine. In medical romances (chapters 7 and 8), the workplace is eroticized, and the heroine's choice of a partner is constructed in terms of career conflicts and choices. In a climate of national anxieties about standards of breeding (chapter 3), the country house romance mobilizes the resources of the working heroine to save the nation's heritage (chapter 4). Finally, the 'bad girl' (chapter 9), the nearest equivalent to an Angry Young Woman, can be seen as a figure who rejects the new model of femininity, based on work and social obligation, as much as she transgresses more traditional notions of the ideal woman, based on virtue, chastity, and submissiveness.

It is certainly the case that the popular women's fiction that is the focus of this study provides hardly any representations of black women workers. This absence is particularly marked in medical romances, which are set within the National Health Service, one of the major employers of first-wave immigrant labour. This absence is probably motivated by both racial and class prejudices, as the professional ethic which career heroines follow places them above traditionally low-skilled work, though only racism could ultimately account for the exclusion of black nurses from hospital romances, as all nurses received the same training and were therefore inscribed within the new code of femininity and citizenship. Though it is not included in this book, the cultural history of black women workers in the 1950s needs telling, as it exposes clearly the limitations of the inclusiveness of the new idea of the modern woman. During the 1950s there was a growing body of sociology and community studies which investigated the causes and manifestations of the 'colour problem' in Britain, though black women's experience was rarely specified.[23]

Nevertheless, the texts looked at in this book challenge received ideas about the relations between gender and work in this period, and voice their right to show the 'other' 1950s of brave new causes for women.

Notes

1. Sinfield also rules out the inclusion of genuinely popular literature in his survey; his focus is on 'high cultural "literature"', charting its development as a partially autonomous practice and acknowledging its contribution to our understanding of ourselves in the postwar period', but rather oddly Sinfield does not rationalize the exclusion of women's or popular texts (pp. 8–9; see also chapter 3, 'Cultural Production'). Other examples of the under-representation of women writers of the 1950s in important literary histories of the period include: Boris Ford, ed., *The Pelican Guide to Literature. The Modern Age* (Harmondsworth: Penguin, 1991; first published in 1961), which only looks at Iris Murdoch and Ivy Compton-Burnett; Robert Hewison, *In Anger. Culture in the Cold War 1945–1960* (London: Methuen, 1988; first published in 1981), which notes 43 women in its index (including references as diverse as Twiggy and the Queen) out of well over 500 entries; Alan Sinfield, ed., *Society and Literature, 1945–1960* (London: Methuen, 1983), which refers to 32 women in a similar length index.
2. See Niamh Baker, *Happily Ever After. Women's Fiction in Postwar Britain 1945–1960* (London: Macmillan, 1989).
3. Barbara Pym, *Jane and Prudence* (London: Jonathan Cape, 1953).
4. Doris Lessing, *The Golden Notebook* (London: Granada, 1972; first published in 1962). See also Lessing's essay 'The Small Personal Voice' in Tom Maschler, ed., *Declaration* (London: MacGibbon and Kee, 1957), where she identifies most 'brave causes' as located in the Third World.
5. See Jenny Taylor, ed., *Reading the Golden Notebook* (London: Routledge, 1992).
6. Olivia Manning, *The Doves of Venus* (London: Virago, 1984; first published in 1955).
7. Iris Murdoch, *The Flight from the Enchanter* (St. Albans: Panther, 1976; first published in 1955).
8. See Bart Moore-Gilbert, 'The return of the repressed: Gothic and the 1960s novel' in Bart Moore-Gilbert and John Seed, eds, *Cultural Revolution? The Challenge of the Arts in the 1960s* (London: Routledge, 1992), pp. 181–99 (p. 183).
9. Ibid., p. 185.

10. Iris Murdoch, *The Bell* (Harmondsworth: Penguin, 1985; first published in 1958).
11. Moore-Gilbert, 'The return of the repressed', p. 195.
12. Monica Dickens, *My Turn to Make the Tea* (Harmondsworth: Penguin, 1972; first published in 1951); Monica Dickens, *The Angel in the Corner* (Harmondsworth: Penguin, 1966; first published in 1956).
13. Ken Worpole, *Reading by Numbers. Contemporary Publishing and Popular Fiction* (London: Commedia, 1984).
14. See David Forgacs, ed., *A Gramsci Reader* (London: Lawrence and Wishart, 1988), section XIV, 'Art'.
15. Stuart Hall, *New Left Review*, Jan–Feb 1960, p. 1.
16. Alison Light, 'Writing Fictions: femininity and the 1950s' in Jean Radford, ed., *The Progress of Romance* (London: Routledge, 1986), pp. 139–65 (p. 144).
17. See Tania Modleski, *Loving with a Vengeance: Mass-produced Fantasies for Women* (London: Methuen, 1984); Janice Radway, *Reading the Romance* (Chapel Hill: University of North Carolina Press, 1984); Amal Treacher, 'What is Life Without My Love: Desire and Romantic Fiction' in Susannah Radstone, ed., *Sweet Dreams. Sexuality, Gender and Popular Fiction* (London: Lawrence and Wishart, 1988), pp. 73–90; Bridget Fowler, *The Alienated Reader. Women and Popular Romantic Fiction in the Twentieth Century* (Hemel Hempstead: Harvester Wheatsheaf, 1991).
18. Vera Wynn Griffiths, 'Something to Talk About', first issue of *Woman's Realm*, 22 Feb 1958, pp. 8–9 (issued as a special 30th-anniversary souvenir in 1988).
19. Maternity leave became available in 1946; see Gail Braybon and Penny Summerfield, *Out of the Cage. Women's Experiences in Two World Wars* (London: Pandora, 1987), p. 246.
20. See also Cynthia White, *Women's Magazines 1693–1968* (London: Michael Joseph, 1970); Janice Winship, 'Nation before Family: *Woman*, the National Home Weekly, 1945–53' in *Formations of Nation and People* (London: Routledge, 1984), pp. 188–211.
21. The author is Sarah Seale, cited in Joseph McAleer, *Popular Reading and Publishing in Britain 1914–1950* (Oxford: Clarendon Press, 1992), p. 109.
22. See Deborah Philips, 'Mills and Boon. The Marketing of Moonshine' in Alan Tomlinson, ed., *Consumption, Identity and Style. Marketing, Meanings, and the Packaging of Pleasure* (London: Routledge, 1990), pp. 139–53.
23. See: K. L. Little, *Negroes in Britain. A Study of Racial Relations in English Society* (International Library of Sociology and Social Reconstruction; London: Routledge and Kegan Paul, 1947); Anthony H. Richmond, *Colour Prejudice in Britain. A Study of West Indian Workers in Liverpool, 1941–1951* (International Library of Sociology and Social Reconstruction; London: Routledge and Kegan Paul, 1954); Anthony H. Richmond, *The Colour Problem. A Study of Racial Relations* (Harmondsworth: Penguin, 1955); Michael Banton, *The Coloured Quarter. Negro Immigrants in an English City* (London: Jonathan Cape, 1955); Michael Banton, *White and Coloured. The Behaviour of British People Towards Coloured Immigrants* (London: Jonathan Cape, 1959); Ruth Glass, *Newcomers. The West Indians in London* (London: George Allen and Unwin, 1960).

3. 'The New People': literature and eugenics in postwar Britain

If the myth of women's domesticated social role in the 1950s can be challenged for what it excludes, notably the importance of work, it can also be challenged for misrepresenting one of its most central features: reproduction. Sets of important discourses about the future direction of British society collided around the issue of how the nation should reproduce itself. Far from being a source of triumphalist celebration, reproduction was a site of controversy, crisis and conflict. Most disturbingly, the theme was permeated by the presence of eugenics, both as an explicit political agenda and as a structuring theme that resurfaces across a range of postwar representations of reproduction and childhood. Explicitly and implicitly, older fears of social degeneration haunted postwar writing. Blockage, abortion and monstrosity were prevalent motifs in both mainstream and non-canonical literary texts. Jimmy Porter's desire for Alison to have a miscarriage in *Look Back in Anger* (1956) is only one of the more famous examples. The pursuit of this theme leads to some unsettling conclusions about the postwar settlement, and remaps the literary and historical terrain in ways that challenge conveniently packaged myths of the state of the nation or the spirit of the age in the 1950s.

Depopulation fears: the 'fading out' of the British people

The immediate postwar period is remembered more for its 'baby boom' than for fears about depopulation. Yet although there was a slight increase in the birth-rate between 1945 and 1947, all measurements indicated that the longer-term trend was downwards. The phenomenon was not new – the decline had begun with the widespread use of contraception among the middle classes at the end of the nineteenth century – but the wartime climate of national emergency and reconstruction was sufficient to generate considerable alarm in the ranks of social investigators and policy-formers. In 1944 the government set up a Royal Commission on Population (which reported in 1949), and in 1945 Mass Observation and the Fabian Society both published reports on the birth-rate situation.[1] These studies concurred in perceiving a threat to national identity and the British way of life. As Mass Observation's *Britain and Her Birthrate* declared: 'Mass Observation has lined up with those who do not want the English people to disappear' (p. 7). After all, these were the very 'people' who had just won the war. This patriotism sanctioned the open expression of eugenicist fears of racial extinction and apocalypse. The problem was not only that the birth-rate was operating below 'replacement' level, the real danger was seen to be 'differential breeding' – in other words that the lower classes were proliferating at the expense of the 'better', higher-quality sections of society. The Royal Commission summed up this fear: 'The more intelligent have smaller families than the less intelligent' (p. 153). The 'innate intelligence of the nation' was seen to be in jeopardy. Clearly, immediate remedies were needed if the middle classes were not to surrender their historic leadership role. The establishment of the Welfare State was applauded for its provision of maternity support services, but the 'eugenicist conscience' (to quote a contemporary Eugenics Society pamphlet[2]) balked at the universality of these benefits. Mass Observation was openly mocking of such socialist measures: 'Direct planning for baby production may well pull up numbers and pull quality down' (p. 231). The pamphlet goes on to mock state policy: 'Let's get ahead with numbers, and to hell with eugenics' (p. 206).

Yet this qualified endorsement of welfare reforms was accompanied by a surprisingly liberal attitude towards the position of women in society. All these reports welcomed the growth in the numbers of working women as an advance of democracy and a bolstering of middle-class social stewardship. If these documents can be taken to represent an official consensus on women's two roles, there was no question of placing women back in the home, despite the anxieties about the declining birth-rate. Indeed, although significant numbers of women who had worked in male-dominated industries were displaced at the end of the war, by 1947 the state was once again actively recruiting women to fill labour shortages. The Royal Commission on Population actually recommended the revival of state-run nurseries to enable women to 'combine motherhood and the care of a home with outside activities' (p. 160). The Fabian study went so far as to accuse 'married women who are not pulling their weight' of being social 'parasites' (p. 25). Nor was there any hostility to the influence of feminism in promoting birth-control – contraception was seen to be essential if the improvement of the national stock was to proceed rationally. So the eugenicist strain in these reports contradicts any notion of a collaboration between a pronatalist, 'baby-booming' Welfare State and the patriotic redomesticating of women. As Elizabeth Wilson has noted, eugenicist discourse could be invoked in this debate as long as there was no hint of compulsion in the aftermath of the knowledge of Fascist practices.[3] In eugenicist terms, 'positive' eugenics were preferable to 'negative' eugenics: incentives to breed, such as better services and allowances, were the democratic route to improving the nation's stock. Draconian state intervention to prevent breeding by undesirable social or racial groups was too reminiscent of Fascist atrocities or American steriliza-tion programmes. However, there were limits to this liberalism. Two particular groups were the target of an unreconstructed 'negative' eugenicist hostility: black immigrants and 'mental defectives'. For eugenicists, the greatest danger of the birth-rate decline was that it would suck into Britain a low-grade colonial stock. The Fabians were in no doubt that 'The eugenics of immigration cannot be overstressed' (p. 50). They recommended that only white Europeans who were between 20 and 30 years old and 'physically and mentally sound' should be allowed into the new Britain. The Royal Commis-sion noted that the 'supply of suitable immigrants' was 'meagre' (p. 225). Racist fears of miscegenation expressed in eugenicist language were nothing new, but by the time the Royal Commission on Population reported, Britain had developed what can only be described as a semi-planned immigration policy. Black workers, mainly from the Caribbean, were invited to Britain to fill labour shortages (usually in low-skilled jobs) in the newly expanded public-sector economy. As Gail Braybon and Penny Summerfield have noted, black labour was regarded by the state as 'docile, unambitious, and cheap'.[4] The contradictions of this policy were evident from the beginning. The state made little attempt to enlighten the British public about the process of importing labour, and virtually no social support was provided for black workers. There was also a failure to challenge racist perceptions of black immigration as a 'problem'. Despite the fact that the 1948 Nationality Act gave Commonwealth citizens a British passport, there was no supporting validation of their Britishness. As the *Empire Windrush* docked in London in that year, the Colonial Secretary Creech Jones was heard to remark that this first cohort of black immigrants 'wouldn't last one winter' – a cutting Darwinian comment.[5]

A measure of the remarkable respectability of eugenicist thought in the postwar period can be seen in the publication of Eva Hubback's *The Popula-tion of Britain* as a Pelican Special in 1947.[6] The dust-jacket informed the reader of Hubback's seat on the Council of the Eugenics Society as just one more credential alongside her feminist career in the promotion of family planning. Nor did the accompanying profile of the author offer any apologia for some of Hubback's more grisly recommendations, such as that the 'voluntary sterilization of those mentally defective, subnormal or diseased should be permitted by law' (p. 284), or that family-planning clinics should give advice on 'whether any given couple should or should not have children on eugenic grounds' (p. 282). The argument for such a policing of the gene pool was to prevent 'the fading-out of the British people' (p. 14). A few years later, Aldous Huxley was to join in the eugenicist chorus crying down the Welfare State's camouflaging of 'insufficient organisms'.[7]

Whether or not the genetic enemy within could be expelled, an intractable problem remained in that the middle classes ('those parents who are above the average physically, mentally and morally' (Hubback, p. 284)) were simply not reproducing at 'replacement' rate. The culprit was not perceived to be birth control; this was merely a device to limit the economic and social burdens that having children placed on parents. The driving force behind smaller families was economic progress. This was a tough nut to crack, as even eugenicists realized that a high standard of living was fundamental to middle-class culture, and it would be futile to threaten it. Moreover, the middle classes were blazing a trail for national prosperity and recovery. In his 1947 essay 'The English People', George Orwell summed up this philosophy with his characteristic pith: 'children matter more than money'.[8] Roy Lewis and Angus Maude's book *The English Middle Classes* (1949) also attacked 'the vigour which leads to infertility, and the ambition which sacrifices parenthood to progress in the social scale'.[9] On the one side lay the monstrous dereliction of reproductive duty, on the other side a memory of Malthusian recklessness and immiseration.

Contemporary literature also participated in these anxieties. Angus Wilson picked up on the theme in his collection of short stories, *Such Darling Dodos* (1950).[10] Three of the stories deal with disturbing failures of genteel reproduction. In 'Necessity's Child', a boy called Rodney has vengeful fantasies of murdering his neglectful, hedonistic parents. His mother regards him as their 'greatest mistake' (p. 95). He represents the curse of what one contemporary study of childlessness called 'one-child sterility'.[11] He is farmed out to public school, and resents his parents' exhibitionist, post-Kinseyan displays of erotic affection. Oedipally, he watches his father 'running his hands down [his mother's] breasts' (p. 105). He is sacrificed to their pleasure: 'We like having fun and we like having it together,' says his mother (p. 95). Rodney is all set to become a rebellious teenager or a delinquent, though the story breaks off at this point.

In 'Mummy to the Rescue' the theme of debased reproduction is worked up into something more sinister. In this case, a daughter has been deserted by her mother and left to the care of genteel grandparents. From the narrative voice, in which the heroine dreams of being reunited with 'mummy', we assume her to be a young child. But the ending of the story has a macabre twist; her dream turns into a nightmare, in which her mother strangles her. It transpires that Celia is not a child but a mentally retarded invalid who has been throttled by her bedclothes. Her 'childish idiocy' (p. 159) began when her mother abandoned her. Celia is the monstrous result ('thirteen stone at least – she had put on weight ever since her twenty-fifth year') of irresponsible reproduction. The story even countenances at a metaphorical level the possibility that her mother has returned in ghostly form to eliminate her 'defective' offspring.

'A Little Companion' is the most directly Gothic of the three tales. An 'old maid', Miss Arkwright, is haunted by a repulsive demon child, an apparition which taunts her lack of progeny. Eventually the demon disappears, only to be reincarnated during the war as a 'cretinous and adenoidal' East End evacuee child (p. 37). The allegorical writing is on the wall: while Miss Arkwright's type becomes extinct – she personifies 'the pattern of English village life' (p. 23) – the 'cretinous' working class is seen to inherit the postwar world. The truly monstrous act in these stories is the refusal of a woman to be a Good Mother. Wilson's stories convey the fear and terror generated by the possibility of women opting out of a reproductive and nurturing role.

As the 1950s progressed into the 1960s, depopulation fears seem to have faded away, only to be replaced by their opposite. As the 'winds of change' for decolonization grew stronger, Aldous Huxley revived the old eugenicist alarm at proliferating 'low-grade' populations in the developing world. In *Brave New World Revisited* (1959), he declared that the 'grim biological background' of over-population was the 'central problem of mankind' (p. 19), leading to poverty and dictatorship. It comes as no surprise to find that in his last, Utopian, novel, *Island* (1962),[12] the secluded Palanese people have instituted strict population control. Any couples wanting a third child are strongly urged to use 'AI' (artificial insemination) for eugenicist reasons: 'it's more moral to take a shot at having a child of superior quality,' explains the heroine (p. 195). A more Swiftian solution to the Malthusian dilemma is imagined in Anthony Burgess's Dystopian novel *The Wanting Seed*, published in the same year. Here, the state has thrown its weight behind the promotion of homosexuality, while unwanted children are turned into phosphorous fertilizer.

Social mobility: the perils of hypergamy

One postwar reform of the new Britain seemed to provide a solution to the eugenicist problem of national decline. The depleted national stock could be replenished by all the bright beneficiaries of the 1944 Education Act. The new scholarship boys (and to a much lesser extent girls) were to be the symbols of meritocracy and social mobility, successfully rising through a selective education system based on intelligence testing rather than privilege. After all, the ruling classes had always recruited from below when necessary. Now this had become state policy. This meritocracy became the embattled cultural territory of the Angry Young Man, who has become a defining myth of the period. The rebellious 'anger' of Jimmy Porter was, and continues to be, celebrated as an indictment of the sterility and complacency of British society. In generational terms, British culture had discovered its own rebel without a cause. In gender terms, Jimmy Porter represented a new masculine vigour, a rejection of effete, patrician notions of high culture. In social terms, the new hero exposed the pains of individual social mobility in an obdurately class-ridden society. Far from being liberated by higher education, the regional or working-class hero felt trapped in an alien culture – 'uprooted and anxious', in Richard Hoggart's memorable phrase.[13]

If 'anger' meant anything, it was that some 'brave new causes' had better be found quickly. Given that *Look Back in Anger* has become such an emblematic text of its time, it is strange that the crucial theme of reproduction has been neglected by critics, especially as it structures the play's dramatic climaxes. Act 1 ends with Jimmy's malevolent wish for Alison to miscarry, Act 2 concludes with the announcement that she is indeed pregnant, and the play ends with the news that she has lost the baby and cannot have another. Alison is summarily punished for her class position with infertility. Jimmy's curse of barrenness must constitute some of the most offensive lines in the play:

> If only something – something would happen to you, and wake you out of your beauty sleep. If you could have a child, and it would die. Let it grow, let a recognizable human face emerge from that little mass of indiarubber and wrinkles. Please – if only I could watch you face that. I wonder if you might even become a recognizable human being yourself. But I doubt it.[14]

On hearing that Alison is in fact pregnant, Jimmy rails: 'I don't care if it has two heads' (p. 73). There are a number of ways in which these outbursts can be interpreted: self-hatred, repressed homosexuality, a displaced loathing of his mother.[15] But none of these views can explain why Alison not only miscarries but is also left sterile: 'It's cost him his child, and any others I might have had!' (p. 95). We can only understand this nemesis in social terms: the cross-class marriage is sterile. Alison has defected from her class and must be punished – there can be no son-of-scholarship-boy to contaminate the gene pool. Jimmy will remain a social and intellectual anomaly; the possibility of class reconciliation is disrupted by the loss of the next generation of the marriage.

The play reminds us that it has never been wholly acceptable, at least at the level of literary representation, for the middle classes to recruit from the working classes. The literary record is consistent on this issue. No fictional proletarian aspirant has been allowed to reproduce successfully. In Hardy's *Jude the Obscure* (1896), Jude and Sue's children are murdered. Leonard Bast in E. M. Forster's *Howard's End* (1910) is killed while his illegitimate son (Bastard) is spirited off to the Wilcox's ancestral home to be reared by the middle classes. The autodidact mining hero of A. J. Cronin's *The Stars Look Down* (1935), David Fenwick, is cuckolded. Monica Dickens's *The Angel in the Corner* (1956) deals with a doomed marriage between the middle-class Helen Martin and an 'angry' Anglo-Italian Joe Colonna. He kills their (already frail) baby by 'accidentally' dropping it down some steps. The heroine of Angus Wilson's short story 'Once a Lady' (1957) is also stricken with infertility for eloping scandalously with a working-class man.[16] So too is Sheila Downey in James Hanley's *An End and a Beginning* (1958).[17] Sheila's family are Irish gentry, and when she marries a Liverpool trade union leader her mother 'dreaded a child of that marriage' (p. 212). Joe Lampton, the ruthless social riser of John Braine's *Room at the Top* (1957), discovers in the sequel, *Life at the Top* (1962),[18] that his wealthy wife Susan has cuckolded him; the daughter he dotes on is not his. Meanwhile, his son has been appropriated by the 'middle class sausage machine' of preparatory school (p. 13). Even a modest social advance is rigorously genetically policed. In Stan Barstow's *A Kind of Loving* (1960) Vic Brown marries his pregnant girlfriend Ingrid, who represents the newly affluent working class of suburban estates and televisions. Vic feels ambivalent about abandoning his more traditional roots, and his conflict is realized, inevitably it seems, in Ingrid losing the baby. In the 1960s' sequel, *The Watchers on the Shore* (1966),[19] we learn that the miscarriage has damaged Ingrid's fertility and their marriage remains childless. Vic embarks on an affair with a London actress. When she becomes pregnant, the paternity of the child is left unresolved, a symbol of Vic's contradictory position: 'it's going to be a bit trickier than normal to produce,' he ponders wistfully (p. 17).

These blighted alliances are all examples of what Geoffrey Gorer, in an important contemporary essay, called 'The Perils of Hypergamy' (1957).[20] Gorer borrowed the word 'hypergamy' from anthropology, to refer to marrying up the social ladder. Gorer believed that the 1944 Education Act had 'enormously speeded up' the process of social mobility for 'brilliant young men of working-class origin' (there is no mention of scholarship girls). What used to take several generations now only took one generation (pp. 329, 332). According to Gorer, the postwar scholarship boy was ill-equipped psychologically to deal with this displacement. His emotional outlook had been forged in a working-class environment which regarded high culture as effeminate. In jumping 'three or four social classes' he was therefore 'being unmanned, turned into a cissy' (p. 332). To compensate for this emasculation, he treated his middle-class wife with traditional chauvinist contempt. But the profound contradictions of his position may explain the prevalence of unproductiveness in literary representations of hypergamous alliances.

Another important study which questioned the social and psychological security of working-class mobility was Michael Young's *The Rise of the Meritocracy* (1958).[21] Young believed that educational selection was bleeding the working class of its best talent. This may have been a 'boon' for individuals, but for the class as a whole 'this victory was a defeat' (p. 140). Like Hoggart, Young was concerned that authentic working-class culture was being eroded by the superficial attractions of affluence and modernity. To Young, meritocracy was an insidious form of social divisiveness: 'every selection of one is a rejection of many' (p. 15). He berated Attlee's government of 1945–51 for not abolishing public schools and preferring selective to comprehensive state education. The 1944 Act had merely created an invigorated ruling bloc: 'the principles of hereditary and merit are coming together' (p. 176). This danger was in fact foreseen by Ellen Wilkinson, Attlee's Minister for Education. She saw selection in education as a means to preserve class barriers and supply unskilled labour to the economy. She is reported as saying, 'Don't worry how we got India, let's go and do some nice work at the forge.'[22] From this perspective, behind the apparent social Darwinism of meritocracy (the idea that the best will become dominant) may have lain a deliberate act of social engineering, to consolidate the distinction between the classes.

The atomic state: monstrous children

There were further reasons to be nervous about postwar reproduction. The young of the postwar years were the first generation to grow up in the shadow of Hiroshima and Nagasaki. As the Cold War surfaced, Britain became an atomic power. The decision was initially taken in secret, but later the nuclear programme masqueraded as an investment in 'clean' energy production. This propaganda was designed to divert public attention away from both military policy and the dangers of radiation contamination (a possibility which particularly alarmed eugenicists as well as the burgeoning peace movement).[23] Nevertheless, the prevailing anti-Communist hysteria of enemies within fuelled popular fantasies of radiation monsters, a new generation of Frankensteinian prodigies rising up to destroy the society which created them.

C. P. Snow captured this mood in his novel about the development of Britain's atomic programme, *The New Men* (1954).[24] The narrator of the novel is Lewis Eliot, a senior Civil Servant in charge of the project to build the atom bomb. His brother Martin also works at one of the government's secret research establishments. When Martin presents an amount of plutonium to Lewis, the triumphal moment becomes a bizarre annunciation that is an omen to the next generation:

'Touch it,' he said.

I put two fingers on the bag – and astonishingly was taken into an irrelevant bliss.

Under the bag's surface, the metal was hot to the touch – and, yes, pushing under memories, I had it, I know why I was happy. It brought back the moment, the grass and earth hot under my hand, when Martin and Irene told me she was going to have a child. (p. 184)

The nuclear child is the incarnation of nature's terrible and thrilling secrets. Lewis's sexual *frisson* signals the dangerous attractions of the 'hot earth'. When Hiroshima and Nagasaki are destroyed, Martin wants to resign. He realizes he has fathered a beast, not a messiah.

Writers were quick to imagine the possibility of a nuclear holocaust and its aftermath. In John Wyndham's *The Chrysalids* (1955)[25] the primitive society which has emerged from the destruction is ruthlessly eugenicist. All new-borns are inspected for genetic defects. 'Mutants' are immediately sterilized and exiled to the 'Fringes', a savage wilderness. But one 'Deviation' (or genetic defect) has emerged that cannot be so easily detected. The story follows the fortunes of a group of telepathic teenagers, a new super-intelligent race. Radiation poisoning has propelled them to the next stage of human evolution. Hunted down by the 'Norms' (or ordinary people), their destiny lies with the 'Zealanders' (inhabitants of New Zealand), who are similarly gifted. In the nick of time, a Zealand helicopter rescues the super-brood and takes them to the land of 'our kind of people' (p. 200). But the happy ending is marred by the flagrant supremacism of the 'New People'. Their helicopter massacres everyone who saw it arrive. This is done not only to preserve secrecy but because these 'inadequate' people 'would have bred with the carelessness of animals until they had reduced themselves to poverty and misery' (p. 157). When one of the 'chrysalid' girls falls in love with a Norm he is murdered. She is told 'marriage to a Norm would be intolerable in a very short time' (p. 92). Another member of the group is horrified at the thought of sex with one of 'Fringe' savages: 'It would be outrageous – like an animal' (p. 172). The new world is shown to be as rigorously selective and hierarchical as the old. Even more disturbingly, the superior physique of the New People is clearly Aryan. When the helicopter lands, the first figure to emerge is a dazzlingly beautiful woman:

> But more than anything it was the lightness of her face that made us stare ... We found it hard to believe that any real, living person could look like that, so untouched, so unflawed. (p. 192)

The novel assumes a natural equation between moral superiority and physical appearance. The narrative does not comment on the sinister and ironic resonances of this description. When we situate the novel in the context of the real, colonial history of 'Zealand', this ending is still more chilling.

The 'Norms' were given their chance for revenge in Wyndham's second, contemporary treatment of the theme of the super-gifted child, *The Midwich Cuckoos* (1957).[26] The narrative perspective is reversed here: the brood of young telepaths become an evil force threatening world peace. Their arrival is an act of extraterrestrial parthenogenesis. An egg-like spaceship lands in the sleepy English village of Midwich and seals the place off with a force-field. When it departs, it leaves every woman in the village pregnant. The result of this collective Virgin Birth is a group of golden-eyed 'cuckoos' who have the power of mind control. Similar broods have been deposited around the world – a universal realization of the fantasy of the enemy within. Eventually, Midwich's 'advanced species' (p. 200) is outwitted and exterminated by the genteel hero. Given the contemporary setting of the story, it is difficult not to interpret the cuckoos as fantasized juvenile delinquents. One of their most terrifying features is that they appear to be a 'child-adult combination' (p. 196), an image reminiscent of contemporary sociological studies of rebellious youth as 'pseudo-adults' suffering from a consumer-led 'acceleration of adolescence'.[27] The ovarian-shaped spaceship could also be read as a metaphor for the nannying, pronatalist Welfare State which has marginalized 'real' parenting (if the novel's chronology is strictly observed, the children are born in 1948, at the height of birth-rate scares). Finally, the cuckoos can be seen as postwar orphans seeking revenge on their parents' generation. Their extermination wipes the slate clean, and purges the angry generation.

The most famous monstrous children of this period are, of course, the marooned schoolboys of William Golding's *The Lord of the Flies* (1954),[28] which also uses the backdrop of a Third World War. The novel is not free of an implicit eugenicist logic. The first boy to die, in a bushfire, is notable for a 'mark on his face' (p. 60). Piggy, the bespectacled, overweight, bright working-class boy, is also killed by the 'pack', which seems a reversion to 'natural' Darwinism.

Freakishness in social terms was also the theme of David Mercer's television play *Where the Difference Begins* (1961).[29] Mercer used the device of a reunion of two brothers to personify and bring together the themes of 'defeated' working-class hypergamy and the perils of the nuclear state. Richard and Edgar Crowther meet at their mother's funeral. Richard is a failed 'angry' painter. Having lost his inspiration, he has turned to teaching. His marriage to a 'well-bred' woman (p. 50) was childless. His girlfriend Gillian is pregnant, but she almost loses the (illegitimate) child from shock when Richard's wife Janet turns up unexpectedly. Reproduction has been less fraught for his brother Edgar, a Tory nuclear scientist. He has two healthy children and seems a model of meritocratic assimilation. But he is now impotent, which his wife attributes to radiation poisoning. His mere presence is sufficient to make Gillian fear for her genes, 'scared stiff she'll have a baby with two heads' (p. 28). Richard sums up the problems of being a social cuckoo: 'In families like ours the children are alien' (p. 48). Significantly, Mercer claimed he wrote the play to express his own feelings of being a 'stateless' and 'dispossessed' working-class intellectual (p. xx).

Pronatalism: angry infants, freakish mothers

It is clear that, far from being universally celebrated in this period, the literary record provides evidence that reproduction was a site of public anxiety and tension. Even the famous postwar pronatalist ethic ('baby booming') has been misrepresented. This is probably because of the fame of its main publicist, John Bowlby. He coined the term 'maternal deprivation' to describe the damaging effects of any mother devoting less than her whole energies to childrearing. In fact, Bowlby's main concern in *Child Care and the Growth of Love* (1953)[30] was with postwar illegitimacy rates and the dangers of institutionalizing orphans. But his warnings about the social dangers of broken homes have been remembered selectively. His recommendation that the young mother needed a generous family allowance so that she 'should not be free, to earn' (p. 108) has been seen as solid evidence that popular psychology conspired to put women back in the home. But as Denise Riley has shown in her book *War in the Nursery* (1983), there was no such coherent policy.[31] The appeal for full-time mothering was driven as much by the media's popularization of forms of psychoanalysis as by reactionary patriarchal ideology. The British psychoanalytic establishment was at this time (and continues to be) heavily influenced by the theories of Melanie Klein, who believed that innate aggression was a primary psychic drive. According to Klein, the separating of the infant from the mother's breast caused it to have violent and sadistic fantasies. This developmental picture was particularly bleak, as Klein saw the infantile responses as predetermined, and her ideas also marginalized the role of the father.[32] It was left to D. W. Winnicott, who distanced himself from Klein's position, to try to reassure the 'ordinary good mother', though even he still invoked the image of the nursery as a battleground.[33] As he put it in a radio broadcast, the infant is 'a bundle of discontent, a human being to be sure, but one who has raging lions and tigers inside' (pp. 11–12). This might seem an alarming situation, but 'all you need to do is to keep the home together, and to expect anything' (p. 78).

It did not take long before women writers began to explore this tangled matrix of anxieties about reproduction. The conflicting demands of the 'dual role' inspired a number of postwar narratives about single mothers. Yet the obstacles in the way of a candid treatment of this theme were still formidable. An indication of its controversial nature was expressed socially in the fact that abortion was still illegal (until 1967), and illegitimate, 'unwanted' children could be regarded as eugenicist state fodder. It was still official policy to export healthy children from 'Homes' to far-flung corners of the British Empire, so as to ensure the continuation of 'good' white stock in areas of 'low-grade' population. This practice had been carried out since the eighteenth century; in the 1950s and 1960s children in care were being told that their parents were dead as a pretext to export them to former colonies where they could begin a new life.[34]

Some women writers struggled to integrate the themes of reproduction and mothering into their narratives. Doris Lessing's semi-autobiographical *In Pursuit of the English* (1960)[35] looks back to her arrival in England from Zimbabwe (then Rhodesia) in 1949: 'when England was at its dingiest, my personal fortunes at their lowest, and my morals at their lowest. I also had a small child' (p. 14). The narrative charts Lessing's climb out of this proletarianized condition to become an author, but the heroic struggle omits any further reference to the 'small child'. In narrative terms, the child is 'aborted' from the text. The theme of the 'dual role' is craftily modified so that 'home' involves adjusting to the insecure life of lodging houses, but not to mothering. The child's existence functions grammatically in the quotation just cited almost as an afterthought, as if it is an additional burden and an index of Lessing's 'lowest' point which she strives to transcend. Perhaps, unconsciously, Lessing felt it had been difficult enough coping with making ends meet and being subject to the accommodation colour bar (p. 40).

Two other well-known novels about single mothering were written on the brink of the emergent sexual freedoms of the 1960s: Lynne Reid Banks's *The L-Shaped Room* (1960) and Margaret Drabble's *The Millstone* (1965).[36] Both novels pursued the theme of the single mother by reinventing the Victorian fallen woman, the traditional, demonic antitype of the Angel in the House. The heroines are successful career women who become pregnant after joyless sexual encounters. Jane Graham in *The L-Shaped Room* is a high-salaried public relations officer for a large hotel, Rosamund in *The Millstone* is an academic researcher. These privileged circumstances make their transgressions more heinous and their redemption more likely. The novels reveal the pressures and anxieties produced by the 'dual role'. In Jane's case, she loses her job as soon as her pregnancy is discovered, but in the nick of time a distant aunt leaves her a cottage – a literary nod in the direction of Jane's predecessor Jane Eyre, who also inherits 'fairy gold' after many tribulations. The property plot is also summoned up in *The Millstone*. In addition to the bountiful availability of post-Robbins Report higher-education grants, Rosamund is conveniently provided with her parents' comfortable central London flat while they are on a lengthy working trip. She does, however, acknowledge, 'I would not recommend my course of action to anyone with a shade less advantage in the world than myself' (p. 112).

But however much they are cushioned from material deprivation, Jane and Rosamund have a brush with the nemesis of postwar population anxieties. Jane is offered an illegal abortion by a doctor, who puts his case in the specific language of the dual role: some women cannot be 'breadwinner and nursemaid, all at once' (p. 32). Having refused his offer, she later tries to terminate the pregnancy herself by going on a 'curry debauch' (p. 150). This episode is redolent with the eugenicist imagery of degeneration. After gorging down the exotic 'poison', she wanders through fog-bound streets in her melodramatic 'lost' condition. She regards her tragic plight at this stage as punishment, not only for sexual sin but for something more unexpected: 'killing my mother by being born' (p. 24). In the language of contemporary psychoanalysis, she can be seen as atoning for her Kleinian, matricidal origins. The novel also gestures towards the possibility that she might transmit an inherent flaw or 'shortcoming'. She imagines her unborn child as 'a face blackened by my own dark rebellious anger against it' (p. 84). Jane also contemplates the horror of producing a homosexual son, another image of unproductiveness.

In *The Millstone*, Rosamund's child is born 'flawed' with a hole in its heart, which Rosamund interprets as providential: the child was conceived in 'heartless' circumstances. Though beautiful in appearance, nothing can conceal the fact that the child is a social and sexual 'freak' (p. 122). Because Rosamund is 'at heart a Victorian' she is paying 'the Victorian penalty' (p. 18).

While Jane and Rosamund wrestle with the moral legacies of Victorian social control, their transgressions look tame when compared with the experience of working-class Jo in Shelagh Delaney's play *A Taste of Honey* (1958).[37] She commits the most extreme forms of eugenicist crimes: under-age sex, miscegenation and illegitimacy. While pregnant by a black Liverpool sailor, she sets up home with Geoff, a homosexual art student who proves himself to be a better mother than her own, and a better likely mother than she is herself. But Jo, and the play, are not ready for such a Bohemian resolution, despite her own budding artistic talent. While the play broke new ground in its portrayal of social and sexual minorities,[38] it could not find a satisfactory answer to its central dilemma: what should become of Jo's baby. With the father conveniently absent, the possibility of a mixed-race relationship is elided. Geoff is dismissed by Jo's feckless mother Helen, and with him goes the possibility of an alternative family structure. Helen's racist humour is the best the play can offer as a cathartic release for the underlying tensions: her proposal for the baby's future is to 'put it on the stage and call it Blackbird' (p. 87) – to exploit the child's 'freak' potential.

The fictional children in these narratives are metaphorical indicators of some central tensions in the new social relations of postwar society. As cuckoos, blackbirds, minstrels, freaks, these monstrous progeny act as reminders of some of the submerged anxieties about the role of reproduction in the new Britain.

In contrast, popular literature for women offers an optimistic countervision of female achievement and social progress. It is the genesis and exploits of this new type of heroine that the subsequent chapters of this book will explore. Romance fiction usually ends with the heroine's marriage, which means that the problem of coping with children does not have to be addressed. Nevertheless, the career heroine of popular romance faces many of the same problems of the 'dual role' as her anxious and blighted counterparts in more mainstream literature. In popular narratives, however, the resources of the workplace and the professional ethic are often the means to a solution rather than an obstacle to progress.

Notes

1.   Mass Observation, *Britain and Her Birthrate* (London: John Murray, 1945); Fabian Society, *Population and the People. A National Policy* (London: George Allen and Unwin, 1945); *Report of the Royal Commission on Population* (London: HMSO, 1949).

2.   Eugenics Society, *Aims and Objects of the Eugenics Society*, 1944, p. 3. According to a recent book on the history of the Eugenics Society, the demise of the movement had more to do with postwar egalitarianism than Fascism. Once the idea of the working class as undesirable paupers was abolished along with the Poor Laws, there was an unsuccessful attempt to shift eugenicist anxieties on to 'problem' families, but the *Eugenics Review* folded in 1968. See Pauline M. H. Mazumdar, *Eugenics, Human Genetics and Human Failings. The Eugenics Society, its Sources and its Critics in Britain* (London: Routledge, 1992), pp. 250–2.

3.   Elizabeth Wilson, *Only Halfway to Paradise. Women in Postwar Britain 1945–1968* (London: Tavistock Publications, 1980), p. 26.

4.   Gail Braybon and Penny Summerfield, *Out of the Cage. Women's Experiences in Two World Wars* (London: Pandora, 1987), p. 285.

5.   *Forty Winters On: Memories of Britain's Postwar Caribbean Immigrants* (Lambeth Council, 1988), p. 8, cited by Peter Hennessy in *Never Again. Britain 1945–1951* (London: Vintage, 1993; first published in 1992), p. 440.

6.   Eva M. Hubback, *The Population of Britain* (West Drayton, Middlesex: Penguin, 1947). See also Richard Titmuss, *Essays on the 'Welfare State'* (London: George Allen and Unwin, 1958): 'men and women, with impaired health and handicaps … will be exposed to the hazards of married life and child-rearing. Formerly, this segment of the population … might not have entered matrimony' (p. 100).

7.   Aldous Huxley, *Brave New World Revisited* (London: Triad Panther, 1983; first published in 1959), p. 32.

8.   George Orwell, 'The English People' in Sonia Orwell and Ian Angus, eds, *The Collected Essays, Journalism and Letters of George Orwell* (Harmondsworth: Penguin, 1970), vol. 3, pp. 15–56 (p. 50) (the essay was written in 1944 but did not appear until 1947).

9.   Roy Lewis and Angus Maude, *The English Middle Classes* (Harmondsworth: Penguin, 1953; first published in 1949), p. 183.

10. Angus Wilson, *Such Darling Dodos* (London: Granada Publishing, 1980; first published in 1950).

11. Lawrence Galton, *New Facts for the Childless* (London: Victor Gollancz, 1954), chapter 1, *passim*.

12. Aldous Huxley, *Island* (Harmondsworth: Penguin, 1970; first published in 1962).

13. See Richard Hoggart, *The Uses of Literacy* (Harmondsworth: Penguin, 1958; first published in 1957), chapter 10.

14. John Osborne, *Look Back in Anger* (London: Faber and Faber, 1976; first published in 1957), p. 23.

15. This interpretation is put forward by Michelene Wandor in her feminist study of postwar British drama, *Look Back in Gender* (London: Methuen, 1987).

16. The story appears in the collection of short stories, *A Bit Off the Map* (Harmondsworth: Penguin, 1968; first published in 1957).

17. James Hanley, *An End and a Beginning* (London: André Deutsch, 1990; first published in 1959).

18. John Braine, *Life at the Top* (Harmondsworth: Penguin, 1966; first published in 1962).

19. Stan Barstow, *The Watchers on the Shore* (Harmondsworth: Penguin, 1968; first published in 1966).

20. The essay first appeared in *New Statesman and Nation*, 4 May 1957. It was reprinted in Gene Feldman and Max Gartenberg, eds, *Protest* (London: Quartet, 1973; first published in 1959), pp. 321–9.

21. Michael Young, *The Rise of the Meritocracy* (Harmondsworth: Penguin, 1967; first published in 1958).

22. Cited in Hennessy, *Never Again*, p. 159.

23. See the *Eugenics Review*, 50(2), July 1958, for the claim that 'radiation may be raising the mutation rate for hereditary diseases' (p. 105).

24. C. P. Snow, *The New Men* (Harmondsworth, Penguin, 1959; first published in 1954).

25. John Wyndham, *The Chrysalids* (Harmondsworth: Penguin, 1985; first published in 1955).

26. John Wyndham, *The Midwich Cuckoos* (Harmondsworth: Penguin, 1973; first published in 1957).

27. See T. R. Fyvel, *The Insecure Offenders. Rebellious Youth in the Welfare State* (Harmondsworth: Penguin, 1966; first published in 1961), p. 218.

28. William Golding, *The Lord of the Flies* (London: Faber and Faber, 1973; first published in 1954).

29. David Mercer, *Where the Difference Begins*, in *Plays: One* (London: Methuen, 1990; first broadcast 15 Dec 1961; first published 1961).

30. John Bowlby, *Child Care and the Growth of Love* (London: Penguin, 1983; first published in 1953).

31. Denise Riley, *War in the Nursery. Theories of the Child and Mother* (London: Virago, 1983).

32. See Juliet Mitchell, ed., *The Selected Melanie Klein* (Harmondsworth: Penguin, 1986).

33. D. W. Winnicott, *The Child and the Family. First Relationships* (London: Tavistock Publications, 1957).

34. See Philip Bean and Joy Melville, *Lost Children of the Empire* (London: Unwin Hyman, 1989).

35. Doris Lessing, *In Pursuit of the English* (London: Grafton, 1989; first published in 1960).

36. Lynne Reid Banks, *The L-Shaped Room* (Harmondsworth: Penguin, 1962; first

published in 1960); Margaret Drabble, *The Millstone* (Harmondsworth: Penguin, 1971; first published in 1965).

37. Shelagh Delaney, *A Taste of Honey* (London: Methuen, 1987; first published in 1958).

38. Colin MacInnes was one of the first critics to perceive the play's innovative social agenda. In a review first published in 1959, he called Delaney 'this splendid young prophetess'. See *England, Half-English* (London: Hogarth, 1986; first published in 1961), pp. 205–7 (p. 207).

4. Half-crown houses: the crisis of the country house in the postwar romance

> Brideshead today would be open to trippers, its treasures rearranged by expert hands and the fabric better maintained than it was by Lord Marchmain.[1]

In his 1959 Preface to *Brideshead Revisited*, Evelyn Waugh locates his 1945 novel as an elegy for the doomed English country house, but is wise enough to acknowledge that he had constructed a myth of upper-class extinction:

> It seemed then that the ancestral seats which were our chief national artistic achievement were doomed to decay and spoilation like the monasteries in the sixteenth century. So I piled it on rather.[2]

Nevertheless, the myth that postwar socialist planning had sounded the death-knell of the country house was widely accepted throughout the decade of the 1950s, and recurs in discourses about the countryside, national heritage and the fate of national 'treasures'. A 1952 guidebook to the newly accessible 'half-crown' houses did acknowledge the tensions, but still argued for a democratic preservation of heritage:

> the civilization which created the English country house ... was one of the main factors in the building of England; and whether we admire it or not as a whole, it is a good thing that its finest legacy should be preserved for posterity. Changing social conditions, greater mobility and perhaps, a wider general sense of artistic and historic appreciation have combined to bring the English country house into a new position of prominence.[3]

For popular literature, *Brideshead Revisited* became a model for narratives in which the central character, the focus of romance, is neither a hero nor a heroine but a house. Waugh's novel can be identified as a precedent for a specific sub-genre within the field of romance fiction, which can be termed 'the country house romance'. In these novels written by and for women, it is the country house and the tradition it represents that is as much an object of desire for the heroine as the hero. Wherever the novel may actually be set, whether its location be Cornwall, Scotland, Wales or Ireland, the geography of the landscape is less important to the narrative than the house itself, which consistently stands as an emblem of 'Englishness', of a British tradition that must be secured and maintained.

Such novels articulate an anxiety about the possibility of sustaining the traditions embodied in the country house, which was widely perceived to be threatened by the onslaughts of the war and of taxation, bureaucracy and death duties imposed by an unsympathetic postwar Labour government. This is a position articulated by Osbert Lancaster in an impassioned state-ment written as late as 1959:

> the architecture of the past was steadily reduced by the activities first of the Luftwaffe and then of the Church Commissioners, the Ministry of Transport and other bureaucratic juggernauts ... At the same time a worthy eagerness, not perhaps in every case entirely unconnected with economic developments, inspired an ever increasing number of stately homeowners to share, on certain days, their treasures with the public at large.[4]

Lancaster's expressed fear of the invasion of the 'day trippers', bewailed by Waugh too, is embodied in the title of Helen Ashton's 1956 novel, *The Half-Crown House*,[5] which articulates many of the themes and concerns that recur throughout these novels: the survival of an upper-class ethos and the main-tenance of the family country house . The phrase 'half-crown house' (which was popularized in magazine and newspaper articles concerned with the demise of the country house) refers to the fee charged by aristocratic families who were obliged to open their houses to the general public for payment, and whose estates could no longer be sustained solely as places of private privilege. In fact, the half-crown entry fee charged for opening up the country house to the general public was one of the terms of government subsidy for the repair and maintenance of stately homes, but that subsidy is a notable absence in this text, as it is in the majority of these novels. State support is not referred to except in terms of a set of bureaucratic restrictions and demands upon an already impoverished upper class. Instead, the narrative offers an embattled aristocratic family engaged in an entirely private struggle to maintain the standards and tradition of their inheritance.

Although the 1945 Labour Party election manifesto did apparently represent a real threat to that privilege in its declaration that 'Homes for the People must come before mansions',[6] it was not (as Waugh recognized) a threat that was ultimately to represent any real challenge to the 'owners of great houses'. This was a phrase from the Gowers Report, published in 1950, but commissioned in 1948, to investigate the fate of the British country house. The report recognized the notion of 'stewardship' of the national heritage by the upper classes and acknowledged, in language very close to that expressed by the heroes and heroines of romance fictions, that:

> the owner of a great house who lives in it today and admits the public to see it has a burdensome, anxious and in some respects uncomfortable way of living, which few would choose except under the influence of a sense of duty.[7]

This sense of the 'duty' of stewardship recurs in romance narratives centred around a 'great house'. The desire to keep the house in the family is expressed not as a wish to hold on to the privileges of inherited wealth, but more as a service to the nation, an obligation which only those born and raised to it can properly undertake. As one heroine remarks, ownership of the house is understood as an inherited and genetic obligation: 'House of the Pines was in our blood. It wasn't so much that it belonged to us. It was more that we belonged to it.'[8]

The ideology of 'stewardship' was made material in the form of tax relief on death duties if these private houses were opened in some form to the public, on condition that they became 'half-crown' houses. The principles of the Gowers Report meant in practice that the families who inhabited such houses were given a substantial subsidy to enable them to continue to live in and maintain them. The Historic Buildings and Ancient Monuments Act of 1953, passed on the basis of the Gowers Report's recommendations, allowed for grants and loans for listed buildings and their acquisition by the nation if the owners really could not finance their upkeep. The Town and Country Planning Act of 1945 had already instituted a policy of preservation; the houses and gardens shown in these fictions to be in jeopardy were in fact protected by sets of orders for the preservation of trees, woodlands and buildings of particular architectural or historic interest. While it may indeed have been true that country estates were hedged round by bureaucracy, as they are depicted in the country house romance, much of this red tape was actually beneficial to the class who inhabited them.

The appointed guardians of the English country house were by no means the embattled and impoverished stewards of heritage, burdened by the duties of maintaining a national asset unaided by the state, that are represented in romance fiction and in much contemporary comment on the problem of the country house. As early as 1939, the 'Country House Scheme' had made provision for the family and heirs of a country house to remain in residence while the National Trust took over responsibility for its maintenance. The death duties which are so consistently invoked as the doom of the English country house in fact allowed, in a series of Finance Acts, for generous exemptions on condition that property, land or treasures were nominally handed over to the state. This could mean allowing the general public access, or turning the house to some form of public use, while the family continued to enjoy most of the benefits of their inheritance. As Harry Hopkins wryly observed in 1964:

> Though the great house, which had once discreetly figured in the background of some family portrait by Gainsborough or Zoffany, might now be an agricultural college, a research headquarters, a school for handicapped children, congeries of flats, or a prison-without-bars, if one made one's way round to the back, one might come upon the lord and lady of the manor very comfortably ensconced in the old coach house or 'converted' stables ... With luck one might even donate one's family seat to the National Trust and go on living there, rent and Schedule A and B tax free. Or one might participate more directly in the new society by joining what the newspapers were calling 'The Stately Homes League', jollily refloating one's fortunes on a flood of half-crowns, motor coach parties and 'set teas'.[9]

The future of the country house had in fact been in economic jeopardy for decades before any possibility of a Labour government or the hordes of 'trippers' that so frightened Waugh, Lancaster and the authors of popular romances. The long-term decline of the country house had come about because it had been an economic anomaly since the Industrial Revolution. Such houses were no longer sustainable by the agricultural estates for which they had been built, and had required forms of subsidy since the late nineteenth century. The Gowers Report in fact takes a very similar position to that of Waugh, in recognizing that the importance of these houses was largely cultural, and lay in their status as evidence of a 'national artistic achievement'. Both Waugh and the Gowers committee recognized that the English country house could no longer rely solely on aristocratic privilege and survive autonomously.

The 'Country House problem', as G. M. Trevelyan termed it in writing of the National Trust,[10] actually focused a much wider range of discourses. In the writings of government, journalism and fiction, the fate of the country house was bound up with discussions about the future of the aristocracy and English heritage in the 'brave new world' of the 1950s. In fiction, the house becomes a metonym for both a national heritage and a particular ideology of 'English' class values, as Robert Hewison recognizes:

> The country house stands for a pre-war society of established values and social relations; its very fabric is the product of a uniquely English artistic tradition and its occupants, in their family relationships, employment of servants, and ownership and rule over the surrounding countryside reflect a secure social order. That the great days of the country house were over added a sealing touch of romantic nostalgia, so that it was admired with passive regret rather than as a positive image of life for the present.[11]

Hewison's examples are all drawn from mainstream literature and are almost entirely male writers; in popular romances, however, such 'romantic nostalgia' is rigorously resisted in favour of a campaigning optimism in which women are seen as the salvation of the country house. The middle-class women writers of romance fiction by no means passively 'regret' the passing of the aristocratic lifestyle, but rather represent a Darwinian struggle for its continuance. In plots which chart a heroine's battle to keep the house, she must fight and adapt to change in order to preserve her inheritance; the 'feminine' is offered as the 'proper' guardian of that heritage.

Romantic fiction is a unique cultural form in that it offers a woman-centred perspective; in the country house romance novel, women are situated at the centre of a perceived national dilemma. Romance fiction by its very nature is concerned with marriage and courtship and, by extension, with inheritance and continuity. The spur of the narrative in these novels is the new structures of property relations in a postwar world, and they all acknowledge in one way or another that the country house and the class who inhabit them as if by right can no longer continue to function in the same way. Although the war may have made it difficult to keep the appropriate staff for the maintenance of the house, and the inherited land may no longer provide the capital to keep up the estate, these narratives offer modes of adaptation which ensure that the house and its traditions can be kept in the 'proper' hands. As one hero, acknowledging his duty of stewardship while faced with the need to turn the gardens of his house into a commercial flower-growing business, puts it:

> In order to hold on to Voecke we have to make it self-supporting ... It isn't only a question of making a decent income. I want to hand on the

place in a better state than I found it. That's what my father did. It's what every Voecke tries to do ... Isn't Voecke worth preserving and handing on to a son?[12]

If male primogeniture remains largely unquestioned, it is the heroine's intervention that allows for a preservation of tradition and offers a feminized solution to the crisis of the English country house. These novels can be read as 'state of the nation' novels, addressed to a female readership, in which the country house, be it farm, stately home, mansion or simply a large house that has remained in one family for generations, stands as a fictional metaphor for tradition and class privilege. It is a woman, in the figure of the heroine, who becomes the means of saving the house (in the sense of both an actual house and a family); it is femininity and romance that are here shown to manage the negotiation of a new historical conjuncture and to reprieve English heritage in the postwar Welfare State. The generic devices of the romance form are redeployed in these novels as a reassurance that the values impacted in the fictional country house can be sustained. The country house romance novels can be seen to address the necessity for the upper classes to adapt to the circumstances of a new agenda, and yet simultaneously demonstrate that they can maintain their class continuity. Their narratives grapple with the question of how the major historical shift of the war and its aftermath can be assimilated into an ideology of tradition and stability.

These narratives do invariably recognize that an irrevocable change in the structure of Britain has happened, but are anxious to represent that transformation as natural and inevitable, and able to be assimilated into an unchanging construction of 'Englishness'. Romance thus becomes a means of naturalizing and mythologizing new sets of economic relations; if the romance novel is inevitably concerned with new alliances, those alliances can be depicted as the consequence of 'natural' impulses and their historical specificity mystified. The romance genre requires that the heroine is confronted with an erotic choice; in the country house romance, her choice of hero is contingent on the acquisition of the means (which may be financial or cultural) to salvage the house which is just as much an object of desire. And if 'falling in love' is represented as an unconscious process, as it invariably is in these texts, then the heroine can be absolved from any agency in making an economically beneficial marriage.[13] The heroine of a romance novel is constructed as less fixed in her class position than a male character, and her potential for class mobility is fully utilized in these narratives as a mythological resolution to the dilemma of who should inherit the house. In the context of the postwar 'Country House problem', that narrative raises, by extension, the question of who it is who should own the nation's heritage.

Romance narratives always situate marriage as a mythical means of ensuring continuity, but in the country house novel a marital alliance also becomes a signifier of adaptation to new circumstances which will preserve the house as both family and building. In these novels, a woman becomes central to the resolution of that crisis, but in order to enable a heroine to become the focal point of an inheritance story that does not challenge male succession, a number of plot devices become necessary. One invariable feature of these narratives is the absence of the patriarch of the family and house, through death or some other circumstance (like Lord Marchmain in *Brideshead Revisited*, there are a number of fathers who have left their familial responsibilities behind and settled abroad). This absent patriarch raises the question of who is appropriate to take over the stewardship of the house and the heritage that it represents. The recurrent narrative device allows for an articulation of the disruption of primogeniture; because there is no 'natural' inheritor, there is an awareness that new configurations are necessary in order for the upper classes to maintain their position in a postwar world.

These novels offer marriage and romance as a reassurance that some form of continuity can be restored, the equilibrium of the country house fictionally articulated through an alliance of breeding and wealth. And the agency of women is central to that restoration. The heroine has to select an appropriate partner, and her choice represents not only romantic aspiration but also a means of acquiring and maintaining the house, her mission to save 'traditions' is a means of allaying any suggestion of debased motive. The source of a potential husband's wealth is central to her choice; the 'appropriate' match and the salvation of the country house are seen to be achieved through an alliance of the tradition of cultural and class heritage with new commercial sources of wealth.

As in all romance narratives, the plot is organized around obstacles in the way of the hero and heroine. The male or female rivals who represent alternative romantic choices and threats to the heroine's 'true' destiny are the standard ingredients of the romance plot. In the context of the country house novel, the romantic rivals may offer wealth or tradition to the hero or heroine, but the rivals are consistently seen to be inappropriately matched to the attributes of the house. These putative marriages represent threats not only to the heroine's potential union with the hero, but also to the house, the family and their traditions. Female rivals are most frequently depicted in these novels as having wealth but lacking the taste and 'proper' sense of heritage required to maintain these values. As one heroine remarks, 'she hasn't an inkling of country life or of how to behave'.[14]

The half-crown house

The heroine of Helen Ashton's 1956 novel *The Half-Crown House* has more than an inkling of both country life and how to behave. Henrietta exemplifies the attributes required of a female curator of heritage. She is the widowed daughter of the house, and has the values and attitudes of her class position; she is gracious to servants and mindful of class and family tradition, she sleeps in 'her old schoolgirl bedroom, with ... the worn carpet, the dented golden-ash furniture, the school photographs, the gymkhana ribbons and medals cherished from childhood' (p. 14).

While Henrietta has a great affection and loyalty to the house and all that it represents, it is constructed in the novel as a relic of the past. The novel begins with a history of the 'Fountain House' from its foundation as an abbey, but then situates it next to an American airbase. It is a household that has lost most of its servants and several male members of the family to two world wars (in fact by 1951, only 1.2 per cent of private households had any domestic servants). The house itself demands enormous sacrifices from the heroine; it is a burden which has become her responsibility. Fountain House is literally eroding, the damage to its fabric an image of the irrevocable harm done to the class and tradition which inhabited it:

> death watch beetles had established themselves in the beams above the Chestnut Staircase, gnawing and ticking quietly at night; woodworm tunnelled the furniture in the attics; dry rot and fungus had a firm hold behind the skirting boards in several rooms on the third floor and behind the minstrel's gallery in the old ballroom. All this quiet eager life fulfilled itself yearly, ignoring the human owners; some day it would inherit the ruined house. (p. 22)

The heroine's struggle to keep the house going is demonstrated as a losing battle, despite her efforts to convert her upper-class skills into money-making enterprises; her cultural capital enables her to set up a small antiques business, her hostessing skills are employed in showing groups of visitors around the house. Henrietta has the traditional attributes of her class, she is stalwart and inventive in a time of crisis. These virtues are shown as having some kind of use value as she doggedly defends her estate, and they go some way in attempting to justify her position of privilege, but even here they are shown to be inadequate to the demands of a new historical conjuncture. Finally, Henrietta resigns herself to the loss of the house, but is unable to conceive of it without the family in residence:

> we shall have to face it, the thing's over and done with. The house has

been a burden on all of us, for years and years; times are changed, it had to go ... In a way, I'd rather see the place destroyed than have it cut up and turned into something it was never meant for. I don't really want anybody but the Hornbeams to live in Fountain Court. (p. 251)

It is significant that the only members of the family left to run the household are ageing women. The heroine, it is implied, is past child-bearing age. The remaining titled family member is the heroine's mother-in-law, who is characterized as an aged, useless and demanding presence. Lady Hornbeam (whose name in itself connotes rigidity and ossification) spends the novel incarcerated in her bedroom, a sinister presence who evokes the madwoman, Bertha Mason, in *Jane Eyre*. As the narrative unfolds it becomes clear that she is also a feckless spendthrift who is responsible for the squandering of the family fortune in keeping up a standard of living and set of values which no longer have any place. It is not the heroine who cannot adapt to new circumstances, but she is shown to be hampered by anachronistic attitudes from other members of the household who are unable to accept their loss of class position. The servants are not the reliable family retainers that they once were, but relics themselves, keeping up appearances that can no longer be sustained. The eighteenth-century dinner-service that the butler lovingly polishes and maintains becomes a metaphor for this process; its beauty and uselessness are an image of the heritage that it stands for, it is a place setting for dinner parties of a scale and lavishness that will never again take place.

While *The Half-Crown House*, like *Brideshead Revisited*, is nostalgic for the values and mores of an aristocratic class and offers an elegiac representation of their lifestyle, its structure and characterizations also raise questions about the viability of such a class in the postwar reconstruction. Ashton's novel is more sophisticated than many others in the genre; it was published by Fontana (the paperback imprint of Collins, which prided itself on being a 'literary' list) and is less formulaic than those produced by Mills & Boon. As with *Brideshead Revisited*, the novel carries with it the recognition that the country house and the class which inhabits it can no longer be sustained in its previous form; there are marked traces of class insecurity and displacement. The romantic resolution that seems to hold out some kind of hope for both heroine and house is ultimately a chimera. Unable to accept the suit of an American millionaire or a parvenu antiques dealer, both of whom offer the capital she needs to sustain the house, the heroine finally marries a member of the family, a cousin who offers the tradition and familiarity that her other suitors lack. While this alliance might suggest a consolidation of class position, the imperfect hero has been crippled in the war (his wound suggests an impotence that has echoes of Mr Rochester in *Jane Eyre*). His amputated arm is an image of castration effected by the war, and the narrative makes it clear that such a marriage will have no progeny. The novel's end does hold out an apparent resolution in which hero and heroine plan to transform the house and its estate into a commercial market garden and so make it financially independent. This dream is shattered when the house and its contents are destroyed by the crash of an American fighter plane from the local airbase, an image of the irrevocable impact of the war on Britain's world status (the novel was published in the year of the Suez Canal invasion). The dinner-service that had been lovingly maintained by this fictional English family for centuries is finally shattered, the values that it stands for literally broken into pieces.

As a 'middle-brow' romance, *The Half-Crown House* admits more contradictions than many other novels in this genre, but finally it cannot allow for an optimistic resolution of the crisis of the country house. More popular romance fictions do however tend to maintain that a romantic resolution to the class and historical tensions of the time is possible, and they employ various strategies to argue for and represent the continuity of the aristocratic lifestyle. These strategies can be divided into several variations, which feature three identifiable types of heroine; they act as narrative devices which serve to indicate that there has been a disruption in the 'natural' order of succession and the inheritance of the country house.

The dispossessed daughter

The Half-Crown House shares a structure with one identifiable popular romantic plot centred around a country house: a narrative in which the aristocratic daughter of the house is forced by circumstance into acknowledging the economic constraints of postwar Britain. This plot offers a version of the Cinderella story, in which a daughter inherits the house (itself suggesting a break in a 'natural' order of male inheritance), but no longer has sufficient capital to sustain it; the heroine must therefore make an economically beneficial marriage in order to restore her 'true' social and economic status. The first-person narrator of Jan Tempest's 1946 novel *House of the Pines* is typical of this pattern. She has lost her house, inheritance and fiancé because of her father's irresponsibility. Now dead, he was an abstracted academic who, enclosed in his study, had failed to recognize the depletion of the 'nice little fortune' inherited from his grandfather (p. 12). His daughter has grudgingly taken up the position of secretary to an interior decorator; once again, her upper-class attribute of taste proves to have some commercial value. The house is rented to the erstwhile fiancé who, having deserted the heroine for the 'only child and heiress of an international steel magnate', has acquired the wealth to keep up the house. The hero and his new bride lack the cultural capital and taste of the class that once inhabited it, and in his plans for redecoration and modernization the House of the Pines is threatened with the taint of new money. Nature itself is, however, invoked to remove the interlopers, who have no 'natural' place in the House of the Pines; the house is personified and makes its dislike felt, driving the *nouveau riche* wife to the edge of a nervous breakdown; in a dramatic conclusion, the faithless fiancé is swept out to sea. The 'firm sands' (p. 8) on which the house had stood at the novel's opening have been eroded, and can only be shored up by the commercial wealth of an American paint manufacturer; his marriage to the heroine's younger sister represents an alliance of cultural and commercial capital that can maintain the house in the manner to which it has been accustomed. It is his two children by the younger daughter of the house who, through a series of narrative accidents (evoking the inheritance plot of *Howard's End*), will ultimately become the rightful inheritors of the House of the Pines, the line of inheritance sustained through their mother.

Vera May's 1956 novel *A Path There Is*[15] also typifies the narrative of lost inheritance, and its title suggests that there can be a way forward for the disinherited upper class. Diana is left penniless by the death of her father and has been displaced from the family home, Willow Chase, into a small house on the estate. Diana attempts to maintain her class position by keeping her horses. As the heroine of *The Half-Crown House* turned her cultural capital to profit with an antiques business, Diana similarly employs her upper-class skills to make a living, by founding a riding school. This suggests that the skills and knowledge of a privileged class can have a function in a newly democratic culture. However, this bourgeois ethic is shown to be insufficient; the only real means of maintaining the house and the standards of an upper-class lifestyle is through the injection of new capital. This can no longer be exclusively derived from inherited wealth, and is shown to be accessible through marriage. As a proud and beautiful member of the upper classes, Diana has several suitors, each of whom offers different kinds of capital investment. One rival for her affections is the son from the neighbouring farm, who seems to be a suitable partner in that he too is landed gentry and, as a childhood friend, in a similar class position. However, like Diana's father, he has not modernized his farming methods, and it is clearly signalled that it is because of this inability to adapt to new historical circumstances that such an alliance can hold no future. A marriage of old estates cannot survive without a new injection of commercial enterprise and capital.

The most appropriate alliance, as both narrator and reader can identify, although the heroine takes some time to recognize the 'true' hero, is the man who has already taken possession of the house. He is the son of one of Diana's father's friends, who has inherited cultural capital if not wealth and, unlike Diana, is in a position of relative economic strength as a newly profession-alized gentleman farmer. He also recognizes, as Diana and her father had failed to do, that modernized farming methods are essential if the estate is to survive.

Diana herself is set in opposition to a female rival for the affections of both men, Evadne, the daughter of a self-made millionaire. Evadne is sternly characterized as an 'unworthy' inheritor of the culture and heritage that are embodied in Willow Chase. She lacks Diana's spirit, 'her character and breeding', and represents unacculturated new wealth. Nonetheless, Evadne represents a significant threat because she has access to the wealth necessary to the survival of the house. Fortunately for Diana, Evadne's father loses all his money in a stock-market crash, firmly indicating that 'new' money is an unreliable option. Moreover, a marriage between Evadne and the hero would represent an alliance of newly acquired wealth with the professional classes, and this is not, within the bounds of these texts, a possible com-promise; one part of the alliance must be identified as a bearer of tradition. In a final scene of reconciliation, the heroine employs the skills of her class and demonstrates her 'innate' knowledge of the landscape by rescuing the hero from a riding accident. As in *The Half-Crown House*, the hero is wounded and becomes dependent on Diana's ministrations and rural expertise. The middle-class professional cannot maintain the standards of an upper-class lifestyle without the aid of the 'natural' abilities of the class above him, and the heroine cannot re-enter her inheritance, the house, without the stability of earned income.

The outsider

The inverse of the dispossessed daughter narrative can be seen in those novels which are organized around a female protagonist who is not born to inherited wealth but becomes the inheritor of the house. The heroine of these narratives is geographically and socially an outsider; she lacks the class training to be a chatelaine, but 'proves' herself, becomes a 'naturalized' and spiritual daughter of the house, and eventually comes to inherit it through marriage. Such narratives have their generic origins in such novels of female virtue rewarded as Richardson's *Pamela*, *Jane Eyre* again, and Daphne du Maurier's *Rebecca*, but in the postwar period the heroine is no longer an impoverished waif waiting for wealth and social status to be conferred upon her by the hero, but a competent professional woman. There is invariably a great emphasis upon her professional capabilities, and it is firmly indicated that the aristocratic family she arrives to serve is in need of precisely these skills and qualities. This heroine represents a reversal of the narrative of the impoverished aristocratic heroine who has to turn the skills of her class to professional ends. Here, the heroine's middle-class pragmatism and competence bring order to a disrupted upper-class household. This is literally the case in Denise Robins's 1955 novel *The Unshaken Loyalty*,[16] in which the middle-class housekeeper heroine, 'a first-class cook with a diploma in domestic science' (p. 7), is shown as necessary to the smooth running of a household threatened by a feckless younger son. It is her good sense and professionalism that expose his potential for destruction and earn her a marriage to the displaced eldest son. The heroine can slide from the position of paid servant to become the chatelaine of the house with no apparent difficulty, in a neatly effected ideological alliance of bourgeois pragmatism and aristocratic privilege. This slippage also allows for a convenient evasion of the heroine's status as a working woman; as the lady of the house, she can become an ideal housekeeper whose loyalty and function extends beyond the domestic. As the chatelaine of a great house, her trained competence in housekeeping skills is shown to benefit the local community and, by implication, to be of importance to the nation as a whole.

The Girl from Van Leyden's (1959)[17] has another heroine whose professional skill and judgement expose the machinations of an aristocratic and decadent younger son. Prunella's class origins are in fact in trade; she is the daughter of a firm of antiquarian booksellers and is employed by the hero to restore the library in his mansion. Although she may come from a background in commerce, the nature of her family business is in valuing, both economically and culturally, the heirlooms of the upper class. Moreover, she is elegant, has 'naturally' good taste and a first-class degree in English from Cambridge. Although Prunella may not be to the manor born, she is shown to have acquired the necessary attributes of upper-class manners and so has become a fit partner for the eldest son and inheritor of the house and its contents. She has a proper recognition of aristocratic privilege, demonstrated in her ability to value and to appreciate the contents of the library. As she reflects, 'Times change, democracy strides on, but there are certain things that are still England ... Prunella's sense of the past was strongly developed and she knew that without roots real growth was impossible' (p. 64).

As a member of the new meritocracy, and with her understanding of the 'roots' of tradition, Prunella is in a position to reaffirm the status of her upper-class hero and narratively achieves a renewal of the family's class identity in her uncovering of the 'bad seed' younger brother. Marilyn, the heroine of the 1954 novel *Enchanted Valley*[18] is still more socially mobile than

Prunella; she is an orphan whose class origins are left deliberately vague. The novel opens with the heroine at a point of transition, in search of employment after acting as companion to a great-aunt, an occupation that has taught her the etiquette and manners appropriate to upward mobility. Her first reaction to the house marks her as its spiritual daughter; it has an erotic charge that precedes (and anticipates) any suggestion of romantic involvement with its owner:

> It was like being hurled abruptly into a new and alien world ... she felt as though she had stumbled by chance on a forgotten, enchanted valley. The sheer beauty of it seemed to reach out and enfold her. (p. 62)

Such moments, in which the heroine falls in love with the house and landscape, are recurrent in these narratives of the outsider who is eventually to become a part of the house and family; they signify her worthiness and appreciation of their heritage. There is a faint hint of postwar democracy in Marilyn's initial suggestion that there might be something unjust in such beauty remaining in the private hands of one family: '"It's incredibly beautiful – and it all belongs to you?" she said, almost accusingly. "It doesn't seem fair"' (p. 97). But this potential challenge to class privilege is rapidly dispatched, and Marilyn is reconciled as she becomes a member of the family. The house and estate are shown to be sharing their treasures; in the transition from private estate to commercial market garden, its flowers are made publicly available. The orphaned heroine is herself finally embraced by both the enchanted valley and its owner, who bears the same name as the house.

The romantic and ideological consummation of all these romances is the acquisition of both hero and house. The resolution of the 'outsider' narrative offers an alliance between a masculine cultural inheritance and the dynamism of a feminine middle-class work ethic. Upper-class heritage is seen to be saved by these heroines from potential decadence and archaism by virtue of their proven qualities of professionalism, competence and work, tempered with a proper respect for tradition.

The unexpected inheritrix

A variant of those narratives which construct women from the upper or middle classes as the saviours and continuance of the stately home and, by extension, upper-class tradition and national heritage, is the unexpected inheritrix. These novels combine elements of both the dispossessed daughter and the outsider narratives, and offer a still-neater resolution to the dilemma of class dislocations: the heroine is always a working woman who reclaims or discovers her blood connection to a world of inherited wealth. These novels offer a narrative inversion of a more usual romance structure, in that they begin rather than end with an inheritance. However, the plot is again focused around the question of how that inheritance and the heritage that it represents can be properly managed.

The title of the 1958 novel *Model Girl's Farm*[19] encapsulates the problem of reconciling a democratic working heroine with a family legacy, in its suggestion of a misalliance between the heroine's profession and her landed inheritance. The plot, however, demonstrates that she, like her sister heroines, the outsiders, is able to prove her suitability for the position of lady of the house. Sandra, a leading fashion model from London, has to lure the affections of the hero away from a country lady, Cynthia, who initially appears to be the more suitable class match, their very names signifiers of class difference. Sandra's worthiness and appreciation of her inheritance and the countryside are, however, finally validated when she assists in rescuing a wounded animal. Duly 'blooded', and so demonstrating her 'natural' allegiance to the land, she achieves the respect of the hero.

The title of the 1955 novel *Dear Intruder*[20] again invokes a threat to the traditions of the country house. The heroine is a working woman employed in an architect's office who inherits a large house in Ireland from an uncle and feels, like the dispossessed heroine, a strong sense of duty, an 'unwritten obligation' to the house and family. Her sense of responsibility is such that rather than follow her initial inclination to sell the estate, she turns it into a nursery and cements her loyalty to the land by marrying a local naturalist. The future of the house assured, the class intruder of the title can finally be welcomed with affection.

The unexpected inheritrix is a heroine who offers reassurance that although she may not initially demonstrate the skills and attributes of her class, she can come to learn them. She is a narrative device which allows for the assimilation of 'modern' principles into an enclosed world of privilege and tradition while ensuring, through her blood connections (however remote these may be), that the principle of inherited wealth is not disrupted.

The heroines of all these romances, whatever their class origins, offer an image of women as the saviours and guardians of the English country house and the hereditary principles that it embodies. This can be achieved, if she herself has the attributes of the upper class, through the Darwinian selection of an appropriate mate who will ensure the maintenance of the estate. If she initially appears to lack the appropriate class position, she is ultimately shown to be an asset to the family and the house, in that she is able to curb the worst excesses of a potentially decadent upper class. In either case, the house and family are 'adapted', often expressed in terms of the 'modernization' of the estate, to the demands of the postwar world.

The country house romance is a genre that persists throughout the 1950s and focuses a wide range of discourses around national identity, working women and a contemporary cultural hegemony. As a popular genre, the resolutions offered in these narratives can appear as impossibly idealized and naïve. Nonetheless, they represent a coming to terms with a real postwar transition, and if the romantic resolution is put to one side, they offer sharp insights into the ideological contradictions of class relations in the period. The economic transition from landed gentry to commercial enterprise is seen in these novels to be ameliorated by the 'civilizing' influence of femininity. Whatever class she may initially come from, these narratives depict heroines who prove themselves to be the naturalized and worthy inheritors of the English 'great house'. While acknowledging that an irrevocable historical shift has occurred, these novels deny any state intervention or support. Instead, they wistfully offer up romance and marriage as a means of holding on to traditional class values and validating them. It is acknowledged that in the context of a new Britain such values have to be adapted and modified, but these popular romances demonstrate the tenacity of an ideology of class privilege and tradition, and go some way in accounting for its persistence.

Notes

1. Evelyn Waugh, Preface to *Brideshead Revisited* (London: Penguin, 1988; first published in 1945), p. 8.
2. Ibid., p. 9.
3. Barbara Freeman, *Open to View: English Country Houses You Can Visit and How to Find Them* (London: Ernest Benn Limited, 1952), p. 5.
4. Osbert Lancaster, Introduction to *Here of All Places, The Pocket Lamp of Architecture* (London: John Murray, 1959), p. xiii.
5. Helen Ashton, *The Half-Crown House* (London: Fontana, 1956).
6. *Let Us Face the Future*, Labour Party election manifesto 1945, p. 7.
7. Gowers Report, 1950, quoted in Roy Strong, Marcus Binney and John Harris, eds, *The Destruction of the Country House* (London: Thames and Hudson, 1974), p. 187.
8. Jan Tempest, *House of the Pines* (London: Mills & Boon, 1946), p. 40.
9. Harry Hopkins, *The New Look. A Social History of the Forties and Fifties in Britain* (London: Secker and Warburg, 1963), p. 182.
10. G. M. Trevelyan, Introduction to *The National Trust: A Record of Fifty Years Achievement*, ed., James Lees-Milne (London: Batsford, 1943), p. 4.

11. Robert Hewison, *In Anger. Culture in the Cold War 1945–1960* (London: Methuen, 1988; first published in 1981), p. 75.

12. Tempest, *House of the Pines*, p. 97.

13. See Tania Modleski, *Loving with a Vengeance: Mass-produced Fantasies for Women* (London: Methuen, 1984), chapter 2, for a fuller account of this argument.

14. Tempest, *House of the Pines*, p. 21.

15. Vera May, *A Path There Is* (London: Mills & Boon, 1956).

16. Denise Robins, *The Unshaken Loyalty* (London: Arrow Books, 1955).

17. Hermina Black, *The Girl from Van Leyden's* (London: Romance Book Club, 1959).

18. Jan Tempest, *Enchanted Valley* (London: Mills & Boon, 1954).

19. Fay Chandos, *Model Girl's Farm* (London: Mills & Boon, 1958).

20. Jane Arbor, *Dear Intruder* (London: Mills & Boon, 1955).

5. 'A generation of inheritors': the career girl novel

What are you going to do, my girl
Now that the time is near
When away on wings
Flutter childish things
And you have to choose a career.

(Noel Streatfeild, *The Years of Grace*, 1950)

In June 1953 a short notice in the *Times Literary Supplement* announced the launch of 'a series of entertaining, well-written novels for older girls, with much useful and authentic information, by authors who have made a special study of life and conditions in a particular career'. The series was the Bodley Head Career Books for Girls, a genre that was 'very new indeed'.[1] The range of professions promoted in the early sets of titles indicated the optimistic sense of vocational prospects ahead for the 'older girl' in postwar Britain: in 1953, *Janet Carr, Journalist*; *Jane Grey, Fashion Student* and *Air Hostess Ann*; in 1954, *Jane: Young Author*; *Jane Goes Farming*; *Pam Stevens, Secretary*. By the end of the decade, the series – and the choice of careers – had expanded substantially to include professions as diverse as medicine, library assistant, advertising, television work, policewoman and teacher. An even stronger sense of opportunity was expressed in a rival series issued by Chatto and Windus in 1954 under the aegis of 'Mary Dunn Career Novels'. By 1960 the young female reader of these books was encouraged to think of a choice of career as: nurse, social worker, musician, teacher, cook, fashion buyer, secretary, broadcaster, gardener, continuity girl, antiques buyer, electrical engineer and even racing driver. These series of novels for young female readers are emblematic of an ideological investment that postwar British society placed in the idea of the trained, successful woman worker. As well as constructing a 'practical future' for their readers,[2] the novels also built upon an expectation that the contemporary ideal of womanhood now incorporated a professional career. The standard heroine of a career novel is ready to leave home to embark on professional training.

As the *Times Literary Supplement* noted, the genre was targeted primarily at the 'older girl' on the threshold of choosing a career (many novels begin with the heroine taking her exams at 16 or 18) and about to participate in what the contemporary feminist Viola Klein called a 'social revolution'.[3] The burgeoning series of career novels went hand-in-hand with the growing professionalization of careers advisory work, most notably in the form of the Youth Employment Service. While such bodies may have helped to normalize the idea of the career girl, there were other organizations, such as the Women's Employment Federation, which saw no room for complacency and maintained a campaigning spirit for the ongoing conquest of the professions. In one of the Women's Employment Federation's pamphlets providing lists of 'openings and training for girls and women' (which also carried a full-page advert for the Mary Dunn career novel series), there is a striking example of the persistence of a powerfully fused rhetoric of suffragette history, wartime 'mobilization' and the bourgeois ethic of national service:

> The early pioneers of the women's movement fought against ignorance, prejudice and custom to obtain for girls the right to education, and the opportunity to use their gifts in the service of mankind. You belong to a generation of inheritors. Don't let your inheritance be stolen from you by sloth, indifference or the pursuit of false values.[4]

As well as reminding 'older girls' of their obligation to history, these elevated reference points lift the issue of work from merely technical or material concerns. The sense of mission or 'calling' also gives a weighty social underpinning to a literary genre that might otherwise be discarded as very minor. If the heroines of career novels are unaware of their full inheritance, they are nearly always aware of their social obligation – careers are rarely seen in purely individualist terms. But crucially, a career is also a source of new pleasures and opportunities for self-development, and this dimension of the narratives provides what Freud has called the 'aesthetic forepleasure' for new tensions and anxieties.[5]

I want to be . . .

Career novels were not the only popular postwar literary genre which extolled the virtues of a working life for the young female reader. Girls' comics and annuals throughout the 1950s included stories, articles and even strip cartoons about choosing a career. A striking example of this popular endorsement of careers for girls is an article called 'Science as a Career for Girls' which appeared in the *Daily Mail Annual for Girls* in 1957:

> In the 1914–18 war there was a poster addressed to young men which said: 'Your Country Needs You!' Now we are saying this more urgently than ever to girls; we need you to do all the things you do already, and we desperately need you also, thousands and thousands of you, to take up test-tubes and spanners and form a great new army of women scientists and engineers! (p. 100)

No longer capitalism's reserve army of labour, girls are now seen as the new model army of technological revolution.

The popular *Girl* magazine published a weekly 'strip' of career stories, later collected in the 1957 *I Want To Be ... A Girl Book of Careers*.[6] As the Introduction explains, the weekly strip cartoon had proved so popular that a decision had been made to gather all the stories in a more permanent form. The language of the Introduction, written by two careers experts with strings of qualifications after their names, clearly articulates a sense of vocation and new citizenship for women in postwar Britain:

> The aim of many girls, when they leave school, is to take up work which will be 'useful' in one way or another when they get married. This is a good thing to do, but sometimes it leads to a great many possible careers being overlooked. (p. 8)

Girl clearly saw itself as a regular forum for advice on these matters, as the male editor of the annual encouraged readers to 'write to me at *Girl*' for more information (p. 5). Clearly, the magazine expected a good deal of interest to be generated by the stories. The 'strips' followed the fortunes of young heroines seeking a wide variety of careers, and negotiating the various stages of attending interviews, exploring training opportunities and assessing necessary qualifications. The choice of careers is not limited to traditionally 'feminine' occupations such as beautician, secretary, nurse and fashion model; there is also promotion of the then conventionally 'masculine' occupations: doctor, dentist, banker, radiographer, chemist and journalist. Even conventional 'girls' careers' are invigorated with a new ethic of ambition and achievement. For example:

> The secretary's career must not be regarded as a last resort for girls who

cannot decide what to do. It may lead to a career in business, journalism and many other professions. Many successful business women started as secretaries, and from there seized all opportunities for promotion. (p. 10)

The narrative format of the stories focuses attention almost exclusively on the acquisition of a career, while romantic matters are pushed to the periphery. In 'I want to be a Fashion Artist' the final frame shows a young man inviting the heroine on a date, while she exclaims 'I'm sorry, Simon, I'm off to Paris in the morning' (p. 51). For Richard Hoggart, the comic strip was representative of modern mass culture's debasement of authentic British youth culture:

> The 'strips' spread like a rash, take over a page of their own and still crop up here, there and elsewhere. There has to be some verbal guidance to the action, but descriptive comment is kept to a minimum; the aim is to ensure that all necessary background information is contained in the dialogue which bubbles out of the characters' mouths.[7]

In fact, what 'bubbles' out of the mouths of career heroines is the effervescent spirit of a new deal for women in a newly constructed idea of Britain.

The work of the popular children's writer Noel Streatfeild (who is still remembered fondly by many women today) shows the new mood of optimism very clearly. In novels such as *White Boots* (1951), Streatfeild presented heroines engaged in exciting and glamorous pursuits: ballet, acting, journalism, show-jumping and ice-skating. But Streatfeild's writing was not confined to novels. She also edited books directly concerned with redefining the discourse of contemporary femininity: *The Years of Grace* (1950) and *Growing up Gracefully* (1955).[8] These are seemingly rather old-fashioned books of etiquette and advice on growing up for the young girl, but of the five sections of *The Years of Grace*, the most substantial is 'Careers', warranting more pages than 'You', 'Your Home', 'Leisure' or 'Sport'. Potential careers included musicianship, film-making, teaching, the Civil Service, retailing, nursing and farming. *Growing up Gracefully* has a chapter called 'Manners at Work' which clearly assumes that the reader will be working or about to work. The chapter ends with a ringing endorsement of female ambition: 'Remember you won't always be at the bottom. We hope the day will come when you are the employer' (p. 104).

Streatfeild is perhaps best remembered for her story about ballet, *Ballet Shoes* (1936). In the 1950s, Streatfeild continued to champion ballet as both a profession and a pleasurable hobby for young women. In volumes such as

Noel Streatfeild's Ballet Annual she reinforced the popular appeal of a glamorous heroine who is also a working woman. The ballerina is probably the most frequently evoked heroine in 1950s' popular fiction for girls, as evinced in Lorna Hill's novel *Veronica at the Wells* (1951), or in the cartoon strip 'Belle of the Ballet' in *Girl* magazine. The appeal of the ballerina no doubt had much to do with her ability to reconcile the imagery of old and new femininities: while representing grace and beauty, her training requires tremendous physical discipline, professional dedication and artistic ability. In Streatfeild's 1951 novel *White Boots*, the focus is on ice-skating, a form of ballet on ice which requires similar talents and sacrifices. At the end of the novel, the two heroines Lalla and Harriet are poised to turn their sporting talents into an adult vocation, and 'grow up gracefully'.

The Church of England also saw an opportunity to turn an evangelical rhetoric addressed to young women to its own ends. Publishers of Sunday School Reward Books (whose popularity is manifested in the numbers that can still be found on the shelves of secondhand bookshops) modernized their appeal by embracing the career novel format. The 'Gateway' series, for example, issued by Lutterworth Press, included Dorothy Marsh's *Pat's New Life* (1954), in which the heroine manages to convert her 'rougher' colleagues in a department store to the Christian faith. In Patricia Baldwin's *Rosemary Takes to Teaching* (1960), published by Victory Press, the heroine draws on her religion to find the inner strength needed to overcome the teething problems of her new job. While these books were able to offer a spiritual resolution to the heroines' difficulties, they also extended the cultural range of the image of the career girl, reinforced its modernity, and gave added authority to its function as a site for the dramatization of feminine identities.

Career novels

The genesis of the career novel can be traced to the popular American nursing stories featuring Cherry Ames and Sue Barton. Though written originally in the 1930s with an American setting, these novels were reprinted frequently in wartime and postwar Britain. While they suggested that the world of work offers infinite opportunities to a young woman for personal growth, adventure and romance (each novel of both series involves a move into a different type of nursing), the new British career novel narrowed the narrative focus onto the period of professional training. Given that this is also the period of adolescence, the career novel can also be seen as a form of *Bildungsroman*, in which that genre's major structural features – conflict within the family, a series of personal crises for the hero or heroine, the quest for a mature identity – are modulated into phases within the process of career choice and training. Initiation into work, usually a very minor phase in the conventional *Bildungsroman*, becomes the vehicle for personal development.

This is seen at its sharpest in the treatment of romance. The heroine's erotic choices, normally the closure of her story, arise from the workplace and are articulated in terms of her career options and their relation to definitions of femininity. The hero usually enters at a late stage in the narrative, and the proposal of marriage is often on the final page. However, any expectation by either the hero or the reader that the heroine will give up her career for marriage is quickly quashed. The heroine either postpones any romantic decision until she is fully trained (making the hero wait is a striking expression of a new empowerment) or she marries a colleague to form a working 'partnership' (some of these novels contain an emergent New Man who actively encourages the heroine to continue her career). The latter solution conveniently collapses the dual role's 'antithesis' between work and home and between private and public spheres. The evangelical feminist thrust of the genre is clear – romance must not divert the heroine from her quest for a successful career nor hinder her achievement of a meritocratic position in society. This appeal of the narratives is underpinned by the use of unsentimental realism and the factual accuracy of the details of training (as the dust-jackets make clear, the authors were often qualified in the career represented). While the novels inhabit a new generic territory as thinly veiled training manuals, their fictional dimension provides the narrative resources to negotiate and resolve new tensions and contradictions within discourses of contemporary femininity.

While Viola Klein and Alva Myrdal stated in *Women's Two Roles* (1956) that the professionalization of women's work had only created a 'revised version' of the traditional distinction between 'feminine' and 'masculine' occupations (the latter still often closed to women), the evidence of career novels is that both spheres of work are firmly within women's grasp and that femininity can be 'revised' accordingly. For example, Jean Llewellyn Owens's *Margaret Becomes a Doctor* (1958) deals with one of the most traditionally 'masculine' professions: medicine.[9] The heroine has the advantage of support from her country doctor father, but she must overcome the hostility of her childhood sweetheart and 'intended':

'Don't believe in women doctors,' commented George grumpily.
'You Victorian!' Margaret jibed, 'I suppose you think women shouldn't have the vote, either?'

In the end they scrapped quite seriously, Margaret being shocked to find that George honestly believed a woman's place was in the home.

'A woman's job is to be decorative, and not mix herself up with the sordid side of life,' was his final pronouncement. (p. 15)

George personifies, in Caroline Haslett's words, those 'last remaining barriers of Victorian prejudice' to the idea of working women.[10] The novel's self-conscious engagement with 'Victorian values' shows its determination to enlighten the young female reader about her feminist heritage. There is a recurrence of an older vocabulary of woman's experience. At the point where Margaret decides to break with George (thus giving her the 'final pronouncement' about their relationship), she determines to become an 'old maid' rather than abandon her training for a life as a 'chatelaine' (p. 98). In fact she meets Donald, a senior registrar, and agrees to marry him on the basis that she will return to a career in Public Health after having children. Her destiny is to conform to an emergent professional life cycle identified by contemporary sociologists: training, work, childrearing, and a return to part-time or full-time work.[11] Determined 'never to become a career woman to such an extent that she became unfeminine' (p. 68), Margaret has therefore negotiated the problem of motherhood, but a more severe test of her dissent from traditional notions of femininity comes from her family. When her father falls ill, her mother insists that Margaret return home to help nurse him. The obligation to help a loved one and the subsequent guilt of refusing the calling of feminine 'duty' poses a major dilemma. Margaret's solution is to reconfigure the idea of duty, to socialize it by applying to it the ideology of career training:

> Where did her duty lie, she wondered, as she took the stairs slowly. If at the beginning she had been doubtful on occasions, now, after three years, she was convinced that a doctor's life was the only one for her. It would be an awful waste of money and training to give it all up now. Some day, provided she qualified, she would be able to help hundreds of people. If she stayed at home, she would help only two, and when they no longer needed her, she would have no career to follow. (p. 88)

As well as clarifying that medicine is 'part of me' (p. 188), Margaret evokes the language of national service (helping hundreds) and public investment – to abandon her career would be economically wasteful. The language of social obligation is necessary, as Margaret, like so many adolescent heroines before her (notably Jane Eyre), faces the wounding charge of selfishness and ingratitude. Having found the discursive resources to defend herself, the plot vindicates her completely, as she saves her father's life when he has a heart attack.

Examples of two traditional (but less ancient) 'feminine' and 'caring' occupations are librarianship and teaching. In *A Library Life for Deborah* (1957), also by Jean Llewellyn Owens,[12] we see the 'plucky' heroine (p. 16) rejecting a job as a secretary (generally the most despised female occupation in these novels) and progressing through the professionalism of librarianship to a tentative (and more glamorous) career as a writer. Throughout all the details about in-service training and career options there is also a strong language of desire. As she becomes more financially independent, Deborah secures control over her sexual destiny. At the end of the novel she contemplates the choice between her two lovers:

> Her own mouth curved into a smile. No girl with an interesting career found it easy to give up her independence. But she was beginning to think it might be rather nice to have someone to lean on, someone to boss one occasionally. (p. 138)

While career novels could never dwell too explicitly on sexuality, given their intended readership, Deborah's triumphalist smile is highly provocative. The excitement of career success is conflated with that of erotic awakening. This moment is even more charged in Owens's *Sue Takes Up Physiotherapy* (1958),[13] where the heroine 'tore open the stout envelope' containing the news of her qualifying and the prospect of 'dozens of attractive posts' (p. 181).

A similar triumphalist crescendo occupies the whole of the final chapter of Louise Cochrane's *Marion Turns Teacher* (1955).[14] The chapter title 'The Great Debate' refers only secondarily to the dilemma of whether Marion should marry. The primary reference is to an annual contest between the debating societies of Marion's all-female and a rival all-male teacher-training colleges. The debating topic, 'Is the Married Woman's Place in the Kitchen, or the Classroom?', is a transparent narrative device providing an occasion for a collective feminist victory. The line of attack of 'the men' is to paint a 'gruesome and highly ridiculous' caricature of the chaos caused by the dual role 'where women rushed off leaving washing-up to husbands, and who corrected exercises in the evenings when their mates wanted to go the pictures' (p. 131). The men's argument is that in the long-run, a career is both disruptive to harmonious family life (the implication is that husbands washing up is both unnatural and effeminate), while in the short-term it is abstinent and dowdy. Both traditional, domesticated femininity, and – more strikingly – an emergent modern femininity (the consumerist, glamorous leisure habits of the proto-teenager) will suffer. Marion's most heroic moment is to clinch victory for her team by cleverly reinterpreting the 'shiny' image of the modern housewife:

> 'Schools are shouting for science teachers to help train a new genera-
> tion, able to understand and contribute vigorously to solving some of
> our problems. Surely women graduates who can teach science are
> wasted when they spend their time scrubbing floors? Besides, clever
> men, like yourselves' – Marion bowed slightly to the opposition and
> caused a titter –'can devise wonderful new and shiny gadgets to ease
> the burdens of housekeeping. Surely trained younger women should
> not be sitting about lazily while all the extra work of our time is done by
> men.' (p. 132)

Marion skilfully steers the value of labour-saving domestic 'gadgets' away from contented motherhood to the career woman's social obligations (the 'work of our time'). To complement her success, her journalist-lover pro-poses marriage in the most respectful terms imaginable, offering to 'sacrifice a bit so his wife can have an interesting life too – a profession if she wants one' (p. 134). Considering that the employment bar against married women teachers had been abolished in the 1944 Education Act, and that there was a national shortage of teachers, the future for the Marions of society looked rosy indeed.[15]

Louise Cochrane's *Anne in Electronics* (1960) is one of the best examples of the career novel's Utopian mapping out of a new social territory for women, in one of the modern 'masculine' professions.[16] Indeed, Anne is constructed explicitly as a pioneer. She is one of a group of female apprentices hired by a northern engineering company called Electra (the reference to the powerful woman of classical legend must be intentional). The company have embarked on a programme of what might now be called positive discrimina-tion or affirmative action. For Anne, the move to Starrington (a new firmament where she can shine?) is like a journey into the wilderness. In an opening that echoes Joe Lampton's arrival at Warley in John Braine's *Room at the Top* (1957), Anne steps off the train into a new world:

> The noise and confusion were baffling compared with the complacent
> middle-class dignity of Linford, where Anne's home was. The view
> from the station was one of an endless vista of terraced houses encrus-
> ted with soot and dirt. (p. 9)

Electra's personnel officer reminds the recruits of their responsibilities in gendered terms:

'The point is that you are being trained for positions of greater importance to the industry as a whole, positions previously predominantly
held by men. You have to prove that you are entitled to hold them, just
as the first women doctors had to prove that they were worthy of that
profession.' (p. 23)

Anne is in the vanguard of a 'generation of inheritors' of the feminist mantle.
The novel explicitly connects a feminist history with the cutting edge of
modernity in its most material form, a new mode of production. Anne is
possibly the nearest female equivalent in these novels to the figure of the
'angry' Arthur Seaton at his lathe in Alan Sillitoe's *Saturday Night and Sunday
Morning* (1958). She may not have his iconic rebelliousness, but her feminist
inheritance invests her with a considerable cultural authority. *Anne in Electronics* is not only a fictional induction into electrical engineering; it also reads
like thinly veiled propaganda for the Women's Engineering Society, founded
by Caroline Haslett in the 1920s. The Society's journal, *The Woman Engineer*,
was a tireless source of practical support for the cause of the woman
engineer. At the end of the Second World War the journal announced that
'the real fight is beginning in earnest' as male engineers reclaimed their jobs:
'Women must still work at the "men's jobs" if there really is to be a better
world.'[17] A year later, as the government's recruitment drive put an optimistic gloss on the situation, the journal even went so far as to tackle the issue
of whether work debased femininity, declaring a woman engineer to be
someone who is 'essentially feminine, but has no worry about the prospect of
having dirty hands and wearing greasy overalls'.[18] At a conference hosted by
the Women's Engineering Society in Coventry in 1957,[19] one speaker
remarked that a woman engineer 'need become neither unfeminine nor
unglamorous' (p. 13), while Iain MacLeod, then Minister of Labour and
National Service, saw women engineers in terms of the needs of the national
economy 'in a fiercely competitive world' (p. 61).

Both the personal and social dimensions of a career are worked over in
Anne in Electronics. As she embarks on her training, Anne quickly becomes
aware that workplace sexism puts her in a seemingly impossible situation.
Male peers condemn her for choosing an 'unfeminine' career, while also
demonizing any 'glamour' in her role as conventional female wiles. 'Female
charms aren't going to get you out of any of the hard work' says one male
colleague, noting her 'seriousness' (p. 35). With the support of company
policy, however, Anne qualifies as an engineer and 'felt rather proud to be
following in the footsteps of the great women pioneers in engineering like
Dame Caroline Haslett' (p. 129). In a direct anticipation of modern feminism's exposure of the sexism in everyday language, the Electra employees are

referred to at one point as 'skilled workpeople' (p. 81). Outside the work-place, Anne receives the blessing of her local vicar for her decision to marry a colleague and continue working: in his eyes, the couple will have 'a mutual professional interest' (p. 137). These are also the terms in which her lover proposes to her, 'to be true to yourself and all those years of training' (p. 134). Work is now a defining feature of self-identity, and the personal has become professional.

Nancy Martin's *Jean behind the Counter* (1960) is a rare example of a career-girl heroine from a working-class family.[20] Like her 'angry' male counterpart Jimmy Porter, however, Jean's social trajectory is away from her social roots. Jean has to overcome the obstacles of social prejudice in addition to patri-archal attitudes. Her entry into the middle-class code of professional training immediately separates her from other 'shop-girls' who have a job but no career – the 'two roles' are less of a problem for other working-class girls in the novel. An early scene in the department store highlights Jean's difference and her resolve:

> 'Think you're going to like it here?' asked Susan, with a lift of her thin eyebrows.
> 'It's what I've always wanted to do,' replied Jean.
> 'Career girl, eh?'
> Susan's tone annoyed Jean, and there was an edge to her voice when she replied:
> 'I don't see why not. What about you?'
> The other girl shrugged her thin shoulders expressively.
> 'It's something to do till I get married.' (p. 10)

The 'edge' to Jean's voice is thematized in the novel. The frictions created by her social aspirations centre on the issue of spoken English, because it is the one demand of her training that will most obviously separate her from her community:

> Until she had come to Stacey's she had never bothered much about how she or anyone else spoke. Now it was different. She knew her own family did not speak well, and although she was just as fond of them as ever, she wanted to be different. Her old slipshod ways must be improved if she were to make any headway. (p. 71)

It is difficult not be reminded here of the contemporary theories of the linguist Basil Bernstein, who claimed that the working class spoke in a 'restricted code', while the middle classes used an 'extended code'.[21] In order to 'extend' her professional and social prospects, Jean must 'speak well'.

There is also a persistence of evangelical language here, as Jean must leave behind her 'old slipshod ways'. Much like Joe Lampton, Jean requires some cultural training in bourgeois disciplines, but while Joe receives his from a middle-class lover, Jean learns the rules from her career training and from a friend's middle-class family, who effectively adopt her. The narrative recognizes very real social tensions, but these are contained by the fact that Jean's aspirations and code of self-improvement are strictly professional and exonerate her from materialism (to capture a husband or acquire wealth). Only when her training is complete does Jean begin a romantic involvement. The end of the novel demonstrates (to the point, almost, of parody) that the career girl can indeed be 'glamorous' and professional. The final page carries an illustration of Jean and her lover at the office ball, but the text reveals that this Cinderella is more excited by the prospect of promotion than she is by the hero. He makes the mistake of assuming that the 'something good' on her mind must be marriage. The disjunction between image and text alerts the reader not to make the same mistake.

Moie Charles's *Eve at the Driving Wheel* (1957),[22] which has the wittiest title of all these novels, eroticizes the heroine's professional skills in a career that is both 'masculine' and glamorous. The driving wheel becomes a central narrative motif which shows, quite literally, the passing of power and control from the masculine to the feminine (the modern usage 'steering wheel' loses the pun). Eve is first 'called' to the profession when her boyfriend (who holds the Victorian view that women are 'decorative') loses control of his car and 'knock[s] himself out on the driving wheel' (p. 8). He becomes the first of a series of emasculated male characters in the novel, and it is difficult not to see a feminist nemesis at work. Eve gets her first whiff of power when she rescuscitates the stunned boyfriend (the kiss of life she gives him is replete with mythic and erotic connotations) and feels the desire to become a driver. Her next boyfriend takes her a step closer to the glamorous world of fast machines; he is a test-pilot who wants 'to feel power under my finger tips' (p. 16). He finds Eve's restatement of that desire – 'I also want the control of power in my finger tips' – a 'lot of nonsense' (p. 17). He should perhaps have chosen his words more carefully, for we are told in one brief sentence that he dies breaking the sound barrier, while Eve goes on to win a Grand Prix. It seems that Eve's ambition for glamorous yet professional power generates a castrating gaze. After securing a job as a chauffeuse, she gives a lift one night to her future husband, an ex-RAF pilot who lost a leg in the war:

> We talked and talked, Pete and I, through that night and suddenly I was conscious that he was watching my hands on the wheel. Months afterwards, he told me that this was the moment he fell in love with me.

I didn't know then that he had been quite a well-known racing driver before he had joined the R.A.F. (p. 86)

Pete is both disempowered by and sexually attracted to Eve's 'hands on the wheel'. Their role reversal is consolidated when the couple establish a motel business in which he stays home to manage the domestic space while Eve supplements their income by competing in rallies. He also learns how to use a false limb, and the point at which he becomes proficient coincides with Eve being offered a major contract with a racing team. But she turns this offer down and establishes her own rallying team with Pete.

While the story is still very much a career novel (containing, for example, six solid pages of a rallying log), the book is most memorable for its imagining of postwar society's primary fetish and icon of masculine prowess, the car. The novel's representation of female control over the car runs against the grain of dominant media images of the sexy 'woman driver', who is usually shown in such a way as to fuel male fantasies of possession and domination. For instance, while she is watching the greatest *tour de force* of Italian rallies, the Mille Miglia, Eve reconfigures the allure of cars from the perspective of a female gaze:

I only saw one woman driver. Naturally I was more than intrigued by women drivers. I'd always pictured them as being tough and leathered. This one certainly wasn't. She was small and elegant, and while she was waiting for her petrol, all she did was to put on lipstick. (p. 63)

The professional woman is glamorized and eroticized with a vengeance. But this is only half the picture. The description continues:

But the one thing that came over from all the drivers was their non-chalance and the way they dismissed everything – the danger, the fatigue, the stamina needed for this long-distance, high-speed driving. It made me realise what skill it needed, skill whittled down to such a precision point that only the worst of bad luck allowed accidents to happen. I was learning.

The glamour may be cosmetic; the skill is not.

This scene can also be compared to a key moment in Braine's *Room at the Top* (published in the same year),[23] where Joe Lampton is 'called' to his ruthless quest for social mobility. The revelation occurs when Joe observes a swanky young man and his girlfriend getting in to a sports car:

I wanted an Aston Martin, I wanted a three-guinea linen shirt, I wanted a girl with a Riviera suntan – these were my rights, I felt, a signed and sealed legacy ... I was going to collect that legacy. It was as clear and compelling as the sense of vocation which doctors and missionaries are supposed to experience, though in my instance, of course, the call ordered me to do good to myself not others. (p. 29)

Braine's scene is a classic example of 'angry' rhetoric. Lampton's drive to inherit middle-class property is powered by rabid individualism, materialism and sexism. The residue of class-consciouness ('my rights') is debased into an anti-heroic parody of the work ethic and self-improvement. While the novel's retrospective first-person narrative makes it clear that Joe has been devitalized by attaining the goal of a leisured lifestyle (he compares his successful self unflatteringly to a 'lacquered' American Cadillac, rather than a thoroughbred English sports car), it is the abrasive, 'angry' voice that has so prominently defined the cultural terrain of the 1950s. In the corresponding scene in *Eve at the Driving Wheel*, there is a neat inversion of 'angry' rhetoric. Eve's ambition is expressed as a wish to belong to a meritocratic profession.

In career novels it is high levels of skill and professional dedication that bring the rewards of glamour and excitement. While it is true to say that these novels largely evade the issue of class, this omission could be a function of their feminist orientation, which sees gender rather than class as the prime source of social inequality and the major obstacle to progress. The novels may not directly challenge existing social structures, but the stories do point to new opportunities for young women within postwar British society.

Notes

1. *TLS*, 26 June 1953, p. v; *TLS*, 26 November 1953, Special Supplement on Children's Literature, p. vi.
2. *TLS*, 28 May 1954, p. x.
3. Alva Myrdal and Viola Klein, *Women's Two Roles. Home and Work* (London: Routledge and Kegan Paul, 1956), p. 183.
4. *Careers. A Memorandum on Openings and Trainings for Girls and Women* (18th edition, Women's Employment Federation, 1958), p. 7.
5. Freud's essay 'Creative Writers and Daydreaming' was first published in 1908.
6. *I Want To Be ... A Girl Book of Careers* (London: Hulton Press, 1957).
7. Richard Hoggart, *The Uses of Literacy* (Harmondsworth: Penguin, 1958; first published in 1957), p. 164.

8.   Noel Streatfeild, *White Boots* (London: Collins, 1951); *The Years of Grace* (London: Evans Brothers, 1950); *Growing Up Gracefully* (London: Arthur Barker, 1955).

9.   Jean Llewellyn Owens, *Margaret Becomes a Doctor* (London: Bodley Head, 1957).

10.   Caroline Haslett, *Problems Have No Sex* (London: Hodder and Stoughton, 1949), p. 82. George's views echo that brand of condescending 'protective' sexism expressed in its purest form in John Ruskin's 'Of Queen's Gardens' (1865), a text that is now central to feminist demonology. See Kate Millett, *Sexual Politics* (London: Virago, 1983; first published in 1971), pp. 89–108.

11.   See Myrdal and Klein, *Women's Two Roles*, chapter 10. Of course the 'new' pattern was in one sense only a professionalized version of the traditional experience of many working-class women.

12.   Jean Llewellyn Owens, *A Library Life for Deborah* (London: Chatto and Windus, 1957).

13.   Jean Llewellyn Owens, *Sue Takes Up Physiotherapy* (London: Bodley Head, 1958).

14.   Louise Cochrane, *Marion Turns Teacher* (London: Chatto and Windus, 1955).

15.   The revelation of Judith Hubback's *Wives Who Went to College* (London: Heinemann, 1957), that many married middle-class women were desperate to 'escape' from an unfulfilling domestic routine, could only boost the aspirational appeal of Marion's example (the study is cited in Elizabeth Wilson, *Only Halfway to Paradise. Women in Postwar Britain 1945–1968* (London: Tavistock Publications, 1980), pp. 55–7). It is possible that career novels helped to transmit to the new generation of 1960s' feminists the expectation that women had a right to a career. The frustrations of women graduates denied any other career except marriage was the theme of Betty Friedan's *The Feminine Mystique* (Harmondsworth: Penguin, 1965; first published in 1963), the book that is usually credited with heralding the emergence of modern feminist consciousness in the West.

16.   Louise Cochrane, *Anne in Electronics* (London: Chatto and Windus, 1960).

17.   *The Woman Engineer*, 6(6), Spring 1946, p. 82.

18.   *The Woman Engineer*, 6(9), Summer 1947, pp. 140–1.

19.   'Careers for Girls in Engineering' (Women's Engineering Society Conference, Coventry, July 1957).

20.   Nancy Martin, *Jean Behind the Counter* (London: Macmillan, 1960).

21.   According to Alan Sinfield, 'Bernstein was upset when critics said the restricted code implied a humiliating uniformity.' See Alan Sinfield, *Literature, Politics and Culture in Postwar Britain* (Oxford: Basil Blackwell, 1989), p. 257.

22.   Moie Charles, *Eve at the Driving Wheel* (London: Chatto and Windus, 1957).

23.   John Braine, *Room at the Top* (Harmondsworth: Penguin, 1969; first published in 1957).

6. Bachelor girls: the glamour of work in the postwar romance

'I blame the war for all that's gone wrong with the women ... Turned a lot of them barmy, in my opinion ... equality of the sexes they call it, don't they? It's the vote that did it. We ought never to have given them the vote.' (Daphne du Maurier, *Kiss Me Again Stranger*, 1953)

The 'Woman Question' was on the agenda for the postwar reconstruction in a range of conflicting ways, at once demanding of 'woman' that she should contribute her new skills and experience to the new social order, while often simultaneously insisting that she should be the custodian of traditional values and ways of life. As Marjorie Tait, author of a study of the education of women 'for citizenship', acidly noted at the time:

We have focused a good deal of attention over this period on women – or rather, on Woman. Much has been said by both men and women about Woman as a person, a wife, a mother, a citizen; her creative abilities or lack of them; her mechanical aptitudes or lack of them; her administrative capacities or ... and so forth. In all this there has been some folly, much prejudice and some wisdom. It has not all, of course, been talk. Women, always encouraged and helped by some men, and usually opposed by more, have experimented in many fields. One way of putting it is to say 'They have tried on new clothes.'[1]

The popular fiction written for women at this time can be understood as offering readers one forum in which to try on the 'new clothes' of different forms of work. Many of the most popular novels centre around a nurse as heroine, but the worlds of work which are offered in romance fiction include an unexpectedly wide range of potential careers for women: artists, circus performers, cartoonists, vets, engineers, doctors, film technicians, farmers, advertising executives and archaeologists are all to be found among the heroines of novels published by Mills & Boon alone in the 1950s. In negotiating the search for an appropriate marriage partner, the heroine also has to reconcile differences in class, education, status and income that are newly structured in the postwar New Jerusalem, and to resolve the conflicting demands made upon the 'New Look' woman of the 1950s. As Alison Light has pointed out, romance fiction offers its readers:

> a world of fancy and faery inspired by an extravagant longing to go beyond what we have and what we know to be the case, to transform our workaday selves through the enhancements of adventure or the giddy metamorphoses of love.[2]

Many of the popular fictions for women written in the 1950s depict the everyday world of work as an adventure in itself, with the heroine a working 'bachelor girl'. The 'fancies' offered in these romance novels give expression to women's desires and aspirations which are not answered anywhere else in that contemporary culture. And when that society is one of postwar reconstruction, explicitly committed to change and the fulfilment of social dreams, the acknowledgement of these aspirations becomes still more important. The war had brought about significant change in patterns of gender and work; there had been a very real increase in the numbers of working women and a profound shift in the range of work available to women, which was to continue throughout the 1950s. If these postwar working 'bachelor girls' are notably absent from contemporary writings by men, and also from popular memory, they are very significant for the popular fiction written by and for women readers.

The pleasure of work

Romance novels, like career novels written in this period, manifest a real sense of new opportunities and doors opening up for the young single woman, the requisite heroine of the bachelor girl romance. As Joseph McAleer has pointed out, the postwar Mills & Boon heroine:

> is wholeheartedly a representation of the contemporary woman, rooted in the time and often struggling with such matters as money, managing a household and holding down a job ... Although the unmarried heroines dream of finding Mr Right and settling down, they do not waste time worrying about it, but are out and about on their own.[3]

The potential that work can offer and the pleasures and excitement to be found in professional achievement are consistently and powerfully evoked in these novels, as in the *The Way is Long* (1950):

> What did she want from life? Was music an end in itself or was she urging towards fame – excitement – adventure? That frightening but oddly exhilarating nervousness before one went on to the platform – the intoxicating relief when the performance ended in a spontaneous outburst of applause! Travelling up and down the country – an American tour maybe . . . Paris – Brussels – Rome! Meeting interesting people – wearing lovely clothes![4]

In its sense of the possibilities that can come with work, this is typical of the opening pages of such novels. Although it might appear to be a particularly glamorous example (the heroine is an aspiring concert pianist), she herself is resolutely unglamorous and repeatedly described as 'down to earth'; she works as a farmer when not playing her piano. Many (although, importantly, not all) of these narratives do imagine a cosmopolitan and artistic lifestyle, but a recurrent characteristic of the heroine is that she is unimpressed by the allure of fame and fortune; her main objective is a satisfaction in her own professional competence.

These narratives repeatedly stress that however apparently desirable the career, it is a form of work like any other; Hettie Grimstead's 1951 novel *The Twisted Road* is set in the film industry, but the narrative is at pains to demonstrate the insecurity of the work and to underplay its glamour: 'it's not so glamorous as people always seem to imagine. You have to put in just as much hard work in a studio as in a factory.'[5]

Despite the constraints and expectations of the romance genre, there is a dominant style of social realism in these texts which deliberately downplays the glamorous elements of a job, and which often employs actual names and a fund of technical detail in order to claim a professional knowledge and familiarity with the field. The majority of these texts do focus on aspirant and creative forms of work (art, music, cinema, theatre), but the Mills & Boon list of the period includes an enormous range of careers and professions for their heroines. And the careers invoked in these novels were not entirely aspirational; Ministry of Labour figures for 1949 show steadily increasing numbers of women applicants for training in every one of the fields covered by these texts.[6]

Woman as citizen

The postwar reconstruction and women's new relation to the world of work brought with it a new language of 'citizenship'. As Elizabeth Wilson has pointed out, there was:

> a real attempt to build consensus, to bring the whole nation within the wide circle of citizenship (with the exception of a residual dross of deviants, who were needed to mark the boundaries). And women were central to this scheme.[7]

The discourse of citizenship, the importance of duty and social responsibility is very strongly present in both public rhetoric and in popular fiction for women and girls. This concept of 'citizenship' and social obligation becomes a central component in a contemporary ideal of British femininity, and consequently in the characterization of the romance heroine. Generically required as she is to be single, alone and on the brink of change, the heroine has, in negotiating the devices of the romance plot, also to prove her fitness to be rewarded by the respect and admiration of the hero. In the postwar context, her required qualities quite explicitly include those of good citizenship.

The 1954 Unesco report on 'The Education of Women for Citizenship' was, significantly, written by a British woman, Marjorie Tait, who explicitly construes 'citizenship' as contingent on the world of work:

> As more and more women go out to work, it becomes essential to think of the workplace as one of the learning-situations in a woman's life and do our best to see that it teaches the right lessons. Teachers, welfare and personnel officers, politicians and ordinary working women are all concerned.[8]

It was not only the professional middle classes cited by Tait who were concerned about the impact of women in the workplace. The discourse of citizenship came to inform all kinds of texts addressed to women, and popular fiction was just as concerned to 'teach the right lessons' as any other form of culture.

One of the features that characterize the heroine of the romance novel is her demonstrated willingness to work; women characters who do not work are invariably disdained, and are often structured into the narrative as the heroine's rival. The beautiful but venomous Viola has 'a hand of delicate softness ... The sort of hand that had never performed a useful task in the whole of its life.'[9] The hero may be temporarily swayed by the attractions offered by such a siren woman of a now outmoded leisured class, but by the time of the narrative's resolution he comes to appreciate the sterling qualities of the working heroine.

Professor Zweig recommended in his study of women and work that the appropriate model for contemporary womanhood was 'The type of woman who, more self-reliant and conscious of her dignity, with more opportunity to employ her talents and abilities, is a true partner in the struggle of existence.'[10] The language here is very similar to that used to describe the feminine type celebrated in the heroines of these novels. The heroine is invariably marked out by her quality of 'self-reliance' and a strong sense of dignity; over the course of the romance narrative she manifests her worthiness as a 'true partner' to the hero. The 1957 novel *Partners are a Problem*[11] demonstrates in its title the centrality of 'partnership' to the conditions of romance. As McAleer explains of the required qualities of a romantic hero of the period, 'Companionate marriage and a sense of security are deemed more essential than a good lover.'[12]

Bachelor girls and career women

The 'bachelor girl' is a central figure in a range of discourses around women and the new citizenship. She is a regular character in popular women's magazines of the period, in advertising and marketing. She is also given her own category in the popular 1956 household manual, *The Book for the Home*. *The Book for the Home* has recommendations for 'Budgeting and Household Accounts' which include twelve specimen budgets, of which ten are based on families, the other two belong to 'single women':

> A career girl would describe the owner of this budget. She is a single woman nearer thirty than twenty, and she has a good job as confidential secretary to the managing director of a medium sized firm. She lives in a two-roomed flat at the top of a converted house, which she furnished with the help of her parents three or four years ago.[13]

The 'career girl' is here constructed as potentially feckless; as the female editor sternly notes, she has overspent her budget on luxuries, but she is given good advice on how to prevent this happening in the future. The other budget for the 'single person' is not given for a man, but for an older woman, the 'career woman' who is an older and wiser version of the 'career girl':

It belongs to a woman in her early forties who has a good job as designer to a clothing manufacturer. Holding down a job of this kind needs a certain degree of elegance which is expressed in a high standard of living ... Our designer lives in a comfortable three-roomed flat which has been her background for many years. When she first took it on, her income was lower, and she shared it with a friend. After the friend's marriage she was in a position to run it for herself ... Her standard of living is higher than is apparent from her record of expenditure. Her firm provides her with all the magazines she needs and likes to read, and with theatre tickets ... The firm pays her expenses to see exhibitions of all kinds and for the yearly visit to Paris considered necessary to her work.[14]

Clearly, there are recognized compensations to life without a husband; however, in line with the 1946 Royal Commission on Equal Pay, the 'career woman' is here assumed to be unmarried and childless; as Elizabeth Wilson has noted:

Work and marriage were still understood as alternatives. The Report assumed in fact that there were two kinds of women. You could either be a wife and mother or a single career woman ...[15]

Nonetheless, the lifestyle of the older single woman is presented in *The Book for the Home* as attractive, almost more enviable in its glamour than the family life which is presented as the alternative. And if the working woman is assumed to be alone in official discourse, this is markedly not the case in romantic fiction of the same period; it is by no means assumed that heroines will leave their careers on marriage.

The economically independent woman was, as *The Book for the Home* demonstrates, a significant component in the postwar consumer culture. As Eric Hobsbawm has recognized, young people generally, and young women especially,

had far more independent spending power than their predecessors, thanks to the prosperity and full employment of the Golden Age, and thanks to the greater prosperity of their parents, who had less need of their children's contribution to the family budget. It was the discovery of this youth market in the mid-1950s which revolutionised the pop music business, and in Europe, the mass-market end of the fashion industries. The British 'teen-age boom' which began at this time, was based on the urban concentrations of relatively well-paid girls in the expanding offices and shops, often with more to spend than the boys, and in those days less committed to the traditional male patterns of expenditure on beer and cigarettes.[16]

The Book for the Home acknowledges in a subtitle that 'Girls like to Shop' and assumes that the daughter of a household is likely to be earning her own income and should learn to manage her own finances: 'by the time a young girl is earning money of her own or is given a dress allowance she can be left free to learn to spend wisely'.[17]

If the categories of 'bachelor girl' and 'career woman' were recognized sociological and marketing categories of the period, they were also a largely urban phenomenon. The growth of the tertiary sector, where most young women were to find employment, meant that the new work opportunities were largely to be found in the shops and offices of the city. As another male sociologist put it, 'the career woman and the bachelor girl are both very much London animals'.[18]

Like Joe Lampton in *Room at the Top*,[19] many of these novels position a young woman as newly arrived in an urban setting, her family safely distant in some fictional rural or suburban location despised by the heroine for its lack of opportunity: 'There just weren't any jobs going in Little Derrington, any more than there were facilities for art or any other kind of training . . . It was hopeless!'[20]

Not all the novels lure their heroines to the city, but those who remain in a rural setting are not permitted a life of leisure either. If the heroine is located in a country estate, it is invariably presented as a working stable or a farm. As in the country house romance, the attributes of the upper-class young woman which would have been celebrated in earlier romance fictions are still present, but are transformed into economically productive labour. Riding skills are turned to teaching and show-jumping, the ability to sketch becomes a viable career in cartooning, musical gifts are seen as an entry into becoming a professional pianist, a gifted painter becomes a book illustrator.

Professional training for women is not on the whole emphasized in these narratives. The heroine's training and qualifications tend to be dismissed in a few sentences, her skill presented as a 'natural' asset rather than a result of dedication. This 'naturalization' and dismissal of a newly acquired professional competence in women allows for a form of ideological reconciliation of the conflict between new career opportunities and traditionally 'feminine qualities'. Although it was the profession of nursing that fictionally most neatly reconciled the oppositions of female professional skill and the 'natural' nurturing role still expected of women, the range and representations of the professions offered in contemporary romance fiction similarly managed to reconcile skilled work and womanly 'nature' with no apparent contradiction.

Work and marriage

A great number of the jobs championed in romance novels are presented as if they were extensions of wifely skills. In the 1956 novel *On the Air*[21] a woman television presenter is promoted because she is so good at making life easy for the maverick genius male producer. The children's officer of *Secret Star*[22] displays both her maternal skills and instincts in her professional dealings with her charges (and indeed comes to adopt one of them). Many narratives centre around forms of work which focus on 'traditional' feminine skills and demonstrate the heroine's appropriateness as a marriage partner. Cook-housekeepers and children's nannies abound in these novels and these fictional roles are extended to include restaurateurs, hoteliers and women who run catering businesses. On securing a marriage contract, however, the professional competence and skills that have been valued in the workplace can slip invisibly into the unpaid and unacknowledged role of housewife and mother, a recurrent slippage that continues to structure the contemporary Mills & Boon novel.[23]

Many of these professional skills are constructed as mere developments of childhood talents and hobbies. The ballerina who features so frequently in romance novels for both women and children is the most obvious example, but the same structure operates over a whole range of career options. The lion-tamer achieves her feats in the circus ring because of her affection for her childhood pets, the cartoonist has an aptitude that has simply developed from her childhood sketching, the costume designer is merely extending the talent she demonstrated in making her doll's clothes.

In practice, although it is not referred to at all in these novels, the form of training which could actually provide the route into such careers, and which was available in both urban and in rural areas, was adult education. From 1946 onwards there was a growth in the provision of adult education classes across the country and a great surge in the numbers attending them – particularly of women students. Although adult education did not provide vocational training as such, it could offer a route into qualifications and professionalization. And the numbers of women attending such classes clearly expressed an ambition that was not content with home-making.

In classes of every kind, and in nearly all extra-mural areas, women students outnumber men ... women [are] in an even greater majority on courses on English Literature and the arts, and to a less but consider-able degree in psychology classes. The average age of the woman student appears to be lower than that of men.[24]

The Adult Education Institute or any state support for education and training are conspicuous absences in romance novels of the period. Rather than send their heroine to the local adult education class, the novels employ a set of awkward narrative devices that allow her to experience the benefits of professional advice and training without searching them out. A glamorous male practitioner in the heroine's chosen field was clearly preferable as a romantic hero and teacher to the solid citizenship of a local WEA tutor. The heroine of *Forgive My Foolish Pride* is encouraged in her painting by the famous (and, significantly, 'modern') male artist who happens to have taken up residence in the next village. The celebrated concert pianist of the 1950 novel *The Way is Long*, who trains another heroine in musical skills, is recovering from a nervous breakdown in a convenient quiet country retreat near by. The move to the city that is such a central feature of these narratives could not be allowed for if such training opportunities were presented as locally available. The presence of a professional practitioner also allows for a narrative digression on the trials and tribulations of the potential career path, as the hero advises the heroine of the perils in store. The device also often serves as a means of introducing other women characters who have made their way in the field, such as women opera singers, musicians, magazine editors, and casting agents, who act as both mentors for the heroine and role models for the reader.

If these narratives do not emphasize training, they often do offer practical advice on career opportunities and strategies, in very similar terms to those of the career girl novels, handbooks and magazine articles written for adolescents, as in this 1954 example about working in the film industry:

> Janet had remained behind in London, living in a Y.W.C.A. hostel while she trained at a commercial school. Her first job had been as a junior typist in the Wardour Street offices of a big film corporation. When there was an opportunity of transferring to the studios, Janet had taken it ... Then gradually the fascinating, hectic, topsy-turvy business that was film-making had begun to absorb her interest ... So Janet had formally turned technician and stayed in film production ever since.[25]

Such sequences in the novels can be read as sets of instructions to the single woman reader with her sights set on conquering the big city. These sections can offer advice on accommodation, training and interview technique, and they lay particular stress on appropriate forms of dress. The purchase of clothes is a recurrent feature of romance fiction; new jobs are frequently presented as an opportunity to acquire a new wardrobe, increasingly so in the latter half of the decade, as the air stewardess in this 1959 novel shows:

> she left the London offices of Charter Airborne Ltd. and boarded a bus for the West End ... New clothes were certainly going to be a necessity and she wanted to have plenty of time to find the most attractive.[26]

Such incidences of the heroine's new spending power represent very real shifts in patterns of consumption. The increasing numbers of single working women in urban centres was economically significant; their spending power was sufficient to alter the shape of contemporary consumption patterns, as Elliston Allen noted in the 1960s:

> It was this great concentration of relatively highly paid young girls that set the pace for the nation-wide teenage boom that began in the mid 1950s, a boom which first revealed its strength in fields where girls' purchases were pre-eminent, like blouses and skirts, cosmetics and pop records.[27]

The pleasures of consumption in fiction, however, extend well beyond the purchase of fashion items; the heroine's ability to rent or buy her own domestic space and furnish it in her own taste is a recurrent signifier of her newly acquired independence. This is most forcibly expressed in the 1956 novel *Secret Star*, in which the heroine's pleasure and excitement in her working life in a children's home is evoked in the contemplation of her domestic purchases:

> My very own ... it was the thought to which Janie woke every morning, and, like her pink curtains with their gay pink stripe, it gave a rosy glow to the day ahead, a premonition of delightful things about to happen, exciting people to be met, freedom to think and plan for herself. She let her eyes travel pleasurably over her little top floor flat, ... she had had all the fun in the world furnishing it and each morning when she woke and found her possessions around her, the chubby fireside chair, the table lamp, the cream painted bookshelves, the hooked rugs – why, then she realised a happiness so intense that it made her almost afraid.[28]

Here, domesticity, working life and consumption exist in perfect harmony for the heroine, a source of great pleasure rather than any conflict. The independent living-space for women is also repeatedly invoked as a celebration of modernity and convenience; new domestic consumer goods are seen as boons which allow women more time to pursue their own ambitions. As the cartoonist heroine of *Luck for Lindy* discovers, 'It was absolutely heavenly, she felt, to be sitting here in her very own flat, eating a delicious breakfast she had cooked herself in her up-to-date labour saving kitchen.'[29] In *Romance Goes Tenting*, the heroine finds that she is able to concoct a 'delicious' stew from the new tinned foods in between showing lion cubs and designing costumes for the circus. This is not described with any disapproval (the stew is met with appreciation by the hero), but is instead an affirmation of what Hobsbawm describes as 'the substantial mechanisation of household chores (notably by means of the domestic washing machine) and the rise of prepared and ready cooked foods.'[30]

Many of the romance novels of the 1950s celebrate the pleasures of an independent income, but they also explore the possibilities that such economic freedom can give and the pleasures to be found in work. In *Luck for Lindy*, the heroine is a bored clerical worker, but her sudden pools win suggests not a life of leisure but a new career as a caricaturist.

While Hobsbawm is right to suggest that the majority of these incomes would have derived from shop and clerical work, within the romance genre such work is seen as a stepping-stone to a more exciting and glamorous career. The forms of work available to the majority of women were in fact much less attractive than those fictionalized in romance; as Tait pragmatically pointed out, 'As society becomes increasingly industrialised women provide on the whole unskilled or semi-skilled labour. Cheap labour as a rule.'[31]

Among the fantasy elements of these romances is that of social and professional aspiration; the dream here is also of what might develop from what appears to be a dead-end job. These novels also have moral lessons for the reader: such forms of work are not to be despised, professional competence is required of every job and will ultimately reap its reward. The heroine of *The Flower Box* (1955) begins her working life as a shop-girl (much to the disdain of her class-conscious mother) but she ends as a professional florist and ultimately goes into partnership with the owner, both in business and in marriage. The competent secretaries of *On the Air* (1956) and *Dream Street* (1959) may begin their stories as clerical workers but their efficiency and professionalism eventually see them promoted to production assistants and, in one case, television interviewer.[32]

Extending further than a Cinderella story in which such ambitions are answered by the arrival of a prince, marriage can no longer be presented in these novels as the entire answer to a woman's life. The heroine of the postwar world has to be shown to be making a social contribution to the reconstruction. Even that arch-defender of the traditional womanly role, Barbara Cartland, could not evade the implications of 1945. The heart-stoppingly beautiful heroines of her 1947 novel *The Dream Within*[33] recognize from the opening pages that they must learn to earn a living. Although the vicar's daughters initially see their enforced employment as a temporary state and a means of finding a suitable marriage partner, their search for work is described in practical detail. Each finds pleasure in her work as, respectively, a model, nanny and companion, and they give up their expectations of a leisured life. Their ambitions to marry a 'millionaire and a duke' are also confounded. Dukes are no longer what they once were; the struggling artist hero who reveals himself as a duke in disguise can no longer afford to keep up his estate and its servants. It is the international banker who has the capital to set up home with his new bride in the family country house. All three heroines are clearly expected to be working wives and have to learn to embrace the new democracy. The eldest sister undergoes a conversion to the greater good in the public ward of an NHS hospital, where she comes to terms with the 'common people' and proves herself worthy of her position as lady of the country house.

Upper-class privilege can no longer be assumed in these novels, but must be earned. As in those novels which centre around the country house, the class position of the heroine is central to an understanding of the renegotiations of postwar class relations. A heroine's class position is less fixed than it would be for a male hero, and is ultimately contingent on marriage. What the 'bachelor girl' romance allows for is a period in which the heroine can experience and experiment with the options available in the postwar world.

The heroine of these novels is very often an orphan – a free-floating class status which allows her to take up different positions in her working life and her marriage. For those heroines who are not orphaned, the most frequent occupation for their fictional fathers (mothers are even more likely to be dead than are fathers) is that of vicar, a neat device which gives the family some class ambiguity: a vicar is just as likely to be the second son of an aristocratic family as a member of the professional or educated middle classes.

As in the country house romance, one common narrative structure which propels the heroine into the world of work is that of downward mobility, in which the heroine is removed from a cosy world of class privilege. Fathers have frequently died, leaving their family impoverished and forcing their daughters to work. The wealthy or genteel families who once would have educated their daughters only for marriage are shown as no longer in a position to do so. The daughter with theatrical aspirations cannot be sent to drama school, another is removed from finishing school to become a shop-girl, the concert pianist gives up her career to devote herself to the family farm, the heiress relinquishes her elegant shoes for wellingtons in the circus ring. But here too (as for the heroines of Cartland's novel), work is offered as an exciting and challenging opportunity to acquire new experiences and meet new people; the loss of upper-class privilege affords an entry into a newly meritocratic class structure.

In these romance narratives, the daughter's experience of work can elevate her from a suburban or genteelly impoverished lifestyle into the professional (rather than aristocratic) classes, and fit her for a socially advantageous marriage in the new meritocracy. The working world is shown as a place that can create extraordinary opportunities both for self-advancement and for that enterprise to be affirmed in a marriage. A lowly secretary can gain promotion and become the wife of a successful film director, an orphaned welfare officer can attract the eye of a wealthy landowner during council meetings and gain his vote and his hand in marriage.

Any upward or downward mobility of the heroine must always be counterbalanced by a harmonization with the professional achievements, wealth and class position of the hero. If one is wealthy, talented or upper class, the other must offer qualities which bring a symmetry to their alliance. Thanks to her pools win, Lindy can bring wealth to the marriage, but her hero provides cultural capital with superior heritage and artistic talent. The heiress marries a hard-working but impoverished vet; the committed and orphaned social worker, a wealthy manufacturer. The possession of wealth or position must always be mediated by a meritocratic alliance with hard work and a sense of social responsibility.

The romance structure must generically always offer the possibility of a different kind of resolution; it is required to lay a false trail of alternative (and unsuitable) potential marriage partners for both hero and heroine. The final marriage in these narratives always represents a choice that affirms a con-sensus politics and middle-class hegemony, in a solid confirmation of the professional work ethic. The heroine's mate is selected on the basis of what is often expressed as 'a sure sense of values'. Extremes of artistic temperament (*The Way is Long*), aristocratic presumption (*The Twisted Road*) or theatrical glamour (*On the Air*) are rejected in favour of partnership, professional dedication and a strong, shared sense of citizenship. Urbanity, artistic bril-liance or 'foreignness' are invoked as signals that, however desirable they might appear, such apparent heroes are the wrong choice for the heroine.[34] It is the stable, often unromantic, but impeccably British colleague who most frequently offers himself as the true hero, 'a man whose life was governed by common sense rather than sentiment' in the words of one novelist. And the heroine must acquire the experience and maturity over the course of the novel in order to recognize him as such.

The romantic heroine of the 1950s is repeatedly shown to eschew glamour in favour of the pragmatic; Janet of *The Twisted Road* finally marries her 'prosaic and undistinguished' colleague in preference to the 'romance and glamour and excitement' offered by Sir Charles, an Air Vice-Marshal. She relinquishes the upper-class heritage he represents, and with it the 'air of aristocratic distinction she had found so irresistible, that sense of quiet power and the unspoken assumption that what he wanted he would take'.[35]

Aristocratic privilege is no longer unquestioned or unchallenged; the apparent attractions of a knighthood are no more to be trusted than are the financial expectations of Barbara Cartland's fictional duke. The heroine of *The Twisted Road* is appalled by the false hero's patrician presumption and by his lack of care for 'ordinary' people. Instead, the future lies in a romantic choice from the 'sensible, hard-working, unpretentious world', values which are understood to be much more fitted to the postwar world. The marriage represents a shared commitment to work that offers a bulwark for 'ordinary people' against the seductive but unreliable promises of aristocratic privilege. In a final scene of recognition, the heroine comes to celebrate the continuity and solidity of working people, and her own place within that world:

> the sound engineers, and the make up man and the continuity girl and the camera operators ... her own people with whom she belonged just as Ivor did. This was her background and her place, in this sensible hard working, unpretentious world. Dreams vanished and romances faded, but this remained. (p. 220)

Women and war work

The Twisted Road is one of the few romance novels of this period that directly acknowledges the experience of women during the war: Janet begins her technical career in documentary film-making, the field that had provided such women film-makers as Jill Craigie and Muriel Box with a start in the film industry. And this professional experience is shown to be a direct consequence of women's war work. Janet (and a great many other real women workers in film) worked during the war for a documentary unit: 'They had gone all over Britain recording the national effort, filming farms and factories, docks and ships and Army camps and RAF stations' (p. 14).

The experience of war and of work that women had come to share with men impacted upon the way in which men and women related to one another in romantic fiction. The terms of the fictional marriage contract also had to shift in a new ideal of marital bliss. Marriage is now conceived as a partnership; the endearments have become 'my mate!', 'my partner!', rather than the 'little darling!' that the heroine now often rejects as old-fashioned. *The Book for the Home* expressed this sense of partnership as 'companionship: The essence of marriage is companionship'. It assumed the likelihood of a working wife and advocated that the husbands should take on 'their share of domestic chores': 'If husband and wife each have their own career they must have freedom to pursue it in their own way.'[36] The advice on marriage goes on to assert 'Away With Domination!' and exhorts its married readers to 'respect one another's gifts and talents'. Such recommendations are regularly to be found in the conditions for the idealized marriage of the hero and heroine of romance fiction. An ideal husband is presented as 'a man of her own world and background whose life and friends and interests she could share ... and have her honoured place in his scheme of things.'[37]

The romance heroine's experience of work has given her a purchase on and understanding of her partner's world; she is no longer prepared to be excluded from the language and preoccupations of masculinity. It is the world of work that is shown to offer women the experience to understand and become a fit partner to the male hero, rather than the shared experience of war. Very few of these novels make any direct reference to the war, and yet it is an awareness of the experience of total war that both made possible and compromised this new language of 'partnership' in gender relations. Although an acknowledgement of the war years is a gaping absence in these texts, the legacy of a war in which women were active participants and as likely to suffer deprivation and injury as men, had to leak into the narratives.

The war casts a long, if rarely explicit, shadow throughout these novels. Their narratives are full of damaged men, and there are a disproportionate number of dead fathers. Yet there is a constant insistence that women can now challenge and confront the mysterious world of masculinity. In *The Twisted Road* the war is still a recent memory and the heroine has had her heart broken by the death of her fiancé, an RAF officer. The language that announces his death is impersonal and alien, and offered as an example of an exclusive masculine language which has no recognition of the suffering of women: 'Jet propelled bombers of the RAF carried out long distance test flights ... one of the aircraft failed to return to base ... It carried a crew of four' (p. 15).

Many of the heroes have hidden past lives that the heroine strives to uncover. Lois, of *Romance Goes Tenting*, only discovers by accident what it is that her male guardian does professionally. A circus *aficionado*, his career as a ringmaster has been kept a secret throughout the nine years of his guardianship during the heroine's childhood. The man who eventually reveals himself as the hero also has a guilty secret (an unsuccessful operation on his family dog, as it eventually transpires), which must be shared with the heroine before their marriage can become one of 'companionship'. It is difficult not to read this recurrence of male 'secrets' as an expression of resentment against the silence of men about those aspects of war which excluded women.

Marriage partners

The expectations of a new form of 'partnership' in postwar marriage are articulated in *Partners are a Problem*: the fictionalized marriage between a vet and a doctor initially appears to conform to the contemporary ideal. While the novel does ultimately resolve all the tensions in a requisite happy ending, it also acknowledges that there are strains and the text at points treads perilously close to exploding its own myth of an ideal marriage. *Partners are a Problem* is an unusual text for Mills & Boon because the narrative's starting-point is a marriage in which both husband and wife work. It is the 'accumulation of grievances and resentments' in the attempt to sustain this 'companionship' that fuels the romance structure of the plot. The text makes much play on the term 'partners' as both husband and wife flirt (literally) with the possibilities of new partnerships in both their personal and professional lives.

The central heroine (in a narrative which, unusually, has several heroines, who offer a range of possibilities for the postwar romantic heroine) is a vet:

A wife who had her own profession to consider; a wife who had dedicated herself to her work before she had met him; a wife who had to combine marriage with her professional life. She wasn't always successful. She had to admit that. (p. 128)

While the tensions of combining marriage and career are painfully acknowledged in a chapter entitled 'Marriage and Motherhood', the narrative never questions Ellen's right to continue with her work; her abilities and professional skill are recurrently stressed. Discovering that she is pregnant in the final section of the novel, Ellen grudgingly comes to the practical conclusion that 'If she had a young family to keep her at home, she would have to settle for part-time work' (p. 129).

Along with the final embrace, the narrative resolution of the 1950s romance novel now has to confront the awkward question of whether, or (more often) how, the heroine is to continue her career path after marriage. The marriage between the protagonists of *Secret Star* neatly negotiates the problem in a complete conflation of the professional and personal. The dispossessed orphan heroine marries the local heir to a woollen business; the wool industry is in decline and he must consider an alternative future. The family manor house and grounds can no longer be sustained and can therefore be pressed into the service of the community as a children's home. Their marriage represents the beginning of an enterprise which manages to be both private and public; the heroine runs the orphanage and adopts her favourite orphan as her son. The Welfare State, in subsidizing the home, has given both hero and heroine the opportunity to demonstrate their status as good citizens and forge ahead as ideal marriage partners and members of the community, she as a children's officer, he as a local councillor and potential MP. As in Elizabeth Gaskell's *North and South*, their marriage represents an alliance of benign capitalism and a commitment to the social good, but here it is in the context of the ideals of a new Welfare State.

Young women in the romance fiction of this period are represented as fitting themselves to be New Citizens and a new kind of wife in the postwar democracy. As Marjorie Tait briskly recommended, 'We want them to take their full part in life as women and the colleagues of men.'[38] However, romance heroines can often demand more than simply to be the 'colleagues of men'. These novels expect women to make their own contribution to postwar reconstruction, and also to make use of the perceived opportunities it offers. The hero of *Forgive My Foolish Pride* assures the heroine that the development of her skills and maturity is vital to their future together:

> you and I can live in London – or anywhere else where you can have all the training you want ... Don't you see, darling. I want you to grow to your full stature, and if through marrying me, you failed to, I could never forgive myself. (p. 186)

The 'bachelor girl' novels have heroines who are competent and capable and who work. Whether or not that work will continue after marriage, their working lives inevitably have an effect on the structure of the romance plot: the meeting of hero and heroine is now most likely to occur in the workplace, the heroine to attract the attention of the hero through her professional capabilities. The nature of the final proposal must also now take account of the heroine's working life; the ways in which romance narratives negotiate masculinity, femininity and marriage has to change accordingly. On a number of levels, these novels can be seen to be engaging with much the same problems and promoting a very similar ideology of 'womanhood' to that articulated by the social scientist Marjorie Tait:

> Having shown that as a sex they can learn the same subjects, take the same vocational training and do most of the same work as men, they should now stop, look both around on the world and in on themselves and ask whether they really want to be educated like men and do a man's work. They must also ask whether this is the way they can best contribute to society. (p. 23)

These are exactly the kinds of questions that are set out to confront the heroine of the 1950s romance narrative. While it is undoubtedly the case that the 'bachelor girl' romance has to conform to generic expectation and invariably ends with a celebration of heterosexual love, that cannot detract entirely from their assertion of a female independence.

Unlike career girl novels written for adolescent girls, the romance genre is predicated on marriage as the narrative closure. The 'bachelor girl' can only ever be a temporary position within these texts, and the heroine must finally repudiate her independence for love and marriage. The successful and career-driven advertising heroine of *Dream Street* may be professionally admirable, but she is not allowed to become 'fully feminine' without the final embrace of the hero. But the implications of the bachelor girl's working life, whether it is to continue or not, cannot be entirely erased. What has been said of filmed representations of independent women is also true of the heroines of postwar romance fiction: 'The endings of the films usually involve a "climb-down" on the part of the star ... in a sense, these endings do not matter. What we remember is the independence not the climb-down.'[39]

The world of work has confronted the bachelor girl heroine with other possible partners, allowed her the experience of an independent income and enhanced her standing within the community. The hero's arms are clearly now not the only option available to a young woman. Although these novels must end with an endorsement of marriage, at the same time they cannot escape their celebration of new forms of independence for women. *The Times* reported that the President of the National Federation of Business and Professional Women's Clubs announced in 1956 that the 'trained girl boffin is here to stay'.[40] The heroine of the bachelor girl romance and her experience in the world of work could not but affirm a new woman who was, in the words of one romance writer, 'a modern career girl who had seen so many facets of life and met so many different kinds of people'.[41]

Notes

1. Marjorie Tait, 'The Education of Women for Citizenship: some practical suggestions' *Problems in Education*, vol. III (Paris: Unesco, 1954), p. 10.
2. Alison Light, Preface to *Twentieth Century Romance and Historical Writers* (London: St. James Press, 1994), p. xi.
3. Joseph McAleer, *Popular Reading and Publishing in Britain 1914–1950* (Oxford: Clarendon Press, 1992), p. 121.
4. Jane Beech, *The Way is Long* (London: Mills & Boon, 1950), p. 11.
5. Hettie Grimstead, *The Twisted Road* (London: Mills & Boon, 1951), p. 37.
6. *Further Education and Training Scheme Progress Reports: Women* (London: Ministry of Labour and National Service, 1949–52).
7. Elizabeth Wilson, *Only Halfway to Paradise. Women in Postwar Britain 1945–1968* (London: Tavistock Publications, 1980), p. 2.
8. Tait, 'The Education of Women for Citizenship', p. 51.
9. Margaret Malcolm, *Forgive My Foolish Pride* (London: Mills & Boon, 1957), p. 52.
10. Ferdinand Zweig, *Women's Life and Labour* (London: Gollancz, 1952), p. 157.
11. Fay Chandos, *Partners are a Problem* (London: Mills & Boon, 1957).
12. McAleer, *Popular Reading and Publishing*, p. 122.
13. Marjorie Bruce-Milne, ed., *The Book for the Home*, vol. 1 (London: Caxton Publishing Company, 1956), p. 573.
14. Ibid., p. 584.
15. Wilson, *Only Halfway to Paradise*, p. 45.
16. Eric Hobsbawm, *Age of Extremes – The Short Twentieth Century 1914–1991* (London: Michael Joseph, 1991), pp. 327–8.
17. *The Book for the Home*, vol. 2, p. 165.
18. D. Elliston Allen, *British Tastes: An Enquiry into the Likes and Dislikes of the Regional Consumer* (London: Hutchinson, 1968), p. 53.
19. See also Louise Cochrane, *Anne in Electronics* (London: Chatto and Windus, 1960).
20. Malcolm, *Forgive My Foolish Pride*, p. 7.
21. Mary Burchell, *On the Air* (London: Mills & Boon, 1956).
22. Marguerite Lees, *Secret Star* (London: Mills & Boon, 1956).
23. See Deborah Philips and Alan Tomlinson, 'Homeward Bound: Leisure, popular culture and consumer capitalism' in Dominic Strinati and Stephen Wagg, eds, *Come on Down? Popular Media Culture in Post-war Britain* (London: Routledge, 1992), for an exposition of this argument.
24. S. E. Raybould, 'University Extra-Mural Education in Great Britain' in *Universities in Adult Education, Problems in Education*, vol. IV (Paris: Unesco, 1952), pp. 27–58 (p. 53).
25. Grimstead, *The Twisted Road*, p. 14.
26. Phyllis Matthewman, *Food of Love* (London: Mills & Boon, 1959), p. 6.
27. Elliston Allen, *British Tastes*, p. 63.

28. Lees, *Secret Star*, p. 24.

29. Phyllis Matthewman, *Luck for Lindy* (London: Mills & Boon, 1954), p. 24.

30. Phyllis Matthewman, *Romance Goes Tenting* (London: Mills & Boon, 1957), p. 318.

31. Hobsbawn, *Age of Extremes*, p. 318; Tait, 'The Education of Women for Citizenship', p. 49.

32. Valerie K. Nelson, *The Flower Box* (London: Mills & Boon, 1955); Burchell, *On the Air*; Hettie Grimstead, *Dream Street* (London: Mills & Boon, 1959).

33. Barbara Cartland, *The Dream Within* (London: Hutchinson, 1947).

34. The hero's 'Britishness' is insistently invoked in the great majority of romance novels. It is not until the end of the decade that a literally foreign hero can be countenanced; with the growth in foreign travel, European heroes finally do become acceptable. *Food of Love* (1959) plays with this generic expectation and finally allows the air hostess heroine to marry an Italian violinist.

35. Grimstead, *The Twisted Road*, p. 112.

36. *The Book for the Home*, vol. 2, p. 175.

37. Grimstead, *The Twisted Road*, p. 115.

38. Tait, 'The Education of Women for Citizenship', p. 11.

39. Richard Dyer, *Stars* (London: BFI Publications, 1979), pp. 64–5.

40. *The Times*, 29 October 1956.

41. Grimstead, *The Twisted Road*, p. 45.

7. Starched caps: nurse-heroines

[A] thoughtful study of a nurse who was pulled two ways; by her love for her vital, rewarding job, and by her needs as a warm-hearted woman (Marguerite Lees, *Sister Grace*, Mills & Boon catalogue, 1957)

Women in the health service were particularly well placed to negotiate tensions around work and gender in the postwar period; the nursing profession could fictionally embody all the ideals of the Welfare State and match them neatly to the figure of the postwar working woman. The nurse is employed in an institution dedicated to the social good, her work requires training and education and she is almost by definition a practical, sensible young woman. And it is the nurse who is the subject of more romance narratives than any other profession in the postwar period.

The medical romance was the best-selling popular form of fiction in the postwar period, and it was also the genre which directly led to the expansion of Mills & Boon into a mass-market publishing house.[1] As Mills & Boon themselves now acknowledge in their publicity material, it was the success of the hospital romance that ushered in their own move to the paperback novel and which also confirmed their links with North American imprints of romance fiction; it was for the rights to reprint hospital romances that the Canadian publishing company Harlequin first approached Mills & Boon for the North American market.

The heroine of Denise Robins's 1951 novel *Something to Love*[2] displays all the qualities of the idealized femininity of the postwar period, and these personal attributes are seen to fit her admirably for the nursing profession:

Christie was a practical girl and realized the hardships of training, all the responsibilities attached to the profession. This was the work a Higher Authority had fashioned her for. Strong hands to succour the weak; good health to bear the brunt of the pain and weariness of others;

a smile to bring answering smiles from small, suffering patients.
(p. 61)

The 'Higher Authority' might in this case signify God, but it is clear from the terms used here that the qualities required of the nurse are also those recommended by the nation for its postwar mothers and working women: strength, health, practicality and a professional sense of responsibility.

The fictional hospital offers a paradigm from which to discuss the state of the nation's health, but it is also a means of negotiating tensions in the new Welfare State, and, especially, the place of women within it. If the 'health profession' is a notable absence in canonical texts of the 1950s, as a subject for romantic fiction it has ramifications beyond those of a career and romance trajectory for the heroine. These novels allow for an exploration of women's experience as practitioners and patients in the new National Health Service.

The National Health Service was a plank of the Welfare State which particularly represented modernity and progress; it was a key institution for a contemporary embracing of 'science' and new technologies. As Anne Karpf has argued, 'The 1950s bubbled with therapeutic optimism ... now the system was up and running and the public had to be encouraged to think medical and use it.'[3]

The medical romance entirely endorses this 'therapeutic optimism'; these novels repeatedly express a frank enthusiasm for medical science and technology; as one heroine enthusiastically put it in 1956, 'this was the age of specialisation and progress'.[4]

The National Health Service and the hospital are seen in both official discourses of health and these fictions as only one aspect of the campaign to improve the nation's health; housing, welfare support and education are also recognized as significant factors in the fight against disease. If this is a position enshrined in the National Health Service and the Welfare State, it is the women practitioners in these novels, with their encompassing of the personal and the professional, who are seen as central to this 'modern' approach to medicine and instrumental to the Beveridge 'all-out attack on the "five giants" of Want, Disease, Ignorance, Squalor and Idleness'.[5]

Wartime nurses

Although the National Health Service began with the National Health Service Act of 1946, it finally came into operation in July 1948. The health service during the war years was a forerunner of the structure of the National

Health Service; the war had required 'an integrated national hospital service'.[6] With that integration of disparate branches of health provision came a cohesion and professionalization of both nursing and medical training that continued into the postwar health service.

Nursing services during the war years had been made up of trained and volunteer nurses, as Brenda McBryde (herself a professional nurse during the war) testifies:

the Civil Nursing Reserve was formed of trained and assistant nurses who, in time of war, could be augmented by the nursing detachments of the British Red Cross Society and St John's Ambulance Brigade. Both these voluntary organisations were composed of young women who had undergone basic training in First Aid and Home Nursing and were known by the initials of their office, Voluntary Aid Detachments (VADs) ... Civilian as well as those in the Armed Services, at home and overseas, students in training, the VADs 'in it for the duration' and the Matrons ... in whose capable hands rested the well-being of thousands of casualties.[7]

Whether volunteers or not, these nurses, who represented a great range of different kinds and classes of women, were active in every aspect of the war services and military operations. Many of these (both in fact and fiction) went on to train professionally after the war, as McBryde put it: 'Some of the VADs who had not nursed before the war found so much satisfaction in their chosen war effort that they went on to undertake full training.'[8]

In addition to those working officially as nurses, there were many women involved in a range of civic duties that were close to nursing; as a wartime propaganda leaflet celebrated: 'There are 700,000 women enrolled in the Ministry of Health services alone. They look after maternity cases, crêches and homes for the evacuated.'[9]

The experience of the war is rarely explicit in postwar medical romances; but it is clear that wartime camaraderie and courage have a trajectory into the contemporary crises and demands of hospital life. Warfare breeds a pulling together that is central to the needs of medical staff; this link between wartime experience and the demands of postwar life is made explicit in a 1956 novel, but is here clearly applied to an older generation than that of the young heroine:

Their experience in the Blitz had stood Matron and the senior members of the staff in good stead: the hospital machine slipped smoothly into a quickened tempo, each small cog moving efficiently to deal with ...

sudden and unexpected emergency. To the injured who entered it, Lichester General presented the appearance of well-organized calm ... a haven of peace, after the storm which had gone before.[10]

The National Health Service

The different traditions of nursing that were to come into the National Health Service all had their own ideas of the function of the nurse. As Rosemary White explains,

> three streams of nursing entered the health service in 1948 ... a) The voluntary hospitals were the charitable hospitals and their nurses worked within a Lady Bountiful ethos ... Within this group were the teaching hospitals whose nurses were the elite of the profession ... b) The municipal hospitals were founded within the great public health movement of the nineteenth century and their ideology was consequently derived from that of the medical officers of health, the arch proponents of preventative and environmental medicine ... c) the remnants of the Poor Law nurses and those who worked in the public assistance institutions. These institutions were founded on the less-eligibility principle and the ideology of custodial care and constraint.[11]

The tensions between these different styles and philosophies of nursing are very visible in National Health Service medical novels. 'Nursing' is most frequently invoked in these romances as still in the tradition of the voluntary hospital; the nurse continues the ethos of a Lady Bountiful, but is now also a modern and professionally skilled young woman. There is in medical romances of the period a frequent nostalgia for the independent 'cottage hospital' and small voluntary hospitals, usually staffed by local general practitioners. The 'cottage hospital' is often employed in these narratives as a nostalgic emblem of bureaucracy before the Welfare State, and is recurrently evoked as the ideal small hospital in opposition to the large training hospitals. Nonetheless, the great majority of fictional nurses undertake their training at the élite teaching hospitals, derived from the 'municipal' hospitals. The cottage hospital, as a stern fictional matron reminds a young nurse, 'has limitations for a nurse wishing to prepare for her "State"'; the nurse heroine is presented as among the best and brightest of her generation, requiring more than the charity hospital could provide for the new demands of postwar medicine.

The contribution of women nurses during the war and the restructuring of the health service had focused attention on conditions of work in the profession; as a 1946 commentator noted:

> The position of the hospital nurse has long been unsatisfactory. The work is hard and highly responsible, hours are very long, but the salaries earned by nurses and matrons of hospitals are very low. Plans are in hand for putting the hospital nurse on a financial basis which will compete favourably with that of women in other professions.[12]

Whatever the contradictions of the 'nurse' may be as a career for women, there is no doubt that the establishment of a National Health Service gave the role a greater economic and professional status than it had enjoyed before. Both the training and career structure of nursing underwent a new and formal professionalization as various forms of nursing were restructured under the National Health Service. The 1943 Nurses Act (which preceded the 1944 Ministry of Health White Paper on the National Health Service) had included a clause which prevented Christian Science nurses from using the title of 'nurse', thus establishing by exclusion a new status for the profession. The Nurses Act of 1949 also introduced a package of legislative changes that standardized the financing and administration of nursing training and brought it into the statutory structure of the National Health Service. By 1957, the Nurses Act had introduced a single register of nurses. All these measures meant that nursing enjoyed a greater professional status than it had during and before the war; and nursing became a better-paid form of work for women than it had once been: 'the pay of female nurses was 13 per cent above the average for women in the lower professional groups in 1955–1956 . . . and 68 per cent of the national average wage.'[13]

As the number of nurses in training grew and the organization of a professional structure developed, the demands and requirements of the nursing profession were newly under discussion:

> The early years of the health service did see a once for all expansion in nursing establishments and a levelling up of salaries as a more uniform national approach to staffing and pay was introduced and an attempt made to remedy the pre-war depression in this industry.[14]

Such a rethinking of the conditions of work in the health service was part of a new way of thinking about medicine as a whole. The war had brought with it a new sense of health and healthy living; the 'Dig for Victory' campaign had led to a marked rise in the number of allotments and an official endorsement of vegetables and vitamins as essential to the nation's health. Food rationing had also enforced an awareness of nutrition, as had government-sponsored leaflets encouraging people to eat well. The National Health Service was founded on an increased public awareness of the relationship of health to conditions of living, and on a newly democratic approach to medical practice. Despite the inevitable limitations, even one of its sternest critics could celebrate that 'the National Health Service has unquestionably brought to the people of Britain a system of medical care which ranks as one of the major social achievements of modern times.'[15]

Postwar medical romances share a very similar celebration of the achievement of a postwar public system of medical care. Private medicine is seen to be part of a system of outmoded privilege, and is most often narratively associated with that outdated character (found particularly in the country house romance), the lady of leisure, who is always negatively structured in opposition to the working heroine. Private patients (often derided by the fictional hospital staff as 'pps') are characterized as spoilt and 'pettish'. The romantic hero may be a hospital specialist or a general practitioner, but if associated with private practice in any way, he emphatically has some form of consultancy work within the National Health Service (as the British Medical Association in fact required), which narratively affirms his status and commitment within the Welfare State. A 1957 doctor hero rejects an offer of promotion to a private nursing home, seeing it, typically, as 'a home for women who are not so much sick as bored, afraid of life, anxious to be fussed over and waited upon. I think other people need me more.'[16]

The National Health Service hospital

The National Health Service 'hospital' acts in these novels as a fictional construct which manages to reconcile 'traditional' social values with the modernity of a new Welfare State, and also as an ideological transition from the experiences of a wartime health service to a new postwar health system. The hospital is a place where teamwork is literally a matter of life and death, and it was also the site through which the majority of the population came most directly into contact with the Welfare State. As one medical practitioner commented in 1957, 'Private practice, for all but the most eminent, has become a hazardous way of making a living now that more than 90 per cent of the population use the National Health Service.'[17] The fictional hospital serves as a metonym for the National Health Service (and, by extension, for the Welfare State); it is frequently referred to in terms of a smoothly running machine in which the medical woman is properly (but humbly) aware of her place: 'I'm only a very small cog in a very big machine, but I'm a part of that machine, a necessary part.'[18]

The nursing heroine is shown to be one element in a system of hospital workers that extends beyond nursing staff and doctors; other occupations for women in medicine are frequently cited: almoners, dispensers, dieticians, pathologists, physio, art and occupational therapists are all female characters who are shown to operate within the framework of the National Health Service.

The hospital or health service 'machine' is represented as a key element in the well-being of the community, whether rural or urban, and an indicator of the state of the New Britain. It is also a system that is shown to depend upon the hard work and dedication of a team of workers. The medical heroine is a central and respected figure within this efficient system, which is seen as central to the sustaining of a healthy community and, by extension, the nation: 'Catering for the needs of a large industrial town, Melfield General was a busy place resembling nothing so much as a hive of industrious bees.'[19]

If nursing is shown in these novels to be a newly democraticized profession, there were nevertheless traces of a hierarchy among the hospitals and their trainings, which existed in actuality and in their fictional representations. History and tradition are the most frequently cited signifiers of quality in a fictional hospital. The following description is typical, in that it manages to reconcile all the different branches of medicine before the Welfare State in a new NHS hospital:

> Lichester General was a teaching hospital with a long tradition behind it. Founded in Tudor times as 'a hospice for the reception and treatment of the poor and afflicted', it had gone under the name of one of its present medical wards, St Mary Charity until – raised in the latter part of the eighteenth century to the status of a training College for Apothecaries and Surgeons – its designation had changed ... finally, during the first world war, to the Lichester General Hospital.[20]

The medical romance frequently manages to account for growth in the hospital and the availability of medical services without any reference to a National Health Service at all, the hospital being constructed as having developed naturally and gradually, a part of the fabric of life. 'Merton Hospital' is typical in its representation of a hospital that has become organically integrated into a national system of health care without the assistance of any elections or apparent policy decisions; it has evolved from a rural to an urban hospital, and from private to public health care without any apparent interference from the state. Instead, we are told, it

> had started life as a cottage hospital, serving a small country town not far from London. But gradually the town had expanded ... as the demands upon it grew steadily greater, the hospital had been enlarged ... over the years it had become known as one of the finest general hospitals in the South of England.[21]

If the traditions of hospitals and practices before the Welfare State continued to be celebrated, so many of the old medical hierarchies and gender relations in health and medicine continued to prevail in the fictional National Health Service hospital.

The nursing profession

Nursing was seen in both official and popular discourses as an appropriately feminine and patriotic form of war work for middle- and upper-class women, but the postwar period nonetheless saw a recruitment crisis in traditionally low-paid areas of women's work, of which nursing was one. The championing in these fictions of nursing as a vocation is related to the government recruitment campaigns for nurses in the 1940s and early 1950s; the 1943 film *The Lamp Still Burns* (directed by Leslie Howard and based on Monica Dickens's novel *One Pair of Feet*) was sponsored by the Ministry of Health and firmly locates the contemporary nurse in the heroic tradition of Florence Nightingale and Edith Cavell. The nurse has an ideological function beyond the work of caring for patients. Nursing as a profession, in the blurring of the boundaries between professional and voluntary work, 'feminine' tending and 'masculine' science and technology, neatly encapsulates a wider national contradiction between contemporary ethics of modernity and tradition. The heritage of Florence Nightingale is rarely made explicit in these novels, but it is often invoked, as in this image of a hospital nurse:

> A calm, serene figure in her mauve print dress and white apron with the starched cap on her dark hair outlined against the dull glow of the lamp, a figure of quiet confidence which many a man has seen through the torturing haze of pain, stretching out towards it with a sense of need which he had hitherto barely recognized.[22]

This erotically charged icon celebrates traditional 'maternal' qualities, but at the same time allows for a 'modern' professional competence in women. The same tension operated in contemporary film representations of women nursing; the 1957 British film *No Time for Tears* cast Anna Neagle as the matron of a children's hospital; her previous screen incarnations as Queen Victoria, Nurse Edith Cavell, a British war spy and Florence Nightingale herself gave a contemporary nurse all the heroic and patriotic connotations of her star persona.[23]

The patriotic connotations of the nurse survived beyond the war and into an association with service and national duty in the postwar Welfare State. The nurse is an icon of femininity particularly suited to a postwar merit-ocracy; she is a career woman whose achievements derive from practical hard work rather than individual brilliance. The nurse is an attendant rather than an initiating woman worker who is prepared to work as part of a team rather than in pursuit of individual glory. This heroine is typical in her modest acceptance of her place within the hospital hierarchy: 'Hospital, she thought, was like that. No one person had to take all the responsibility, each was a cog in the big machine, part of a team.'[24] The nursing heroine was a figure around whom a whole contemporary set of discourses concerning femininity could coalesce; as Melosh explains:

> Nurses' increasing skill and influence placed them on a collision course with the postwar ideology of domesticity, later named the 'feminine mystique'. Sources as diverse as nursing manuals, sociological studies and popular fiction all revealed a heightened concern with nurses as women, a new sense of the possible contradictions and conflicts between the demands of work and the claims of gender.[25]

The nurse is a model in which such conflicts could achieve a mythical resolution; the young nursing heroine frequently features as respectful of hospital traditions but is also prepared to challenge outmoded attitudes from a previous generation of matrons and doctors. The nurse offered a reconcilia-tion of the new and contemporary with a respect for heritage and the legacies of the past. This reconciliation had also been written into the plans for the National Health Service: the 1944 White Paper on 'A National Health Service' assured the nation that:

> The record of this country in its health and medical services is a good one ... There is no question of having to abandon bad services and to start afresh. Reform in this field is not a matter of making good what is bad, but of making better what is good already.[26]

The nurse personified a similar reassurance in terms of changing constructs of femininity; she is a figure who gently reforms rather than challenges gender roles. In the brave new world of medical technology, the nurse is a highly skilled and knowledgeable woman, but her role is also one of caring and nurturing. The traditionally 'feminine' qualities, 'warmth of understanding and quiet patience'[27] (two of the most frequently cited qualities required of the fictional nurse) are matched in the postwar nursing heroine with a trained professional competence, as in this 1954 heroine:

> Janet was a born nurse. It was obvious as soon as she came into a room or walked along a ward. There was competence in her erect bearing and a world of serenity in her calm eyes, and the curve of her mouth was generous and kind. She would never lose her humanity in a sea of technical routine nor would she become bogged in sickly sentiment to the danger of her professional skill. She was calm, cool and deliberate, and all through her training she had taken things in her stride.[28]

Janet clearly has a vocation, but it is important to recognize that this is not a requirement for all nursing heroines; many arrive at 'serenity' and 'competence' through their training. The heroine of *The Starched Cap* (1957) begins the novel as a society lady of 'the diamonds and mink set',[29] but by its end has been trained into a democratic devotion to professional duty. Many of these novels centre their narrative on the procedures of nursing training and so demonstrate that the nurse is not necessarily born, but can be made.

Nursing training is shown to instil a practical sensibility, a no-nonsense and democratic approach to work and colleagues. One nurse recognizes another's profession, although both are out of uniform, because she manifests the 'commonsensical' and sensible qualities of the ideal nurse, with her 'matey approach; short nails; shiny fingers; no rings; just the general cut of [her] jib'.[30] Nursing training offered a protected means for young women to experience the world of work and independence; the closed community of the hospital re-creates a family structure. The fictional heroines may have left the family home, but they remain in the position of daughters, with the senior matrons and sisters *in loco parentis*.

The matron is a very important character in the nursing narrative, a reassuring, if firm, maternal presence; she is most frequently represented as firm but fair, stern but with a warmth and empathy at times of crisis. This description is typical: 'It wasn't at all in character for her [Matron] to take anyone's part unless she had cold facts. She was no airy idealist. Quite unexpectedly she smiled.'[31] The matron is a female figure of authority to whom the young nurse is answerable, but she is also a mediating figure between the nursing profession and the demands of the doctors. The matron was in practice a figure who wielded not inconsiderable power; as well as holding the status of an experienced nurse, she was in an important bureaucratic position within the new National Health Service, as Goldman explains: 'The Matron has full authority in matters affecting the nursing staff, and may also supervise domestic services, e.g., cleaning, cooking, etc.'[32]

The training of nurses is seen in these novels as a form of professionalization that can draw on a new generation of educated and ambitious young women. A 1957 fictional matron sifts through the entry of student nurses and finds them to be:

Girls who had made their applications to be nurses for a year or more! Girls who had stayed on in the Sixth Forms of their schools and taken their General Certificates of Education at advanced level! Orthodox young women, most of them, amenable to hospital discipline and anxious to work![33]

Discipline and work in the nursing profession are central themes in medical romances. Despite their generic conventions, these novels are at pains to deglamorize the profession and stress, as the hero of *My Dear Doctor* puts it, that 'Nursing, and the medical profession in general, is sheer hard work, sometimes boring, sometimes emotionally exhausting, always unremittingly demanding' (p. 63).

The daily work of nursing is consistently shown as physically extremely demanding; fictional student nurses spend much of their training in a state of exhaustion. There is an insistent claim to authenticity in all these medical romances; there are frequent references to particular drugs and surgical procedures and a clear pride in the use of technical language and medical acronyms. Many of the writers of nursing romances appear to have been nurses or matrons themselves. Infrequently (as many of these novels are written under pseudonyms, this is not regular publishing practice), references to the author's own professional experience are included in the preliminary pages; author Bess Norton is advertised in *The Quiet One* as 'a State Registered Nurse herself, with experience in hospitals large and small'.[34]

References to hospital hierarchies and positions are important to the narrative, but this knowledge is assumed rather than explained; the reader is expected to work out the importance and significance of rank in the hospital structure, as in this introduction:

When I was last in O.P.D. .... he was Mr Greswolde's H.S., and later he was R.S.O. for a time. I remembered Marty's spell of nights on Women's Surgical, and the evening she and Larry Draycott had gone out to celebrate his Fellowship – but he was a Consultant now I reminded myself. A consultant wouldn't be seen dead hobnobbing with a Staff nurse.[35]

There is much emphasis on such professional knowledge; it is scientific learning coupled with practical nursing skills that are shown to characterize the successful nurse. The heroines of these narratives have a strong sense of professional pride; their desire to nurse clearly demands more than traditional expectations of femininity; their ambition is expressed in very strong terms, and often explicitly challenges gender assumptions:

'I've always thought I'd like to be a nurse, Mark', she said desperately ... 'Most women and girls think that at some time or other', he said absently. 'It's a sort of continuation of their love for dolls, you know. When they grow too old to play with dolls they hanker after dressing up as a nurse and looking after bigger dolls. It's quite natural, and soon passes.' He got up, ignoring her gasp of indignation and her shocked expression.[36]

Such a refusal of traditional expectations of women (Mark later comes to acknowledge his mistake and is thus eventually deemed a worthy hero) are frequent in these novels, and their narratives are consistently at pains to stress the technical and professionally demanding skills of the work. Any glamorous idealization of the profession is considered to be naïve and distinctly unprofessional, as one doctor-hero sardonically notes of the heroine's nursing ambitions:

If you've been seeing a lot of glamorous films about hospital life, then naturally you want to be a nurse – half the younger female population in the country goes through that phase, thanks to the films and the plays written around the subject![37]

The reader is not spared the gritty details of damaged bodies and the tedious and unglamorous tasks involved in repairing them: 'I took out stitches, cleaned cuts, soaked whitlows, spread kaolin and instilled drops.'[38]

This practicality and lack of sentiment are characteristics of the fictional career girl of the 1950s, but in the figure of the nurse they are tempered by a 'feminine' tenderness. A 1956 novel describes its nurse-heroine as having qualities that override the spectre of an 'unfeminine' modern working woman:

There was a sort of melting warmth about her that was not to be found in the usual run of modern young girls. Maybe it was the times and the harsh, post-war tempo of life that were remorselessly grinding it out.[39]

The educationalist and champion of working women, Marjorie Tait, marked out nursing as a different category of profession from others undertaken by women during the war, and saw the difference explicitly in gendered terms:

When in the second world war women in large numbers joined the armed forces of their countries as auxiliaries, they wore a uniform which was a modified version of a soldier's, a sailor's or an airman's. The hospital Nurse also wears a uniform, but it is entirely and often emphatically feminine, part of the tradition of her work, which is traditionally women's work.[40]

The postwar fictional and actual nurse was, despite her entry into the male world of work and science, still expected to uphold the traditional qualities of femininity. The nurse might be a newly professionalized working woman, but the skills and qualities asked of her were also those required of an ideal wife and mother in the era of 'domestic science'. She might achieve professional status, but her role is always narratively defined by her subordination to the higher status of the doctor. As Barbara Cartland (rather improbably) acidly pointed out of the 1950s medical romance: 'They always had the doctor marrying the nurse.'[41]

Marriage and motherhood

The generic expectations of the romance form mean that marriage as a happy ending is invariably the resolution to these medical fictions; and so the nursing heroine has all the qualities expected of the contemporary ideal wife and mother. The demands that an eminent male surgeon makes upon Nurse Janet, in one example, are explicitly close to those of a wife. In a conflation of her roles as professional nurse and fiancée, Janet obediently complies with his demands:

'I shall need some fresh pyjamas and a clean handkerchief or two and perhaps you could bring along a few of my books and any letters there may be waiting for me?' Janet accepted the commission with an almost pathetic eagerness, writing down a list of the few necessities he wished her to buy for him and carrying it across to the Nurses' Home.[42]

Nursing is also explicitly associated with motherhood in most of these novels. A 1957 novel opens with the competent nurse-heroine instructing a young mother in the bathing of a baby, as if to identify the profession-alization of motherhood as one of the most significant aspects of her training. This heroine does experience a trace of envy of the mothers that she treats, 'a pang, a little secret ache of unfulfilment',[43] but such wistfulness is relatively rare. More frequently, the maternal qualities of the nursing heroine suggest that the skills of the professional nurse can slide easily from the public to the private sphere; they are just as appropriate to the mothering of her own family as to the world of work. It is not seen as inevitable that the nurse will continue to work after marriage, but it is assumed that her skills will be redeployed in the service of her own family.

Nursing training and medical skills are seen as unequivocally beneficial in the social sphere. Both the First and Second World Wars had constructed an image of the nurse as an ideal and maternal feminine presence in a brutal world of men. As Brenda McBryde put it:

> [the patient's] intermediary between life as it was and how it will be in the future is his nurse. The bond between them is a kind of physical love. Temporarily, she is mother, wife and sister in one female image.[44]

This 'emphatically feminine' and eroticized image of the nurse carried across and remained current in a whole range of media discourses in the postwar period. Nursing training is seen in these novels as a discipline that is good for both women citizens and their husbands and families. It remains of import-ant social benefit whether that training is employed in the context of work or the home; a 'feminization' of medicine that is professionally and domesti-cally influential:

> That year of discipline had been good for her and taught her to have a will and a mind of her own, which would be a firm foundation for a marriage with so arrogant a young man . . . He was on his way to being probably the most eminent surgeon in the country . . . but Jane would give him a sense of integrity, a balance, a beauty, a deep happiness . . . without which he would never be a completely successful surgeon.[45]

The nurse-heroine often does leave her profession for marriage at the end of the novel, but this is seen as not so much a wasted training as a means of improving the nation's mothers, in that it takes the ethos of the medical profession and the National Health Service into the community: '"Service", Queen Frieda's motto was, but there were all kinds of service, and in the end the best service that most women could do for the community was to care for their husbands and families.'[46] The hospital nurse is seen as a manifestation of the 'womanly' role that can and should be taken into the wider community; through their nursing training, young women are represented as in the process of becoming more rounded people and consequently better citizens. A 1957 fictional matron outlines her criteria for the selection of nurses for training:

> We want girls to go right through with their training, and become useful to the community. That was what the hospital was for – to serve the community ... hospital training was going to do this girl good, and help her to be a more responsible member of society.[47]

The fictional nurse offers an ideal model of the 'partner' that Ferdinand Zweig and others so commended as the proper status for the postwar woman citizen, and her marriage to a doctor (the invariable choice of partner in these novels) represents an appropriately scientific basis for parenting the nation's future generations.

Social mobility

The postwar fictional nurse also functions narratively to resolve potential conflicts around social mobility and class transition. The vocation or training for nursing could allow both for a validation of middle-class working women, and also for the professionalization and training of working-class women. A student nurse 'with a pronounced cockney accent' comes to recognize, in her assessment of an upper-class colleague, that: 'We're all on the same level here – all student nurses. She's no better than I am now, even though I did leave school at fifteen.'[48]

Nursing represents a form of meritocracy that enables young women from a range of class backgrounds to achieve professional status. The hospital is a world in which a fictional nurse from a working-class background can acquire sufficient cultural capital to hold her own in any social circle, and 'the farm labourer's daughter [can become] Sister of Foster Ward'.[49] Nursing training is shown in these novels to be a means of throwing different classes together in a common cause. The snobbish Jane arrives at nursing school as 'an over-made-up creature who talked in such a la-di-da fashion and made fun of those people who didn't have a B.B.C. accent'.[50] The ensuing narrative offers a reconciliation of class difference through a shared dedication to duty, as Jane is trained into a democratic sensibility and comes to respect the importance of a medical 'team'. It is part of Jane's maturing process to learn to overcome her snobbery, while her working-class colleagues similarly have to overcome their prejudices and grudgingly come to respect her profession-alism as a nurse; the hospital is a site of the new egalitarianism.

Romance is also presented as a means of reconciling class difference and decrying aristocratic snobberies. The heroine of *Bachelor of Medicine* (1956) is hardly working class, but she does come from 'honest country stock' and has no upper-class pretensions. She has (as the narrative repeatedly insists) reached the status of sister in a hospital ward through her competence and hard work, but despite her meritocratic achievement, she is jilted by her aristocratic doctor fiancé as not 'a suitable match for the son of Sir Felix Asperley'. This false hero is clearly constructed in the novel as a cad, unappreciative of the practical middle-class qualities the heroine manifests. The heroine finally exacts her revenge by marriage to a doctor of even greater status and medical brilliance within the hospital hierarchy, although it takes a near-fatal car accident and the perfidy of the upper-class false hero to enable her to recognize the unobtrusive but sterling qualities of the 'true' hero:

> Unfailingly reliable, unobtrusively kind and so quiet and undemand-ing that one simply accepted his good-natured presence and made use of him, without any sort of tangible acknowledgement. Joe never asked for thanks, he never asked for anything: he was there when he was needed, and when he wasn't he retired into the background, seemingly content to remain unnoticed.[51]

This hero is clearly a counterpoint to an outmoded snobbish false hero and he reveals himself as the true hero through a proper appreciation of the hero-ine's professional competence. His reliable and self-effacing qualities are also those required of a nurse-heroine; in a celebration of the unobtrusive, their romance blossoms in a shared but quiet commitment to the National Health Service. Both hero and heroine have seized the new opportunities of the Welfare State, and their partnership represents a triumph of egalitarian dedication to duty over the nepotism and old-boy network that are here seen to have once dominated the medical profession.

The romantic hero of the medical romance is repeatedly less likely to be an upper-class surgeon or consultant than a workmanlike colleague to the heroine nurse. A snobbish surgeon is likened in one 1956 novel to Adolf

Hitler in his arrogance and grandiose manner towards the nursing staff.[52] Often the narrative conflict will be structured around an élite and skilled specialist who presents himself as the rival to the more ordinary workaday male doctor actually destined for the heroine. The heroine of *Dear Doctor Everett* rejects the internationally acclaimed 'genius in his profession' in favour of the true hero, who is more suitably modest.[53]

Capable competence

In her dedication and competent professionalism, the nurse's mythical capabilities extend to the tidying up of social ills. Whether inoculating children, bandaging wounds or providing maternity advice, the nurse's professionalism is presented as of medical and social importance. There is a set piece in almost every medical romance (whether based in a hospital or some other kind of medical practice) in which the heroine wins over a small working-class child and convinces him (or, much more rarely, her) of the sense and caring of the National Health Service.

The sensibility of the nurse is seen in these novels as a bulwark against any potential ignorance and lack of care in the community. She is also a figure who militates against the extremes of tradition and modernity. Nurses are shown to be empathetic but professional in the face of death, their medical knowledge offering a protection against the retrogressiveness of outmoded traditions, but also against the potential barbarism of modern youth. The male teenager (the iconic figure of the 1950s) injured in a motor-bike or car accident is also among the recurrent surgical set pieces of these novels. Motor accidents caused by an excess of speed or 'tearaway' behaviour abound in the narratives and are vividly demonstrated as blighting young lives. There is a regular loss of limbs in young male characters; patients who were once active sportsmen, cricketers or footballers are literally and metaphorically emasculated. It is the nurse who patches up their physical wounds, but she also gives them a reason to live by reminding them, often simply by her very presence, of the responsibilities of 'good citizenship'. The scientific and practical common sense of the nurse is shown to assuage guilt and change attitudes; a young man gratefully acknowledges her sensible advice after the death of his girlfriend in a motor-bike crash:

'You really believe that? That it was just plain scientific cause and effect? You think things happen just like that?'
'Yes' I said firmly. 'I do.'
'Thanks ... Thanks a lot, Nurse.'[54]

The hospital is in itself a place of order and organization in a potentially disorderly world, a beacon of cleanliness and tidiness and a defence against the clutter of the modern consumer society. And it is the figure of the nurse who achieves that tidying up, as in this 1956 description of a hospital ward:

> The dark linoleum shone, each of the thirty white-painted hospital beds stood in perfect alignment with its neighbour, coverlets unruffled and blankets correctly tucked in, bedside tables and white enamelled lockers cleared of the litter of cigarette packets, newspapers and pools coupons with which the men normally cluttered them.[55]

The advantages of new technical and medical advances in hospital medicine are constantly championed; the most skilled male doctors (and most eligible heroes) are represented as those who have been to America and have trained in the latest surgical techniques. Modern technical developments and gadgetry in medicine are represented as exciting and positive; in the words of a typical narrative, a dramatic cure is effected by 'all the resources of modern radiological technique'. Technology is benign and helpful in the professional life of a working nurse: one heroine is thrilled by the effects of new antibiotics and a 'new nylon syringe that does speed things up!'

Romantic novels of the postwar period, and not only those set in hospitals or surgeries, manifest a real sense of commitment to a National Health Service. There is a strong sense in these novels that the nurse is supported by a system that trains her in the best medical traditions. There can sometimes be a trace of resentment at the imposition of bureaucracy, but this is more frequently seen as helpful rather than constraining; the National Health Service is frequently shown to finance the heroine's professional expenses. A district nurse is delighted with her allowance for her expenses and undeterred by the red tape involved:

> she had to complete Form F/T6 to claim for her expenses and allowances. It was quite a thing, calculating her mileage for the past month, postage, telephone calls, and all the rest of it. By the time she had it all neatly tabulated and had certified that it was a true and correct statement 'in accordance with the current regulations of the County Council', the morning had slipped by.[56]

The communal benefits of nursing skills are not restricted to the hospital in these novels. Although the majority of medical romances are set in hospitals, nursing heroines are seen to be at home in every aspect of the community. Like their literary predecessors, the popular American heroines Sue Barton and Cherry Ames,[57] the nursing heroines of the 1950s can belong in any number of different environments: general practice, clinics, workplaces and schools. There is a substantial subdivision of the genre which focuses on nurses working in forms of medical practice outside the hospital: *Factory Nurse, Hotel Nurse, Emergency Nurse, District Nurse*, while *Hospital on Wheels* demonstrates the peripatetic possibilities of nursing.[58] Wherever she may be located, the nurse acts as a signifier of new and better living and working conditions and a new nationally efficient health service. In a 1959 novel, a hospital and a factory nurse co-operate to ensure the best treatment for 'a man from the factory up the road, with a sliver of metal swarf in his right eye. The works nurse had sent him with a note.'[59]

The nurse is presented as a conduit for taking the ethos and skills of medicine in the Welfare State to the wider community. She is shown to be part of a health care system which has become integrated into the Welfare State and become part of people's daily lives. Preventative medicine is championed as just as important as the drama of the operating theatre; the school nurse is as intrinsic to the national health as the hospital surgeon: 'She weighs and measures the children and does the sight testing and looks at their feet.'[60]

District Nurse characterizes its heroine as a mediator between hospital training and the outside world; a local doctor describes the heroine as belonging to the local community, and it is her roots there that allow her to disseminate both her skills and her Welfare State compassion. Her qualities are akin to those of a missionary: 'A girl with a job she loves, and with roots deep in the countryside. Someone deeply sympathetic, sure of herself, and able to pass on her faith and serenity to others.'[61] This heroine shares a cottage with the 'young village schoolmistress'; both are young women committed to the education of the local community. Their skills and concern are shown to benefit all generations in the community, who are suitably grateful:

> the people she visited were usually so very thankful to see her ... The burnt child whose dressings she renewed, the tonsillitis patient who was having a daily penicillin injection, the elderly bedridden patients whom she made comfortable – their faces lit up when she came in. 'Oh, Nurse, I'm so *glad* to see you!'[62]

District Nurse also has a complex subplot which moves the novel close to the thriller genre and extends the heroine's role beyond a sphere of merely local influence into one of explicitly national purpose. The hero is a government agent, the nursing heroine his ally in defeating a dastardly plot; her capabilities are here employed to defend Britain in an international context.

Colonizing nurses

If the black nurse is significant by her absence in novels set in a British context, the white British-trained nurse is frequently transported to the former colonies. The travelling nurse is another popular sub-genre of the romance novel.[63] The nurse here becomes a missionary figure who can take the benefits of the Welfare State not only into the British community, but to the world. In her reconciliation of traditional and modern virtues the fictional nurse functions as an effective icon who can facilitate a transition from empire to Commonwealth. Written in 1956, the year of Suez and the year before Ghana and Malaysia were to become part of the Commonwealth, the end of empire is clearly unavoidable for *Nurse Wayne in the Tropics*. Nurse Wayne takes her experience and SRN qualifications to Africa, and brings with her a properly scientific and modern approach to medicine. Over the course of the narrative, she wins the respect of the 'natives' and the hero through the demonstration of her nursing skills, which, like the hero's farming skills, are seen as an appropriate 'civilizing' of African ways. Triss, the nurse-heroine, is explicitly counterpoised to the 'spoilt-kitten life' of her female employer, wife of a cocoa farmer, who stands as representative of an unsustainable colonial past.[64]

The heroine of *The Starched Cap* similarly acts as a reproach to the leisured women of the empire, but in the context of London rather than the colonies. She comes from 'a family with a long tradition of proud administrative service in the Colonial Empire' but chooses to leave her unspecified colonial home for Britain to pursue a nursing training. She is the orphaned daughter of the 'Governor of the territory', a colonial past that is clearly constructed as no longer acceptable to a new democratic work ethic. The hero comments:

> She has had nothing but a life of complete frivolity out here. Dancing, flirtations, tennis, golf and garden parties! ... I am afraid she will go to pieces entirely unless she finds some real worth-while interest in life.[65]

It is nursing that provides the 'real worth-while interest' for this particular heroine, but nursing is repeatedly invoked in these narratives as a career for women that sets itself against the class and empire snobberies of an Old England and represents something of a challenge to colonial constructs of femininity. The nurse, democratic in her training and her attitude towards patients, is 'modern', a representative of all that the war was fought for.

The idealized model of the nurse that persists throughout the 1950s begins to show signs of strain in the novels of the last years of the decade. There are traces of an acknowledgement that recruitment to nursing is falling and that the nurse herself might represent an impossible ideal, even in the context of romantic fiction. The heroine of *The Summer Break* (1960) begins a first-person narrative with plans to leave the profession, uncertain that she can conform to the image of the 'ministering angel' embodied in her colleague:

> Everything Nurse Lonnie did was always done precisely according to the book, which ought to have made her the perfect nurse; ... she was like a cool plastic nurse-doll, gliding about the ward on noiseless castors, and showing very little more human warmth than an electronic computer.[66]

Nurse Lonnie is a recognizable figure from earlier medical romances, but in the age of the 'electronic computer' she is no longer convincing. The heroine offers a resistance to the stringency of hospital regulations which remained unquestioned in earlier novels of this period. The fictional hospital which contains both Nurse Lonnie and the less exemplary heroine is nevertheless named 'The Good Hope', and, as the genre requires, the heroine ultimately finds both love and a dedication to her profession there. If earlier medical romances were at pains to deglamorize the profession, later novels refuse the image of the nurse as 'angel' and thus go still further in curtailing any over-idealization:

> you need good feet, warm hands, and the ability to keep your mouth shut. People talk about 'the noble profession' as though we deliberately set out to be martyrs. We grumble just as much as anyone else, believe me.[67]

The nurse-heroine nevertheless did offer a celebratory articulation of the newly professionalized working woman, and she personified the ethos and hopes of the Welfare State. While the medical romances of the postwar decade are novels which undoubtedly celebrate women's work and skills, their challenge to conventional patterns of gender and work remains, however, strangely muted. In spite of her new professionalization and salary, her competence and skill, the nurse, in her professional status and her role as nurturer and carer, is always subservient to a male superior. If nursing is presented as an opportunity for young women, and the heroine as an appropriate role model for the modern working woman, these narratives allow traditional hierarchies of gender and work to remain largely undisturbed. As Anne Karpf has argued of the representation of women doctors in postwar popular culture:

Women doctors may be problematic to medical drama, but nurses aren't. Drawing on cultural ideas of nursing as a kind of professionalised femaleness, nurses are depicted at best as perpetual geysers of nurturance and intuitive mothers to the world.[68]

It is the woman doctor, whose role and training in the medical hierarchy are not gender specific and whose status is equal to that of a male colleague (which despite all assurances to the contrary, the female nurse can never be), who is actually a much more subversive fictional heroine.

Notes

1. For more on the history of Mills & Boon and the history of the nursing romance, see Deborah Philips and Alan Tomlinson, 'Homeward Bound: Leisure, popular culture and consumer capitalism' in Dominic Strinati and Stephen Wagg, eds, *Come on Down? Popular Media Culture in Post-war Britain* (London: Routledge, 1992).
2. Denise Robins, *Something to Love* (London: Hutchinson, 1951).
3. Anne Karpf, *Doctoring the Media: The Reporting of Health and Medicine* (London: Routledge, 1988), p. 52.
4. Barbara Allen, *Doctor Lucy* (London: Mills & Boon, 1956), p. 18.
5. Brian Watkin, *The National Health Service: The First Phase – 1948–1974 and After* (London: George Allen and Unwin, 1978), p. 14.
6. Robert Dingwall, Anne Marie Rafferty and Charles Webster, *British Nursing: An Introduction to the Social History of Nursing* (London: Routledge, 1988), p. 104.
7. Brenda McBryde, *Quiet Heroines: Nurses of the Second World War* (London: Chatto and Windus, 1985), p. 1.
8. Ibid., p. 230.
9. Arthur Wauters, *Eve in Overalls* (no date; reprinted London: Imperial War Museum, 1995; first published during the Second World War).
10. Alex Stuart, *Bachelor of Medicine* (London: Mills & Boon, 1956), p. 170.
11. Rosemary White, *The Effects of the National Health Service on the Nursing Profession 1948–1961* (London: King Edward's Hospital Fund for London, 1985; distributed for the King's Fund by Oxford University Press), p. xii.
12. Arthur Wauters, *British Social Services – Today and Tomorrow* (no date; British Library Catalogue 1946).
13. Dingwall, Rafferty and Webster, *British Nursing*, p. 112.
14. Ibid.
15. Louis Goldman, *Angry Young Doctor* (London: Hamish Hamilton, 1957), p. 5.
16. Anne Lorraine, *My Dear Doctor* (London: Mills & Boon, 1957), p. 35.
17. Goldman, *Angry Young Doctor*, p. 58.
18. Alex Stuart, *Master of Surgery* (London: Mills & Boon, 1958), p. 103.
19. Allen, *Doctor Lucy*, p. 21.

20.   Stuart, *Bachelor of Medicine*, p. 20.

21.   Anne Lorraine, *Send for Doctor* (London: Mills & Boon, 1958), p. 16.

22.   Jean S. Macleod, *Dear Doctor Everett* (London: Mills & Boon, 1954), p. 19.

23.   Anna Neagle played Queen Victoria in both *Victoria the Great* (1937) and *Sixty Glorious Years* (1938), and the title roles in *Nurse Edith Cavell* (1939), *Odette* (based on the true story of a British woman spy with the French Resistance, 1950) and *The Lady with the Lamp* (Florence Nightingale, 1951).

24.   Macleod, *Dear Doctor Everett*, p. 31.

25.   Barbara Melosh, 'Doctors, Patients and "Big Nurse": Work and Gender in the Postwar Hospital' in Ellen Condliffe Lagemann, ed., *Nursing History: New Perspectives, New Possibilities* (New York: Teachers' College Press, Columbia University, 1983), pp. 157–79 (p. 164).

26.   1944 White Paper, 'A National Health Service', quoted in Watkin, *The National Heath Service*, p. 3.

27.   Macleod, *Dear Doctor Everett, p. 5.*

28.   Ibid., p. 6.

29.   Valerie K. Nelson, *The Starched Cap* (London: Mills & Boon, 1957), p. 6.

30.   Bess Norton, *The Quiet One* (London: Mills & Boon, 1959), p. 129.

31.   Ibid., p. 83.

32.   Goldman, *Angry Young Doctor*, p. 5.

33.   Nelson, *The Starched Cap*, p. 6.

34.   Norton, *The Quiet One*.

35.   Ibid., p. 10.

36.   Lorraine, *My Dear Doctor*, p. 5.

37.   Ibid., p. 63.

38.   Norton, *The Quiet One*, p. 31.

39.   Marjorie Moore, *A Year to Remember* (London: Mills & Boon, 1956), p. 37.

40.   Marjorie Tait, 'The Education of Women for Citizenship: some practical suggestions' *Problems in Education*, vol. VIII (Paris: Unesco, 1954), p. 11.

41.   Barbara Cartland, quoted in Joseph McAleer, *Popular Reading and Publishing in Britain 1914–1950* (Oxford: Clarendon Press, 1992), p. 119.

42.   Macleod, *Dear Doctor Everett*, p. 31.

43.   Marguerite Lees, *District Nurse* (London: Mills & Boon, 1957).

44.   McBryde, *Quiet Heroines*, p. 127.

45.   Nelson, *The Starched Cap*, p. 189.

46.   Ibid., p. 188.

47.   Ibid., p. 65.

48.   Ibid., p. 68.

49.   Stuart, *Bachelor of Medicine*, p. 94.

50.   Ibid., p. 80.

51.   Ibid., p. 42.

52.   Ibid.

53.   Macleod, *Dear Doctor Everett*, p. 20.

54.   Norton, *The Quiet One*, p. 48.

55.   Stuart, *Bachelor of Medicine*, p. 7.

56.   Lees, *District Nurse*, p. 89.

57.   For more on the Sue Barton and Cherry Ames series, see Deborah Philips, 'Healthy Heroines: Sue Barton, Lillian Wald, Lavinia Lloyd Dock and the Henry Street Clinic' in *Journal of American Studies* (forthcoming).

58.   Hilary Neal, *Factory Nurse* (London: Mills & Boon, 1961); Anne Lorraine, *Hotel Nurse* (London: Mills & Boon, 1954); Anne Lorraine, *Emergency Nurse* (London: Mills & Boon, 1955); Lees, *District Nurse*; Anne Lorraine, *Hospital on Wheels* (London: Mills & Boon, 1956).

59.   Norton, *The Quiet One*, p. 19.

60.   Lees, *District Nurse*, p. 68.

61.   Ibid., p. 98.

62.   Ibid., p. 14.

63.   See also Celine Conway, *Rustle of Bamboo* (London: Mills & Boon, 1957); Caroline Tranch, *Nurse to the Island* (London: Mills & Boon, 1957).

64.   Anne Vinton, *Nurse Wayne in the Tropics* (London: Mills & Boon, 1956).

65.   Nelson, *The Starched Cap*, p. 7.

66.   Bess Norton, *The Summer Break* (London: Mills & Boon, 1960), p. 7.

67.   Ibid., p. 26.

68.   Karpf, *Doctoring the Media*, p. 52.

8. 'White-coated girls': doctor-heroines

Doctor Marland ... caught a glimpse of herself, tall, slender in her well-cut white coat. Not even now, after many months of hospital work, could she resist the faint thrill of pride which always came to her when she caught sight of herself in her white coat. To her it was a symbol, the badge which proclaimed her, to the outside world, a qualified doctor. (Anne Lorraine, *First the Doctor*, 1958)

The 1950s spate of medical romances do not centre only on women nurses with male doctors as heroes; there is also a substantial sub-genre of hospital novels in which the heroine is a woman doctor. The doctor-heroine is a figure who comes to represent a new generation of medical practice, and who offers a means of negotiating the new structures and opportunities of the National Health Service.

Like the fictional nurse, the woman doctor offers a mythical resolution to the opposing claims of traditional versions of femininity and the modernity of a new social order; but she also represents more of a challenge to the male-dominated bastion of an ancient profession. While the woman doctor does feature as an option in the career girl novel, she is there positioned as about to embark on a professional and romantic life.[1] The doctor-heroine of the romance novel is already qualified, and her adult femininity is central to the narrative structure. The fictional woman doctor goes still further than the nurse in allying professional training with a middle-class service ethic, and allows for a discussion of the highly trained and educated woman in the Welfare State of postwar Britain.

From 1949, grant applications to the Ministry of Labour from women wishing to train as doctors outnumbered those for nursing or any other form of medical practice. Applications by women for medical training numbered 448 in 1949, and had risen to 10,696 by 1952, a figure larger than for any other form of training for women, other than teaching.[2] The growth in the numbers of women applicants to the health service was a measure of a general draw towards medicine after the war; between 1939 and 1952 numbers in the medical profession rose from 37,429 to 50,574.[3]

The woman doctor does embody the traditional caring virtues of 'femininity', but as a woman with a scientific and professional training she also answers to the 'modern' 1950s aspirations of science and citizenship. In this image from a 1956 novel, the doctors' lodgings neatly place her in an uninterrupted continuum between the old and the new:

> Seventeenth century houses neighboured each other ... dignified and graceful .... Further on the houses were smaller, newer, less dignified, but they made up for it by the picturesque gaiety of their carefully tended gardens each bounded by a low white-painted wooden fence. The doctor's house stood midway between old and new, a small unpretentious timbered place, having something of the charm of both.[4]

This doctor-heroine similarly manages to retain 'the charm of both old and new'; she embodies the 'dignity and grace' of her profession, but the youth and attractiveness which all romance heroines must possess also grant her a 'picturesque gaiety'. The woman doctor is in herself a novelty, but she carries with her the values of a long-standing and worthy male medical tradition.

Professional women

Medical romances very much affirm and celebrate the heroine's justifiable pride in her achievement as a professional woman. The doctor-heroine is invariably represented as academically gifted and successful in her chosen profession; Doctor Lucy is typical: 'The gold Medal – only awarded in exceptional circumstances at St. Christopher's – had been awarded to her, and she was the first woman to have won it since the war.'[5] A qualified doctor is shown in these novels as a role for young women to aspire to, a model of contemporary citizenship in her intelligence and devotion to duty. In the words of an admiring nurse, 'I envy you Miss Royston – being a doctor, I mean, having what it takes to be one. The – the selflessness, the dedication – and, of course, the brains.'[6]

Medicine and meritocracy

The doctor-heroine is marked by an insistently 'ordinary' background, her class origin limited to a range between genteel poverty and the solid professional classes. None comes from a particularly underprivileged family (although this can be the case with a medical hero), but they will emphatically not be wealthy either; the doctor-heroine is a product of a meritocracy. If her father is himself a doctor (as is sometimes the case), he practises in a modest clinic rather than as a hospital surgeon or private physician; although always firmly middle class in her tastes and values, the heroine's habitat is more likely to be unapologetically suburban than 'county' or London: 'Her own people, Marion knew, were much more ordinary. Her father was a chartered accountant, shrewd, worldly, pleasant-mannered; her mother a suburban matron, full of her household and her bridge.'[7] Doctor Marion is that rare figure in postwar fiction, the scholarship girl; her training would have predated the Welfare State (she is practising in 1951). Marion is at pains to explain to a small working-class boy that her status does not derive from social position, but from hard work. It is clearly implied that her scholarships are the equivalent of the new grants for training and that the working-class boy has similar opportunities, now provided by the Butler Education Act: 'I've paid for my own education since I was fourteen. Junior county scholarship, then a senior one, at a secondary school. Scholarship to Cambridge and another to my hospital.'[8]

Class is, however, generally less emphasized for the medical heroine of these narratives than is her gender. Always represented as securely middle class in her tastes and milieu, the new potential for upward social mobility through the acquisition of professional skills is instead often displaced on to male characters. Eminent male surgeons (often titled) frequently reveal themselves to be of working-class origin. One surgeon is the son of a miner; the brilliant doctor-hero of a 1956 novel is evidence of what can be achieved through ability and dedication: 'For a Mill lad to have qualified as a doctor was, in itself, nothing short of a minor miracle – they had had so little, needed so much, and had been offered so few opportunities.'[9] This character's final alliance with the heroine is based on a shared understanding of the difficulties faced in the medical profession on the grounds of both gender and class. It is the male character who offers a means of exploring the conflicts of class prejudice, enabling the woman doctor to trouble, rather than directly challenge, the archaisms and exclusions of an old-boy network.

The doctor-heroine is frequently depicted as distanced from the rich and privileged classes; her rival for the hero's attentions is often from an upper-class background, but she herself is scornful of private patients. There is almost always a scene in these novels in which the heroine is invited to a dinner party at which she feels uncomfortable (but holds her own) among titled guests. The profession of doctor is nevertheless perceived as one that demands respect. Whatever her own class background may be, the woman doctor's ethos and professional skills place her firmly within a middle-class frame, and she is shown to be accorded some of the regard and deference once accorded to the gentry. Her professional status is also represented as giving the woman doctor somewhat more licence than other women, as one snobbish patient demonstrates: 'Mrs Johnson ... didn't disapprove of men drinking unless they were doctors, but, on the other hand, disapproved strongly of women drinking unless they were doctors.'[10]

The health service is itself represented as a crucible for a new meritocracy, in which the opportunity for women and those from different class back-grounds to train as doctors stands for a new egalitarian ideal. The hospital is invariably shown to be making complex medical treatments available to everyone; it is a democratic institution and the woman doctor is in herself seen as a beneficent sign of its progressiveness. Each novel invokes a range of (frequently comic) working-class characters in the wards and waiting-rooms, whose function is to demonstrate both the doctor-heroine's democratic social skills and the new availability of hospital treatment to all. In a 1958 novel, the hospital's senior consultant and the wife of a trawlerman require the same highly technical (and costly, although this is not stressed) operation, in demonstration of the fact that the resources of the National Health Service are available to everyone. In language that brings together a working-class vernacular and an awkward familiarity with the titled classes, the trawler-man is amazed that he now has access to 't'specialists ... Sir Martin Fitzcarron and him they call Sir Somebody Gilmore'.[11]

In the context of this egalitarian ethos, the woman doctor represents a challenge to inherited beliefs about gender and class and embodies a new independence for women; her professional status is not dependent upon marriage or background. If the nursing heroine generally achieves upward social mobility through marriage to a doctor, in a transition from skilled worker to the professional classes, the woman doctor is a professional in her own right. She is already a proven woman member of the meritocracy, whose challenge extends much further than the professionalization of the 'feminine' attributes of nurturing that is so celebrated in nursing romances. A patrician woman character in a 1954 novel is disconcerted by the fact of a woman doctor in ways which would not apply to a nurse. Her discomfort is clearly presented as founded on both class and gender prejudice:

Ah, women doctors ... so unfeminine! ... Surely doctors should be men. Doctor Moir was their brother's employee and colleague. How difficult it was to remember that employees could be socially equal. Now a nurse; she would present no problem, sitting at one's table.[12]

While the snobbery of this position is represented as unacceptably antiquated, there is a recognition in these novels that the woman doctor is something of a pioneering figure for working women.

Doctors and nurses

The doctor-heroine is almost always the only woman of her status and age in the novel and her position as a woman in a male-dominated profession is recognized as fraught with difficulties. As one nurse acknowledges,

It's not very often that we get a woman medical student ... [the consultant] simply doesn't believe that they have a place in medicine ... One of the girls in my set went on and did medicine, but I don't think she had a very easy time. The medical students felt she knew more than they did, and so she did as far as clinical experience was concerned. And oddly enough, the Sisters and the Nurses resented her on the wards.[13]

'Resentment' is a recurrent term in descriptions of nurses' attitudes towards women medical students, and points to the anomalous position of a newly qualified young woman doctor. A woman physician is shown to arouse conflicting feelings, caught as she is between the envy of women nurses and the prejudice of her male doctor colleagues. In an episode which appears in most medical romances in different variations, a heroine begins the novel and her first year of residency in a state of 'melancholy', ostracized by both nurses and male colleagues: 'Was there not a thinly veiled antagonism amongst the nurses, an infuriating tolerance among the doctors?'[14] The 'lady doctor' repeatedly has to prove herself and her professional competence to the nursing staff, who tend not to be individualized and named as they generally are in novels with a nurse-heroine. There is a clear implication that the professional status of the woman doctor is resented by her less exalted colleagues, and that envy is most frequently expressed as a snide denigration of the doctor's femininity.

The 'femininization' of medicine

The doctor-heroine is defined by her colleagues and her family as 'different', in terms which confirm the woman nurse as a more traditional model of working femininity:

> Her parents had tried to dissuade her ... after all, doctoring wasn't exactly what they had hoped for their only daughter ... she could take up nursing instead – wouldn't that do? Nurses seemed to like their job, but they often gave it up when they got married. They hadn't wanted their daughter to be different – to be a bit of an oddity – a girl who didn't even want to get married.
>   'I don't want to be a nurse,' she had explained stubbornly, 'I'm going to be a doctor.'[15]

These are narratives which, like the career novel *Margaret Becomes a Doctor*, endorse that stubbornness and are sympathetic to the ambition of the woman doctor; she is, after all, a heroine. The hospital is seen in these novels as an appropriate site for working women, and the Welfare State as having created new opportunities for women to work. Doctor Anne's father may tell his daughter that 'medicine is still a man's world' (as fathers in career girl novels often do), but his daughter can challenge him with a fervour supported by the ethos and modernity of a Welfare State: 'Don't you know that there are women's hospitals staffed by women physicians and surgeons, and they don't even need a man to tell them what to do next?'[16] Doctor Anne's medical career is paralleled with that of her male childhood friend, Jonathan. Both apply for medical training, but while he comes from a long tradition of male doctors, the heroine's father disapproves of her vocation; a man has the moral support and cultural capital not available to a heroine. Doctor Anne, however, establishes her own contacts in the hierarchy of the medical profession; working temporarily as a typist in the office in the hospital, her efficiency and dedicated interest attract the attention of an eminent professor, and so she gains experience and knowledge beyond that of her male counter-part. Like the heroine of the bachelor girl novel, Anne reaps the rewards of not despising low status and apparently unremarkable work. The heroine's lack of privilege, which necessitated such humble work, is thus transformed into an asset in the career ladder, and her humility is rewarded.

Women doctors in official discourses of health and in fiction are understood to have particularly 'feminine' skills which articulate and enshrine the Welfare State's relationship with the community but which are not shared by their male colleagues. Doctor-heroines are shown to have a special sensibility in their understanding of personal relationships, a sensitivity to the social situations of their patients, and a particular ability in dealing with women patients and relatives, and in comforting children. In an episode which recurs in a number of these novels, a woman doctor reassures a patient's wife, while the narrative comments: 'what man could have dealt with the secret fear haunting the woman's eyes?'[17]

Such scenes are not presented as simply an affirmation of the heroine's maternal skills (although they are certainly that), but also as a specifically feminine asset that is professionally significant and beneficial to the practice of medicine. Doctor Anne's approach to patient care demonstrates that shared female experience can be advantageous to medical diagnosis and the efficiency of the health service:

> she found the women grateful for her gentleness ... There was sincere interest when she asked about their homes, and she made notes for the Almoner when she found them worrying about families left to their own devices when the letter had come calling them into hospital. It didn't take her long to discover that things like these were often the real causes of a puzzlingly slow return to health. What good could the surgeon's skill do when a woman's strength was sapped by the steady fret of whether someone was cooking Bill's supper the way he liked it, and would Mary remember that carrots made Baby sick? At the gentle bidding of Anne's voice their troubles came tumbling out.[18]

The heroine becomes the means through which technological advances in medicine are fused with care in the community, the feminine a way of injecting personal concern into a potentially frightening scientific medical world. Despite their celebration of 'science', these novels betray an unease about the advance of technology in medicine, and a sense that the increasing specialization of its practitioners is a potential loss to medicine. As one male doctor articulates:

> I'm all for specialisation myself – I'm sure it makes for greater efficiency in the long run ... we've got science at our fingertips, we do a good job, but we lack – I don't know, I think it's humanity.[19]

It is the feminine principle, in the person of the heroine, who can mediate these conflicting demands of humanity and efficiency. This is repeatedly required of the doctor-heroine by patients and male colleagues, and is often the foundation for romance. One progressive medical hero asks his heroine to bring her 'womanly intuition, your maternal instincts' to his work as a psychiatrist; he sees her 'femininity' as attuned to the 'spiritual' and thus as medically useful: 'I am quite convinced that you cannot separate any physical disease from the mental and spiritual life of the patient. Doctors are coming to believe this more and more.'[20]

The woman doctor stands as a representative and harbinger of such new approaches to health, but she also heralds shifts in attitudes towards women in the professions in the postwar period. Prejudice against women in the medical profession is coded as part of the ignorance and resistance to change that the Welfare State is designed to abolish. Objections to the woman doctor are frequently displaced on to a minor character who stands as a representative of prejudice, and who is always summarily corrected; 'I don't hold with women doctors myself, do you?' is a typical remark at the beginning of these narratives. The doctor, and particularly the woman doctor, is shown to be a recruit in the battle of the new Welfare State against class deference and 'old-fashioned' wisdoms that no longer have any place. In one novel, an initially hostile nurse comes to recognize the advantages of the woman practitioner, and chides a patient for her ignorance: 'As long as there are women like you in the world . . . we'll need all the women doctors we can get, believe me!'[21]

Welfare State women

The doctor-heroine embodies a belief in progress; in her mission to improve health, she also represents a refusal of a return to the conditions of the 1920s and 1930s. Doctor Lucy is inspired to train by tales of prewar poverty:

> But in the twenties and early thirties, the Mill district had been hard hit by unemployment, and Lucy had often listened to her father's bitter complaints of the conditions there. He had told heartrending stories of the ragged half-starved children and of the filthy insanitary homes in which, somehow, they managed to exist: of their constant struggle against hunger and disease and of the unfailing courage and cheerfulness which characterised them.[22]

Modernity, science and progress are seen as the means of combating such conditions; women doctors and nurses represented a new generation of committed workers for the social good whose training qualifies them to combat poverty and disease and teach their fellow citizens. Resistance to the woman doctor and the new medical professionalism is repeatedly derided in fictional encounters with patients; such scenes function to champion the benefits of the Welfare State and the National Health Service.

The 'white-coated girl' of the eponymous 1955 novel briskly admonishes a patient who harks back to the past and does not appreciate her advantages as a beneficiary of the National Health Service: 'Your grandmother probably managed quite well,' she agreed mildly. 'But it is possible she might have managed even better had she been given the advantages you are given my dear ... What is wrong with baby ... ?'[23]

The National Health Service woman doctor is thus shown to be an emissary of the Welfare State, one who is even more highly trained than the nurse. Her personal ambition is fuelled by National Health Service principles, and her professional training and dedication are a means of bringing its promises to fruition:

> Anne was soft hearted: the poverty she saw and the conditions in which her patients lived moved her deeply, but she accepted the fact that, until she qualified, there was little she could do to be of practical assistance.[24]

The medical practice and principles of the doctor-heroines endorse a position of holistic medical care, dramatized in their response to patients and colleagues, and also in their career trajectories. Their femininity is seen as more appropriate to community medicine, and thus any direct competition with élite male practitioners (often embodied in the hero) is neatly evaded. Although doctor-heroines are shown to be more than capable of undertaking difficult surgical procedures (Doctor Lucy is not alone as the winner of a prestigious gold medal), their professional field at the end of the novel is much more likely to be some form of general practice than the operating theatre. Anne Caxton sets up a community health mobile clinic, while Mary Marland goes into partnership with her psychiatrist hero to develop a clinic for 'psychosomatic illness'. Marion Blake has a general practice rooted in the community where she serves 'a new estate', while Doctor Lucy, who at the novel's opening is preparing for a brilliant surgical career, finally chooses a rural general practice as the appropriate forum for her skills.

The National Health Service Act had created three branches of the health service, of which the second, Local Health Services (which include general practitioners and rural hospitals), is most often seen in fiction as a more suitable job for a woman. This is not only because general practice is characterized as a relatively easy option (although that can be the case), but also because the woman doctor is seen to bring to medicine a broader range of understandings than a purely rationalist science. This 'feminization' of medical science is shown in these novels to be most appropriate to district and community health, where maternity services and care of the elderly are paramount.

This fictional emphasis on the appropriateness of general and rural medicine to the woman doctor is reproduced in the actual figures of a report on women doctors working in 1962 (all of whom would have trained in the 1950s); a large proportion (35.5 per cent) of them did work in general practice. Hospital careers were much less likely to be available on a part-time basis, and were thus a difficult option for working women with children, as the survey's figures indicate: 'single and childless married women were most commonly found in the hospital service ... General practice, on the other hand, absorbed more of the married women with children and widowed and divorced women.'[25]

Whatever her final professional destination might be, the fictional medical student's training is always the best available. Doctor-heroines are invariably students at a large urban hospital, which is seen as an élite medical institution (as they were within the profession). In 1957 there were 36 such hospitals, described by a doctor of the period as 'the medical show-places of Britain'.[26] The medical romance similarly treats the teaching hospitals with great respect; one novel refers unironically to 'the idolised and revered Manderfield's hospital'.

Medicine and motherhood

The professional training of the woman doctor is repeatedly seen in fiction as beneficial to the nation, in producing both a medical practitioner and a properly qualified mother. The woman doctor represents an even stronger ideal of maternity than does the nurse, her 'family' being the community, as one newly qualified young woman articulates:

> I want to heal bodies – is that unwomanly? What does the ordinary wife and mother do with her life, nine-tenths of the time? Exactly what I'm doing, only on a very small, limited scale. She cares for her family ... I want hundreds, possibly thousands of people to care for, to comfort, to help. Is that unwomanly?[27]

Professionally trained in the scientific care of patients, the medical heroine is shown as up to date with new technologies, her healing skills a demonstration of 'modern' approaches towards the maternal. These novels often explicitly suggest that their heroines are a model for a new attitude towards motherhood, both in their interactions with patients and in their own maternal ambitions. The skills and qualities that fit the medical heroine for her work of national and social importance are precisely those championed in an ideal 1950s' mother. The woman doctor, like the modern mother, is required to be practical, commonsensical and scientifically informed. She is also unsentimental; medical heroines invariably have practical, 'no nonsense' names (Anne and Mary are frequent). Doctor Marion is approvingly told that her name is 'A good name. Old English, sensible.'

The experience of organized childcare during the war and the restructuring of the health and welfare services had established a newly professionalized approach to and language for 'traditional' maternal skills, as a woman commentator noted at the time:

We have seen a good deal of change in standards of child care in Great Britain in the last generation, particularly during and since the second world war. One of the many factors contributing to the change has been the provision of day nurseries and crêches for the babies of women at work and the extension of the system of nursery schools during the war. Many people are concerned lest such welfare provision, together with 'free' health and education services, family allowances and other forms of state intervention in family life, may diminish in parents their sense of responsibility for their children . . . but there is already some evidence on the other side which is relevant here. Matrons of nurseries say that . . . in matters of feeding, discipline and so forth, the mothers tend to take the professional standards of child care back from the nursery into the home.[28]

The 'professionalization' of childcare is evidenced in the profusion of male expert advice on bringing up baby that appeared throughout the 1950s. A World Health Organization conference on 'Maternal Care and Mental Health' was the basis for the publication of John Bowlby's *Childcare and the Growth of Love* in 1953, and Dr Spock's *Baby and Childcare* was first published in Britain in 1955.[29]

This official discourse of childcare is echoed – in its belief that women can be educated to be better mothers – in most medical romances, and in all the novels featuring women doctors. Each one has a scene in which a mother and child enter the hospital or practice and through their encounter with the treatments and practitioners of the new National Health Service come to a clearer understanding of their own health and welfare and the benefits of the Welfare State. Motherhood is not structured as a 'natural' instinct, but as a set of skills which can be taught, analogous to a profession; a young (and childless) doctor-heroine 'quietly advises' one of her misguided patients:

> what many mothers find it difficult to believe is that mothercraft doesn't always come by instinct, any more than being a doctor or a dentist or a school-teacher does! We all have to learn, and there's no need to be ashamed to be a pupil to the most wonderful profession in the world, my dear.[30]

Health care is seen here, as in all of these novels, as a matter of good housekeeping; the new educational model of housework as a 'domestic science' informs the language of childcare. Scenes recur in which women doctors or (more infrequently) nurses bring the new ethos of the Welfare State to poor and ill-educated young mothers, and heroines are represented as taking pains not to appear judgemental: 'Doctors have been dealing with babies like George for many a long year, and they know that what kills babies is their mother's ignorance – not their wickedness.'[31] As 'housework' becomes 'domestic science', so medical science can be explained in the practical language of the household; the woman doctor is an extended version of the practical mothering skills taught by the scientific approach of this new domesticity. As the 'white-coated girl' explains to yet another suspicious mother, the care of her baby requires much the same common-sense approach as a new domestic appliance:

> Actually you're treating this young man in just the same way as a careless housewife treats a boiler. You're not giving him enough air to keep his own central heating system working, do you see?[32]

Another doctor-heroine attempts to persuade a young mother that urine is not an appropriate cure for her baby's eye problems, and is told: 'It's an old fashioned remedy. You wouldn't have heard of it. Doctors are all so new-fangled nowadays. But country people have their own ways.'[33] Such episodes function to show the health service and its workers resisting the retrogressive traditions of old wives' tales and moving the public towards a new and healthy scientificism; a benign technocracy in the face of the ignorance of a resistant community.

There are contradictory positions within this discourse of maternity care in the new Welfare State: on the one hand there is progressive support for a system which offers the best health care for those who would have been disadvantaged before the war, but at the same time there is an implicit élitism in the representation of those who are new to it as ignorant and feckless. This position can often veer towards the eugenicist; it is not infrequently sug-gested that there are those among the lower orders who would have been better off without offspring at all. The mother who washes her baby's eyes in urine is shown to have already lost four children to lack of care, and to manifest a singular lack of distress at their demise. The hope that these narratives hold out for such 'unsuitable mothers' (in a recurrent phrase) is that they can be taught proper maternal skills and be improved by the middle-class ethos embodied in the doctors and nurses of the Welfare State.

If women doctors are represented as having the skills required for good parenting, so too are men in the medical profession. A surgeon's (and surgeons in these novels are, with rare exceptions, male) hands are recur-rently described as strong and gentle. Male doctors inevitably identify themselves as worthy heroes for the doctor-heroine in a scene in which they demonstrate their warmth towards a child patient; a false hero often betrays his narrative function by his lack of concern for a child. In his calm but authoritative approach to children the hero signifies his skills as a doctor and as a potential father:

> his voice was clear but quiet, as if fashioned for the sole purpose of bringing reassurance and encouragement to the sick and weary, his hands were strong and well shaped, hands she had seen at work with small children, marvelling at their firm yet gentle touch.[34]

Although, as Elizabeth Wilson has noted, the dominant expectation was that the postwar 'career woman' would also be single and childless, this is markedly not the case in novels which feature the woman doctor.[35] And it would seem that the romance of the hospital or medical school was not entirely a fantasy either; 57 per cent of women doctor respondents to a questionnaire had married doctors. The actual figures of the number of married women doctors trained throughout the 1950s demonstrate that the belief that the career woman doctor should also be single was ideological rather than actual: 54.4 per cent of married women doctors were working full time by 1962. The figures, however, also suggest the very real problems of combining childcare and continuing with a career path: 46 per cent of women doctors with children were working part time in 1962, while 36.6 per cent had given up work entirely. And of those, the survey discovered that: 'There were 1067 women among the 1533 who were not employed who said they wished to work.'[36]

Marriage and medicine

The fictional woman doctor is less likely to leave the medical profession on marriage than is a nurse. The heroine of the 1958 novel *Master of Surgery* (the title is ambiguous: two potential heroes and the heroine herself have claims to the title) is demonstrably more ambitious and able than her hero. She wins a medal in the final examination, while he fails:

> She wanted to get to the top of her chosen profession now. It would be a waste of all these years of study and training – six years now, she had given to it – just to marry Michael and settle down as his wife in a country practice somewhere in some sleepy market town. Michael, she thought, wouldn't get any further than that, he didn't want to, but – she did. She wanted to use the knowledge she had acquired and go on using it.[37]

The narrative here echoes the concerns and the language of professional training and obligation to be found in official discourses about the training of women doctors. The problem for women of reconciling the demands of work and family was not only a fictional dilemma, but one which the 1962 survey of the careers of women doctors identified as a serious national problem:

> The amount of work which professionally qualified women are able to do is a matter of national importance. The training of medical students now represents an investment of public rather than private resources. The community needs doctors ... Nor is the dilemma one for women doctors to resolve individually.[38]

The narrative resolutions of medical romances do attempt to resolve the dilemma individually for their heroines. There is a prim awareness in these novels of the financial cost of medical training and the responsibility of women doctors to make use of their skills and education. A male doctor bemoans the loss of medical women to marriage but is gently corrected by his young woman colleague:

> 'More marriages are made in hospital diet kitchens than the authorities realise. They lose hundreds of nurses that way every year, and heaven knows, staff are hard enough to come by, harder still to train.'
> Vaguely disconcerted by his remark, Lucy attempted to turn it into a joke – 'they don't lose many women doctors'.[39]

There is a strong sense in medical romances that women who have had the opportunity to train and qualify as doctors should not waste the experience, a position that was echoed in official discourse: 'In accepting one of the limited opportunities for training for a profession whose skills are greatly in demand, they incur an obligation to the community which they must do their utmost to discharge.'[40] The fictions do claim that marriage and career are perfectly compatible for a woman doctor. The 'true' hero is able to reconcile 'the doctor and the woman' (another recurrent phrase), and always recognizes the heroine's profession as integral to her feminine qualities:

> I'm in love with the doctor and the woman because I have never known one without the other. I love the two Marys, because in my eyes they are one and the same person – a lovable, completely satisfying entirety. Take away the doctor, and the Mary that is left is unknown to me.[41]

The hero is almost always a medical colleague, and, if not always unquestioningly, does come to support the heroine in her dedication to medicine. The narrative resolution (as frequently in the career girl novel) repeatedly shows hero and heroine planning both a personal and professional future together, their loyalties equally to one another and to the hospital: 'we know that we belong, not only to [Saint] Martha's, but to each other. And that makes it all worthwhile somehow.'[42]

The false hero often displays his character function through the demand that the heroine give up her work for marriage. A fiancé who assumes that marriage will curtail his future wife's medical career is seen as immature and irresponsible, unsuitable as a potential partner and father:

> 'You think more of this darnation doctoring than you do of me,' he had accused her, sulking like a small boy. .... 'If you're going to marry me, what's it matter whether or not you pass the exams anyway? ... Think what a remarkably good mother you'll make for our enormous family, darling.'[43]

A man who fails to appreciate the woman doctor's professional dedication cannot be a hero: 'I can't give it all up, Tony, it's part of me!'[44] The heroine will frequently denounce any such demarcation between marriage and work as 'old-fashioned'; the medical romance narrative promises a 'modern' and managed resolution of the conflicting demands. It is the conflict of a dual role for women that is often the tension fuelling the romance plot, the obstacle in the way of true love, as in this synopsis for a 1958 novel:

> Mary Marland had been brought up to believe that to be a good doctor she must virtually cease to be a woman – give up all ideas of love and

marriage and even the occasional gaieties that make life pleasant. Naturally the time came when she rebelled – yet she still wanted to be true to her work. This is the story of how she reconciled both claims.[45]

These narratives stop short of explaining quite how the woman doctor was to achieve this 'reconciliation'. The romance novel generically tends to leave the heroine at the point of marriage, rather than facing her with the problems of an actual husband and children. Instead, these novels hold out the promise of a magical resolution for the medical heroine, in which romance and dedication to duty will make everything possible.

The medical romance's combination of the two genres of romance and career novel in itself challenges the traditional divide between love and career. The conflict is a recurrent schema in these texts; in a scene which appears in different variations throughout the narratives, a woman with ambitions in surgery is warned by a male colleague: 'I've seen it happen, but it's rare ... look what the women concerned have given up ... love, marriage, home and children. It's a heavy price to pay for a contribution to medicine.'[46] Despite such acknowledgements of the difficulties of career advancement for women, female ambition is sanctioned rather than frowned upon in these novels. Doctor-heroines are frequently shown to resist, if they rarely directly challenge, traditional expectations of their contribution as women, as Doctor Mary Marland demonstrates:

> I was taken on at this hospital mainly, I believe, because it was supposed a woman's outlook might help with women and children patients and that obstetrics needed a woman's ideas, etcetera ... The trouble began almost at once, when they realised I wasn't prepared to stay nicely placed in the particular little rut they had chosen for me.[47]

In spite of such instances of a feminist assertiveness, the woman doctor's 'femininity' is seen as an essential component of her success as a practitioner. Women who have no life outside the hospital environment are sternly rebuked by other characters within the narrative: the medical heroine must leave room in her life for romance. Over-professionalization or extreme dedication to a career path are signalled as potentially damaging to the heroine's 'natural feminine instincts', to employ a phrase which recurs throughout these texts. The figure of the unmarried Matron is often invoked as a terrible warning of what over-dedication to a career can do to a young woman. One young heroine is advised: 'You know, you're heading straight towards a very grim, vinegary spinsterhood, if you're not careful. Just then you looked exactly like our revered Matron, believe it or not!'[48] Young women doctors are repeatedly warned by male colleagues and consultants against losing a sense of their 'proper' femininity. The 'white-coated girl' is advised by her senior (male) tutor, in a conversation which is echoed in most of the novels, to make sure that she doesn't 'forget about being a woman': 'Give Anne Caxton a chance now and then – don't cheat the world by allowing Anne to be swallowed up by that greedy, domineering doctor-woman!'[49]

If the doctor-heroine can initially appear to confound the traditional qualities of the romance heroine in her independence and professional status, she is always given the opportunity to prove her 'femininity'. There is invariably some kind of transformation scene (generally a hospital dance) in which, like Cinderella, she dazzles guests and hero with her beauty and charm. The heroine's youth and attractiveness to men are persistently emphasized as if to quell any doubts about her femininity: 'There were quite a number of women in his profession nowadays, but Ann Royston didn't look like any woman doctor or medical student he had ever seen before. She was quite breathtakingly lovely.'[50] There is a clear anxiety in these narratives that the encounter with the harsh realities of medicine and the professional status granted to the woman doctor could somehow 'defeminize' her. One nurse assesses her female superior as: '"starchy" and dictatorial . . . the kind of female who wears her stethoscope as if it were a row of pearls.'[51]

Many of the narratives play with the romance reader's expectations; both the title and the introduction to the heroine often set out to confound any assumption that a doctor should be male. The 1954 novel *Doctor Dear* opens with the entrance of a doctor into a private house; it is only some paragraphs into the opening and the address 'Doctor Dear' from the patient that reveals the fact that the doctor is a woman and the heroine of the novel:

> So this is general practice, thought Mrs Johnson's doctor as she so often did. This is what really happens on a visit: this is what it is to enter a house as a GP . . . And me a woman too.[52]

The titles of novels with doctor-heroines recurrently juxtapose the professional title 'doctor' with a female diminutive: *White-coated Girl, My Dear Doctor, Doctor Dear, The Little Doctor*. The heroine's rival for the hero's attentions is often structured as either medically brilliant but lacking in 'feminine' warmth, or as an overly 'feminine' creature lacking in any practical skills. The 'truly' successful doctor and woman can incorporate both qualities; the heroine is shown to maintain her femininity in the face of the grim consequences of bodily malfunction, as in this example of a pathologist: 'Fantastic to think of dainty Philippa growing microbes from pus and urine and doing post-mortems, but there it was; she liked the stark truth of it, she said.'[53]

Like the career girl and bachelor girl novel, many medical romances are structured as a form of *Bildungsroman*, in which the young and dedicated medical student learns to temper her professional commitment and ambitions with human warmth and empathy. The progress and lessons of romance are integral to the heroine's process of maturing; her understanding of others is in the interests of both the satisfactory culmination of romance in marriage and her medical practice.

The romance of science

The romance of medical science is central to these novels, as in this romanticized description of a doctor's dedication to her work:

> Marion could not give up practice, with its ardours and its interests – scientific, running like an accompaniment, mathematically exact, behind the human melody of sweet treble and ominous bass: the apparently miraculous recovery of a moribund diabetic when put on insulin, of a weary breathless pernicious anaemia victim after a few injections of liver – both marked for early death but for modern science.[54]

If science and medicine are written about in romantic terms, their actual practice is described in resolutely unglamorous terms: discussions of bowel movements, urine samples, gall-bladders and even piles are frequently cited among the professional duties of the woman doctor. The doctor-heroine is more likely to be shown alleviating the small complaints of ordinary people than using her skills in dramatic life-saving operations. General practice is emphatically not seen as an easy option: the first case for young Doctor Moir is the amputation of the toes of an elderly woman patient.

The medical romance offers a strange combination of a romantic celebration of science with a 1950s' emphasis on social realism and a refusal of sentiment. The generic romance requirements are found in the pleasures of work, the qualities of the men and women who do it, and a shared dedication to the social good. These romance fictions unequivocally champion the National Health Service and demonstrate in their narratives a commitment to a system which even one of its fiercest contemporary critics acknowledged to be remarkable:

All the resources of modern medicine with its intricate tests, expensive drugs and complicated methods of treatment are freely available to every patient in the country. This unique organisation has established itself so firmly in the fabric of the welfare state that a return to any form of uncontrolled medical service cannot be regarded as likely or even desirable.[55]

The principles of the National Health Service and of a newly democratic Welfare State are integral to the romance narrative: false heroes threaten to lure heroines (both doctors and nurses) from dedication to duty and are often attracted to the rewards of private practice; the true hero is committed to a public health service and is a 'partner' to the heroine in championing social and medical reform.

These narratives demonstrate a great measure of respect (bordering on idealization) for the medical profession and for those women who choose to become doctors, but that respect also demands a commitment from their heroines. The fictional heroines of these romances do indeed do their utmost to discharge their obligations; they are dedicated, competent and professional, and romance is shown to benefit rather than detract from their professional commitments. The trajectory of the romance narrative not only unites the heroine with her hero but also serves to reveal her as 'truly feminine', and sets her up as a potentially ideal mother and the hero as ideal father. The doctor-heroine is clearly in a position to take her own skills and the practices of the hospital, and with them the principles of the Welfare State, forward into family life.

The medical heroine belongs to the postwar discourse of the health service and is a significant example of the optimism of the early years of the Welfare State. In the postwar period the figure of the doctor was almost unequivocally trusted and respected, as one study of doctors suggests: 'more and more, during the late 40s and increasingly in the 50s, the feeling grew that at last doctors could do something.'[56]

By 1957, however, the optimism of what the Welfare State and the National Health Service could achieve was waning. The publication of Louis Goldman's polemical *Angry Young Doctor* (a year after the first production of *Look Back in Anger* and the birth of the Angry Young Man) articulated some of the cracks and strains in the system. Although entirely supportive of the National Health Service, Goldman stringently expressed the discontent of many NHS doctors. He acknowledges in his introduction that the young doctors he speaks for may be male or female, but thereafter, throughout the text, his assumption is that the doctor is male and has the sole responsibility for a family. There is no recognition that his appeal on behalf of the 'dispossessed, the frustrated and the despondent in medicine' might apply particularly to women, as the figures for women leaving the profession suggest that they did. Goldman's arguments for greater professional security, for better working hours and a fairer salary, and his complaint that promotion in the medical profession happens through an old-boy network, had, and continues to have, an even greater resonance for women in the medical profession than for male doctors.

Nevertheless, the fictions that celebrate the dedication of the woman doctor continued to hold out the hope that in the postwar world a working woman can have it all: 'Anne stood up. "Bill, a woman can have both. It takes planning, but it can be done".'[57]

The woman doctor, of all the professions, most clearly articulates the conflicts and needs of the professionally trained woman in the postwar world, and of all careers for women, that of doctor is the most idealized in fiction. The woman doctor is highly skilled in the tasks of caring and nurturing, and she is shown in these texts turning her professional skills to her own family, the community and, by extension, the nation. If these are narratives that hold out the hope that dedication to a career and to marriage and motherhood might be made compatible in the new social order, it is not an entirely escapist expectation, but it is one that remains to be answered.

Notes

1. See the discussion of *Margaret Becomes a Doctor* in chapter 5.
2. Ministry of Labour and National Service, Further Education and Training Scheme, Joint Committee of Award Making Departments. Progress Reports: 1949–1952.
3. Louis Goldman, *Angry Young Doctor* (London: Hamish Hamilton, 1957), p. 59.
4. Barbara Allen, *Doctor Lucy* (London: Mills & Boon, 1956), p. 16.
5. Ibid., p. 15.
6. Alex Stuart, *Master of Surgery* (London: Mills & Boon, 1958), p. 104.
7. Josephine Elder, *The Encircled Heart* (London: Lutterworth Press, 1951), p. 90.
8. Ibid., p. 67.
9. Allen, *Doctor Lucy*, p. 93.
10. Mary Bethune, *Doctor Dear* (London: Michael Joseph, 1954), p. 12.
11. Stuart, *Master of Surgery*, p. 174.
12. Bethune, *Doctor Dear*, pp. 24–5.
13. Elizabeth Gilzean, *Next Patient, Doctor Anne* (London: Mills & Boon, 1958), p. 37.
14. Anne Lorraine, *Send for Doctor* (London: Mills & Boon, 1958), p. 15.
15. Allen, *Doctor Lucy*, p. 22.
16. Gilzean, *Next Patient, Doctor Anne*, p. 12.
17. Anne Lorraine, *White-coated Girl* (London: Mills & Boon, 1955), p. 13.
18. Gilzean, *Next Patient, Doctor Anne*, p. 45.
19. Allen, *Doctor Lucy*, p. 22.

20. Lorraine, *White-coated Girl*, p. 10.
21. Anne Lorraine, *First the Doctor* (London: Mills & Boon, 1958), p. 84.
22. Allen, *Doctor Lucy*, p. 9.
23. Lorraine, *White-coated Girl*, p. 10.
24. Gilzean, *Next Patient, Doctor Anne*, p. 9.
25. *Women in Medicine: the results of an inquiry conducted by the Medical Practioners' Union in 1962–63* (London: Office of Health Economics, 1966), p. 16.
26. Goldman, *Angry Young Doctor*, p. 53.
27. Stuart, *Master of Surgery*, p. 104.
28. Marjorie Tait, 'The Education of Women for Citizenship: some practical suggestions' *Problems in Education*, vol. VIII (Paris: Unesco, 1954), p. 28.
29. John Bowlby, *Childcare and the Growth of Love* and *The Roots of Parenthood* (London: London National Children's Home, 1953); Benjamin Spock, *Baby and Childcare* (London: Bodley Head, 1955).
30. Lorraine, *White-coated Girl*, p. 87.
31. Ibid., p. 61.
32. Ibid., p. 95.
33. Bethune, *Doctor Dear*, p. 38.
34. Lorraine, *White-coated Girl*, p. 17.
35. Elizabeth Wilson, *Only Halfway to Paradise. Women in Postwar Britain 1945–1968* (London: Tavistock Publications, 1980), p. 45.
36. *Women in Medicine*, p. 16.
37. Stuart, *Master of Surgery*, pp. 16–17.
38. *Women in Medicine*, p. 16.
39. Allen, *Doctor Lucy*, p. 60.
40. *Women in Medicine*, p. 42.
41. Lorraine, *First the Doctor*, p. 187.
42. Stuart, *Master of Surgery*, p. 184.
43. Lorraine, *White-coated Girl*, p. 27.
44. Lorraine, *First the Doctor*, p. 46.
45. Ibid., synopsis.
46. Gilzean, *Next Patient, Doctor Anne*, p. 65.
47. Lorraine, *First the Doctor*, p. 21.
48. Lorraine, *White-coated Girl*, p. 59.
49. Ibid., p. 18.
50. Stuart, *Master of Surgery*, p. 46.
51. Lorraine, *White-coated Girl*, p. 5.
52. Bethune, *Doctor Dear*, p. 5.
53. Elder, *The Encircled Heart*, p. 18.
54. Ibid., p. 63.
55. Goldman, *Angry Young Doctor*, p. ii.
56. Jonathan Gathorne-Hardy, *Doctors: An Open Look at Doctors' Lives* (London: Weidenfeld and Nicolson, 1984), p. 39.
57. Gilzean, *Next Patient, Doctor Anne*, p. 112.

9. Bad girls: femininity, delinquency and fiction

Bad youth

If the 1950s gave birth to the pleasure-seeking teenager and the career girl, it also spawned an *alter ego*, the juvenile delinquent. It has become something of a truism that there was a sharp increase in youth crime in the postwar period. As the historian Peter Hennessy notes,[1] 'the country felt itself in the grip of a crime wave [of] black market spivvery and juvenile delinquency in particular' (p. 445). The media were apt to sensationalize and whip up moral panics about these new folk-devils. While the actual crime statistics, according to Hennessy, show that 'crime among the young did not really take off until the consumer booms of the late 1950s and early 1960s' (p. 447), there was a widely held 'sensation that standards and civil culture generally were declining' (p. 445). The young criminal was constructed in popular representations as an icon of the disruptive social legacy of the war. The Ealing Studios' film *The Blue Lamp* (1949), in which the kindly policeman George Dixon is gunned down by a new breed of vicious wide-boy-cum-criminal (Dixon was reincarnated in 1955 for the long-running TV series *Dixon of Dock Green*), disseminated powerful images of a Britain trying desperately to cling on to traditional moral values in the face of a hedonistic and materialistic anarchy unleashed by the war's social dislocations. If these images are to be believed, the problem stemmed primarily from the undermining of family life; a loss of cohesion caused by the repercussions of evacuation, absent fathers, divorces (official alarm at the rapidly climbing divorce rates led to the establishment of a Royal Commission on Marriage and Divorce, which reported in 1956), high illegitimacy rates and broken homes. With their moral and cultural identity weakened by this anchorless social existence, the argument went, the young were easy prey for the dehumanizing pleasures of mass consumption, slickly marketed youth culture and the illusory expectation of material success. From this perilous position, it was only a short step to the criminal pursuit of such rewards.

One reason for the intense fear of a wave of youth crime could be that the problem seemed to fester in the very heart of reconstruction. The Criminal Justice Act of 1948 continued a prewar process of the gradual liberalization of the penal system, including the abolition of the flogging of prisoners and the development of a probation service (the House of Commons even voted narrowly to abolish the death penalty for a trial period, although the Bill was later defeated in the House of Lords).[2] To those who had helped plan and implement the New Jerusalem of a more just and egalitarian society, the juvenile delinquent was emblematic of many of the contradictions and lurking dangers in the modern Welfare State. The sociologist Pearl Jephcott summed up this kind of anxiety in her study *Some Young People* (1954),[3] where she characterized the new generation of working-class youth as those who were:

> turned loose from overcrowded homes into noisy, uninspired, undisciplined streets, nourished on popular Sunday newspapers, strip-cartoons, sex-novelettes, the cultural fare of cheap cinema with its fug, noise and lack of standards, and who, ignorant of Christian lore, morality and discipline, and with all the natural instincts of youth starved or perverted, become the inevitable prey of the gang leader or, at best, grow up to lead, despite all the material opportunities of our age, inert, stunted and purposeless lives. (p. 6)

This litany of national decline found even fuller expression and dissemination in Richard Hoggart's *The Uses of Literacy* (1957), most memorably in his portrait of the 'Juke Box Boys', those disaffected youths who frequented milk bars:

> 'living to a large extent in a myth world compounded of a few simple elements which they take to be those of American life . . . these are the figures some important contemporary forces are tending to create, the directionless and tamed helots of a machine-minding class . . . The hedonistic but passive barbarian who rides in a fifty-horsepower bus for threepence, to see a five-million-dollar film for one-and-eightpence, is not simply a social oddity; he is a portent. (pp. 204–5)

By the late 1950s, as Peter Hennessy indicates, affluence had created a more distinct youth culture centred on teenage fashion, music and sexuality. The figure of the amoral teenager could be readily redeployed by commentators as continuing evidence for a general lack of moral standards among Britain's youth, social drift, gullibility to Americanized mass culture and, at the extremes, crime. Anthony Burgess's *A Clockwork Orange* (1962)[4] took Hoggart's 'portent' and projected it forward into a Dystopian future where a corrupt socialist state and a sadistic youth culture exploit each other and the citizenry get caught in the middle. Unlike Jephcott's primitive 'gang leader', however, the novel's hero Alex is addicted to a diet of classical music, and so represents an even more dramatic and insidious threat to cultural 'standards' – far from being able to enlighten its consumers, high culture has been assimilated into a morally corrupt youth subculture. The dress-code of Alex's gang is reminiscent of the Teddy Boys, who famously dressed in a pastiche of the aristocratic dandy.

Not all commentators expressed such patrician distaste for the first postwar generation. T. R. Fyvel's detailed study *The Insecure Offenders* (1961), subtitled *Rebellious Youth in the Welfare State*, was probably one of the first left-wing sociological responses to juvenile crime.[5] Fyvel saw youth crime as a 'proletarian rebellion' against the 'values of the affluent society' (pp. 39, 230). While Fyvel reiterated the familiar diagnosis of the postwar dehumanization of working-class communities by 'soulless' affluence, he emphasized the contradictions between capitalism's promises of social advance and classlessness and the stubborn resilience of class barriers. Youth crime was no longer about deprivation; on the contrary, 'the current unrest of youth is a new phenomenon', to be found in 'most advanced industrial countries of our time' (pp. 13, 21). From this perspective, youth lawlessness was a protest against respectability, conformity and the phoney economic and social goals of mobility and high living-standards. Fyvel redefined the problem of youth crime as a political and ideological failure which led to familiar spiritual symptoms of purposelessness and social disengagement. For Fyvel, the postwar 'consensus' had not taken a sufficient grip on the socially destabilizing and alienating influences of capitalism. Fyvel may have been responding to C. A. R. Crosland's seminal revisionist work *The Future of Socialism* (1956),[6] which argued that most of the goals of socialism had been met through capitalist means. According to Crosland, now that 'traditional capitalism has been reformed and modified almost out of existence', the old socialist agenda of public ownership could be abandoned and attention turned to fine-tuning social mobility and the 'social assimilation' (pp. 61, 132). In an anticipation of some of the Wilson reforms of the 1960s, Fyvel demanded vigorous state intervention in unblocking the channels of social exclusion, such as higher education. Like Hoggart, he feared the obliteration of authentic working-class identity by a 'distorted materialist society without purpose' (p. 12). Until this 'distortion' was sorted out, argued Fyvel, there would always be a significant minority of youth who would turn affluence against itself.

Hoggart and Fyvel were part of a broad intellectual movement at this time which had the dominant aim of analysing the strengths and weaknesses of British cultural traditions (in particular, radical, left-liberal and working-class traditions) under the formative yet repressive regime of industrial capitalism and liberal democracy. Alan Sinfield has coined the term 'left culturalism' to describe this attitude and its mobilization in such pioneering works as Raymond Williams's *Culture and Society* (1958), E. P. Thompson's *The Making of the English Working Classes* (1963), and the *New Left Review* (founded in 1960).[7] Left culturalism had a protective if exasperated attitude towards the contemporary working class. As Sinfield puts it,

> The revolution hadn't occurred because the fundamental oppression of working people was being obscured, and affluence was destroying their dignity and resistance. It all seemed a failure at the level of culture. (p. 245)

Nowhere was this cultural failure more apparent than in the plight of juvenile delinquents and the supposedly misguided youth culture that generated them. From a left-culturalist perspective, one 'purpose' for post-war youth was to achieve the fullest possible class-consciousness, which was being rapidly diluted by the 'purposeless' synthetic pleasures of consumer capitalism and the Welfare State. The insistence that class rather than genera-tion was the true determining factor in the motivation and complexion of postwar youth culture was one of the main aims of left-culturalist sociology in the 1960s and 1970s.

Investigations by the Birmingham Centre for Contemporary Cultural Studies developed the theory that subcultural styles performed a 'resistance through ritual' against consumer capitalism.[8] For Dick Hebdidge,[9] groups such as the Teddy Boys did represent a symbolic force of (in Fyvel's words) 'proletarian rebellion': 'the emergence of such groups has signalled in spec-tacular fashion the breakdown of consensus in the post-war world' (p. 17). Hebdidge is also keen not to romanticize these semiotic class-warriors, and so he emphasizes their racism and aggressive masculinity; nevertheless he believes that in their 'moment' they represented a vital challenge to postwar conformity – in George Melly's words, 'a grey colourless world where good boys played ping-pong' (p. 83).

From the 1950s onwards, most sociologists and cultural commentators have interpreted early postwar youth culture and delinquency as an exclu-sively male phenomenon, in which what Hebdidge terms 'sexual aggressiveness' (p. 83) carried a radical tinge as a defensive, class-conscious mechanism against the forces of national cultural decline. This interpretation has undoubtedly gained some further authority from the fact that it overlaps with the myth of the Angry Young Man, the folk-devil who can be seen as the slightly older or more sophisticated counterpart of the youth rebel. Merging these two significant areas of social and cultural history produces the idea that in the 1950s a transformation of youth masculinity took place – masculinity was reinvigorated to fight off the enervating and dehumanizing effects of individualism, welfarism (the 'nanny state'), National Service (not abolished until 1963), the pacification of the working class, and political apathy in an era of 'consensus'. In 'angry' literature the women characters are always subordinated to the hero's anxieties: Alison irons Jimmy Porter's shirts in *Look Back in Anger* (1956); Arthur Seaton's three lovers (Brenda, Winnie and Doreen) in *Saturday Night and Sunday Morning* (1958) do not have an independent narrative existence; and the same applies to Joe Lampton's lovers Alice and Susan in *Room at the Top* (1957). In those texts where the 'angry' anti-hero is delinquent or criminal, women are further relegated to the margins of the narrative: in Alan Sillitoe's *The Loneliness of the Long Distance Runner* (1959), Smith's feckless mother enters the story in a flashback to the hero's dislocated family background; in Brendan Behan's *The Quare Fellow* (1956) and *Borstal Boy* (1958) the prison setting excludes women completely, as does the boys' school location of Edward Blishen's novel *Roaring Boys* (1955).

As Angela McRobbie and Jenny Garber have pointed out,[10] the experience of girls has been so marginalized in sociological studies of this period that young women of the 1950s have been denied any significant participation in the teenage revolution; their fate has been 'total invisibility' (p. 215). However, while most of the official publications from this time do concentrate almost solely on male crime, most of them provide revealing glimpses into the largely uncharted world of the postwar female delinquent. Moreover, one of the solutions proffered in these reports is to provide such wayward women with a career. While the 'angry' hero could reject the work ethic as a force of false consciousness and conformity (think of Joe Lampton's attitude towards his 'zombie' town-hall job), the bad girl was publicly exhorted to abandon pleasure and seek a career. While these official discourses construct female crime and its punishment as a debasement or exaggeration of femininity, work and a career – rather than marriage and children – are put forward as a route to social salvation and a balanced femininity. It is possible to conclude that the bad girl of postwar reconstruction is the obverse of the career girl, rather than the Angel in the House.

Borstal girls

In 1948 the Borstal girls kept in the detention wing of Holloway prison in London rioted.[11] While this event has almost disappeared from the historical record of postwar women's history (unlike the execution of the glamorous Ruth Ellis, for instance), it is a reminder that female youth crime was a significant problem. Between 1948 and 1960 the numbers of Borstal girls rose from a few hundred to around a thousand – a steep rise that partly reflected the effects of the 1948 Criminal Justice Act, which aimed at avoiding sending young offenders to prison, but which was also in line with the steady increase in male youth crime (on average, there were ten Borstal boys to every Borstal girl).[12] According to official studies and reports, most of these girls had a similar profile: they came from broken working-class homes; their offences were primarily to do with property and sexuality, rather than violence (shoplifting and underage sex being particularly common); and their exclusion from the security of a respectable working-class upbringing and the benefits of the 1944 Education Act made them easy prey for the unbridled pursuit of immediate gratification. In a survey of prisons and Borstals conducted by the Howard League for Penal Reform in 1950,[13] Borstal girls were portrayed as an unstable and dangerous amalgamation of those stereotypical and exaggeratedly 'feminine' attributes, vanity and emotion:

> Though the general idea of the Borstal system is the same for girls as for boys, the former do present certain special problems. They are, for one thing, an extremely difficult type to handle. Practically all of them are over-sexed and they are generally committed for stealing either clothes or jewellery or money to buy such things. Their excessive sexuality is generally linked with other well-defined characteristics. They are usually over-emotional, unstable and somewhat hysterical, but they generally have a strong, if distorted aesthetic sense ... In addition to these characteristics, they are mostly of low general intelligence ... lower than is the case with boys. (p. 17)

Even before the age of affluence had properly begun in the late 1950s, these Borstal girls are personifications of what Richard Hoggart termed 'shiny barbarism', victims of the 'corrupt brightness' (p. 282) of mass-produced, easy pleasure. Just as T. R. Fyvel thought that affluence demanded its young consumer grow up too quickly, these girls are seen to have been tempted into sexual precocity. The Howard League report recommends that an effective way to reform them is to provide a more constructive channel for their rabid desire for 'unhealthy excitement' (p. 18). Responding to the 1948 Criminal

Justice Act's emphasis on corrective training, the report discusses 'The Problem of Suitable Occupation':

> The girls, like the boys, have evening classes, with educational courses, handicrafts and so forth, but, except for the few who are employed on farms or in the garden, the main part of their work is either wholly domestic or in the trades which are closely allied to it, such as machining or laundry work.
>
> Obviously it is right that the girls should be taught the arts of housekeeping since nearly all of them marry and will one day have to run their own home. But it is possible to have too much of a good thing and the Borstal girl is easily bored with too much domesticity ... domestic work is too easily accepted as a general solution of the problem of occupation and too little attention is given to the needs of those who have special aptitudes. (pp. 20–1)

In her study of youth alienation, *Some Young People* (1954), Pearl Jephcott supported this view and suggested that some of the 'more thoughtful' working-class girls

> had a feeling and a conscience that even a girl's job might be one which, as they said, 'would do something for the world' ... the whole business was a wrong to them; and there seemed a strong case for presenting the alternative of marriage or career in not quite such black and white terms. In a sense these girls were pioneers in their own social world and ought not to have had to limit themselves for fear that, if they stood out for a career rather than just a job, they would be disloyal to their own femininity. (pp. 86–7)

A familiar discourse of evangelical feminism resurfaces here, and provides some evidence that the ideology of the career girl permeated all social levels. Jephcott's comments also allow us to conclude that popular narratives about career heroines, in which these anxieties about betraying traditional notions of feminine behaviour are overcome, could have met the aspirations of a socially diverse female audience. For Jephcott, the antidote to the socially regressive wayward girl was the modern career girl. Other commentators saw the issue of a 'suitable' occupation for bad girls as an unresolved problem. Lionel Fox's study, *The English Prison and Borstals Systems* (1952),[14] noted that 'unfortunately, despite careful enquiry, it has not so far proved possible to find trades in which it would be both useful and practicable to train women in prison', but added that even 'domestic crafts' are taught as a trade, so that on release the women can hopefully 'get good work and run good homes' (p. 377) – thus reconciling the conflicting demands of the 'dual role' of work and home.

Training for a career is the constitutive absence in postwar constructions of the bad girl. For Jephcott and other observers of postwar youth alienation, 'soulless' affluence had lured young people away from a commitment to socially useful work by brandishing the superficial and morally dangerous pleasures of socially useless leisure: a 'barren and restricted' lifestyle, according to a 1950 study of 80,000 young people in Birmingham.[15] The study attributed the purposelessness of modern youth culture to society's over-stimulation of pleasure and under-motivation of work: 'no attempt is made to enable young people to see the importance and social significance of the work they do' (p. 177). Taken out of context, it is easy to see such a remark as exemplifying a deeply reactionary public morality; the implication is that young people should see work as a national duty that comes before self-fulfilment. Such pronouncements merely reinforce the idea of the 1950s as a socially conservative decade, the foil to the greater personal freedoms of the 1960s. But once the issue of work is gendered, such an interpretation becomes unreliable; it is not easy to reject the work ethic unless one has a secure place within it, which women have rarely had.

It was recognized by observers of postwar youth that the working mother had led to a reconfiguration and modernization of the family. *Eighty Thousand Adolescents* (1950) noted that 'the emancipation of women is leading to a change in the traditional pattern of family life', but rather than decrying this fact as an undermining of social stability, the study asked for 'an expectation that domestic responsibilities will be shared' (p. 178).[16] Unless marriage becomes more equal both inside and outside the home, the report suggested, the resulting strains could adversely affect family life and the development of the young. The responsibility for adjusting to the new, more democratic sexual division of labour lay equally with both partners. Despite a lingering media anxiety about maternal deprivation, sociological investigations did not, on the whole, saddle working mothers with the sole responsibility for producing delinquent offspring. While T. R. Fyvel felt that the 'exodus of wives into employment' may have led to 'a weakening of family life', he did not blame those women for any socially damaging consequences of this situation. He accepted that 'every contemporary social force is pushing them in this direction', particularly emancipation from 'the old drudgery at the kitchen sink'. He also felt that there had been insufficient social planning for this change, including re-educating young people in the changing structures of family life. He did not accept that there was any scientific evidence for a causal link between maternal deprivation and delinquency. Fyvel gave as much weight to the diminished role of the father, whose masculine status had been undermined by deskilling at work and the need to be more child-centred at home (pp. 127–31).

The cultural significance of the bad girl is not only in her challenge to the restrictive social and sexual codes of the postwar period; she is also the antitype of the New Woman of postwar reconstruction. It is certainly the case that when we read a comment by a contemporary criminologist that the problem of the 'over-sexed female adolescent has no solution',[17] it is tempting to see the bad girl only in terms of female desire and transgressive boundaries. But it is important to recognize that the bad girl is a fugitive from modernized femininity, as well as a sexual prodigy.

Bad heroines

Some of the most shocking sexual details about 'bad' girls were published in a frank account by a middle-class prisoner of her harrowing time in Holloway's women's wing. In Joan Henry's *Who Lie in Gaol* (1952),[18] there is a candid, liberal depiction of the prevalence of lesbianism in women's prisons (sufficiently scandalous, however, to provide a salacious cover for the 1958 paperback version, in which the narrator is cornered by a predatory female warden). In the portrayal of 'Brownies' (under-21 prisoners), however, it is almost as if we are reading offical reports rather than firsthand experience. Noting that many of these young women are 'very highly sexed', we are told that most are from broken homes, cannot hold down a 'steady job' and are not given adequate vocational training: 'men prisoners have far more advantages than women as regards useful employment, and learning a trade' (p. 76).

As this representation shows, the danger posed by the 'highly sexed' bad girl came as much from her social purposelessness, her exclusion from the respectable career-heroine ideal, as from her precocious sexuality. In her most demonized form, she could become a social menace, her 'unattached' energies destabilizing traditional social structures. Such a figure appears in Josephine Tey's popular detective novel *The Franchise Affair* (1948).[19] The novel is memorable not only for its inscrutable adolescent villainess, but for the way her crimes focus sharply defined class antagonisms in postwar English society. Moreover, despite detective fiction's generic convention of narrative closure, the tensions produced by this bad girl's actions are left unresolved.

The novel's title, setting and hero signify that the narrative is as much about notions of Englishness and social progress as it is about crime. 'Franchise' connotes the issue of democracy (in the plot it is the name of a mansion), the location is the village of Larborough in the heart of the English countryside, and the hero is not a detective but a local lawyer, Robert Blair, a pillar of the establishment and defender of tradition. He is asked to defend two respectable gentlewomen, the spinster Marion Sharpe and her mother, who live at the Franchise, after they have been accused of abduction and torture by a 15-year-old orphan, Betty Kane. She claims that they tried to force her to become their servant (a Gothic spin on the 'servant problem'), and when she refused, they starved and whipped her (there are hints here of lesbian abuse) until she managed to escape. Her story seems watertight and quickly becomes a *cause célèbre* in the tabloids. Their inflammatory reporting whips up a local class-war against the Franchise. Graffiti is daubed on its walls accusing the Sharpes of being Fascists, and a riot leads to the house being burnt down.

By this time, however, Blair has broken through Betty's defences. His suspicions of her veracity begin when he first meets her. The waif's appearance is too contradictory; beneath a 'demure' exterior he detects traces of 'savage emotion, primitive and cruel' and wonders whether she is 'oversexed' (pp. 33, 36). Her precocious sexuality is her downfall; his first real clue is some lipstick found in her possession. It transpires that she had a month-long affair with a businessman from the area and made up the abduction story as a cover. All Blair's social and sexual prejudices are confirmed. He discovers that Betty's mother was a 'good-time wife' in the war before she abandoned her daughter (p. 79). Blair remarks, with eugenicist triumphalism, that Betty's crime was 'as plausible as the blood she came of' (p. 166). Betty's foster-parents gave her too much 'unsupervised freedom' (p. 96). In Blair's eyes she is a 'monster' with a 'child-like grace' (pp. 189, 190). Like St George, he has quelled the dragon that threatens the English castle and its damsels. Throughout the incident, Blair is as concerned to rescue the Sharpes's reputation (he is in love with Marion) as to expose Betty's crime. He describes the attack on the Franchise as an act of highly un-English 'mob violence' (p. 131) and he is not averse to punching one of the 'gloating' local gang members (pp. 225–6).

Yet the novel does not fully authorize these nostalgic, chivalric values battling against a vicious onslaught by the debased egalitarianism of a levelling postwar culture. Although Blair is the narrator and hero, Betty's inscrutability escapes his narrative control. Even if her sexual misdemeanour can be explained by the bloodline of her mother's nymphomaniac genes, we never learn why she concocted her fantastic alibi, nor what will happen to her. Elements of her crime, such as the intelligence needed to memorize and convey convincingly all the details of the exterior and interior of the Franchise, contradict Blair's image of her as an instinctual 'primitive'. Blair refuses to think too deeply about the eruption of class hatred in this pastoral setting, preferring to fall back on convenient labels and prejudices. The social antagonisms aroused by Betty's crime remain textually unresolved and socially unplaced. Finally, Blair's expected prize (marriage to Marion) almost slips away. The Sharpes (with Blair in tow) choose to emigrate, the Franchise remains a pile of rubble, and the continuity of English tradition represented by the country house, with all the values of order and hierarchy that Blair set out to defend, is broken.

This ending suggests that the bad girl inhabits a historical space which lies partly within but largely outside the literary and social conventions of popular generic fiction. Appropriate to the requirements of the detective novel and thriller, there are areas of darkness surrounding Betty Kane's characterization and her social disaffiliation that confirm her role as a sinister and enigmatic villainess (she is associated with numerous locations in the story but belongs in none). Yet she is also constructed as a delinquent victim of a determining, unstable postwar world – we learn that she was a war evacuee, has experienced maternal and paternal deprivation, and has grown up socially displaced, with foster-parents, on one of the new housing estates. The narrative that Betty is more significantly excluded from (and that illuminates her deviancy with greater historical accuracy than can the novel's sensationalist gestures towards eugenics) is not the detective novel or thriller but the career-heroine narrative, in which a modernized femininity can aspire to social and – in romances – sexual fulfilment. It is that story which the bad girl narrative represses so deeply; these stories open up in dramatic ways the question of what constitutes 'acceptable' standards of femininity and female desire. Tey's novel is unable to find a solution and leaves a yawning gap between the debased modernity and unassimilable sexuality of the villainess, and the eccentric ruling-class independence and repressed sexuality of the heroine.

The plot of Agatha Christie's *Mrs McGinty's Dead* (1952),[20] though set in a contemporary sleepy English village, revolves around the legacy of the misdemeanours of four bad girls of the 1930s: Eva Kane, a young governess who fell in love with her employer and helped him murder his wife (note the shared surname with Betty Kane); Janice Courtland, whose lover killed her brutal husband; Lily Gamboll, a working-class delinquent from an overcrowded home who killed her aunt with a meat chopper and ended up in an approved school; and Vera Blake, who married a succession of crooks. It transpires that Eva Kane had a son who was adopted by a wealthy woman who knew nothing of his past. He now lives in the English countryside under a different name, but when a newspaper feature on the four bad girls threatens to lead to his accidental exposure, he embarks on a series of murders to silence anyone who knows anything about his true identity. After he is caught by Hercule Poirot, his defence is to plead eugenicist predestination: 'I'm not responsible. It's in my blood. I can't help it' (p. 220). Though Poirot is unconvinced by this argument (the murders were premeditated), the plot does support the idea that, as in Christie's 1949 novel *Crooked House*, bad blood must be purged from the gentry, and the murderer's crooked genes will eventually damn him (in this case, the sins of the mother are visited on the next generation). But as with *The Franchise Affair*, the novel also provides a historical explanation for the eruption of violent crime in an English village: 'The war stirred up everyone and everything' says one character (p. 184). Poirot muses that 'More murders have been committed for respectability than one would believe possible' (p. 105); Kane's son is not the only 'respectable' character with a past to hide. As Poirot's investigation deepens, he discovers a number of genteel women who led 'wild' lives during the war, or who conceal their lower-class origins. The disruptive consequences of the war's emancipation of female desire are being played out in the heart of England. It is likely that the novel raises these anxieties in order to displace them on to Eva Kane's crime of passion, where they can be resolved by Poirot's detection. But the abiding impression created by the tensions of the novel's social setting is that beneath the postwar stereotype of happily domesticated femininity is the unresolved legacy of wartime freedoms.

Crooked girls, plucky heroines

While Betty Kane threatened the bastion of English class privilege from without, a different kind of bad girl was at work within the castle. Ever since Henry James's *The Turn of the Screw* (1898), the figure of the dysfunctional aristocratic child has cast an eerie shadow over the stability of the country house and its cultural authority. The child is, after all, the potential inheritor of the estate, and the female child has an added generational function. If her integrity is in doubt, the means of social reproduction is compromised.

In Agatha Christie's *Crooked House* (1949),[21] these 'dark undercurrents' (p. 129) are charted in a murder-mystery plot that resolves into eugenicist fable. In time-honoured fashion, the problems begin when the impure (and in this case, foreign) values of commercialism contaminate the transcendent virtues of landed wealth. The murder victim is a Greek millionaire, Aristedes Leonides, who made a shady fortune in the restaurant business in the early twentieth century, has married into the British aristocracy and built his 'hybrid' family a country house. His two sons are feckless and make poor marriages, one to a flighty actress, which produces three offspring – the eldest daughter Sophie, the much younger Josephine and a son Eustace; the other son marries a doctor, who is so wrapped up in her career that she is cold and ascetic – it is an indication of the novel's reactionary attitude to working women that this union is childless, implying that no woman can reconcile the conflicts of the 'dual role'. On the other hand, Sophie Aristedes is clearly a good woman who worked at the Foreign Office during the war. Though she has returned to family duties, there is an implication that her patriotic professional training has provided her (like the country house romance heroines) with the necessary resourcefulness to find a solution to the problems of aristocratic succession in a postwar, 'soak-the-rich' epoch (p. 7).

When Aristedes is found poisoned, most of the family members seem to have a motive for wanting him dead, including his young second wife, an ex-waitress (this well-wrought scenario of Christie's detective fiction shows the potential for the ruling class to fracture under the stresses of internal property wrangles and ill-advised marriages). The twist in the plot – both in generic and generational terms – is the discovery that the poisoner is in fact the child Josephine; she has killed her grandfather because he frowned on her aspiration to be a 'bally' dancer (p. 159). While ballet may be an acceptable career for the middle-class heroines of Noel Streatfeild's novels, it is beneath the dignity of Christie's upper classes (the childish spelling of the word emphasizes the vulgarity of the ambition – 'bally' is very similar to 'belly'). In one sense, Josephine is a frustrated career girl who longs to escape from the strictures of aristocratic-class disciplines into dominant bourgeois culture where, as the unravelling of the plot makes clear, she truly belongs. She is among the ruling class, but not of them.

Like Betty Kane's curiously adult expressions, Josephine's physiognomic excesses raise suspicions about her integrity. When the narrator-hero first sees her, he is astounded by her appearance: a 'fantastically ugly child with a very distinct likeness to her grandfather' (p. 58). Given that his ugliness exerted a 'magnetic' sex appeal (p. 14), there is a flicker here of the 'over-sexed' female delinquent, a sexuality that is shown to be deformed in a girl. Josephine is more significant for a precocious intelligence which is 'twisted' into fantasies of revenge on her stultifying relatives. An avid reader of detective stories, she even manages to fake a search of her room in order to cast suspicion on another family member. Like Betty Kane, Josephine is an unreliable sub-narrator. Both girls construct their alibis like crime novelists and vie for narrative control with the male hero-narrator. Josephine's desire to escape from the house suggests that she is aware at some level of her position as a social mutation – one of her most vicious acts is to poison her nurse for calling her a 'changeling' (p. 120). Once her exposure is imminent, the family cannot tolerate the scandalous consequences of a public trial, so the plot musters a heavily contrived 'internal' solution. The sister of Aristedes' first wife, who always disapproved of the match and is terminally ill, takes Josephine for a drive in the countryside and promptly takes them both over a cliff. In all but name, this is euthanasia, social hygiene. There is no question that Josephine's bad blood has to be removed; the unanimous verdict is that she was, in the words of her killer, 'one of the litter who is "not quite right"' (p. 158). The hero adds his own touches to this judgement in his ritualistic summing up:

> with her precocious mental development had gone a retarded moral sense. Perhaps too, the various factors of heredity had met together . . . in her very marrow had run the essential crooked strain of old Leonides . . . she was a pathetic little monster. She had been born with a kink – the crooked child of the little Crooked House . . . in poor little Josephine all the worst of the family came together. (pp. 159–60)

To counter Josephine's destructive influence and preserve the good blood, the estate goes to Sophie. As in the country house romance, the responsibility for guarding the nation's heritage is feminized. The thriller and detective genres, as the example of Josephine's aunt demonstrates, also permit women to act ruthlessly, even criminally, in defence of tradition and conservative values.[22]

In Netta Muskett's *Bring Back Yesterday* (1955),[23] another popular woman's novel about the bad girl in postwar society, a 'crooked' marriage plot plunges the heroine into murder. The novel is a generic hybrid, deploying the conventions of romance, crime novel and middle-brow realism – these formal shifts are required to keep step with the novel's exploration of shifting gender and class relations. The story begins with a highly reactionary portrait of postwar 'levelling-off days' (p. 32), in which the heroine Helena Clurey and her family are forced to share their house with a working-class family. The situation is a consequence of the wartime blitz and the billeting of bombed-out families; but almost ten years later there is nothing that the middle-class Clureys can do to evict the working-class Olivers, who are protected by the law and are shown as determined to milk the situation to its utmost. The petty triumphalism and mean-spirited pretensions of the Olivers make them a caricature of class vengeance: 'Let me tell you, Miss 'Igh and Mighty Clurey, as things is changin'. You've 'ad your day, you an' your sort,' says Mrs Oliver to Helena (p. 12). Damned by her dropped aitches, Mrs Oliver fares no better when she affects a 'pseudo-BBC voice' whenever (which is frequently) she answers the Clureys' telephone. The class hatred that informs Muskett's representation of 'insidious' postwar egalitarianism (p. 8) is as trenchant as anything in Evelyn Waugh. The Olivers are Malthusian, irresponsible breeders. There are 'young Olivers everywhere' – they have 'overflowed', most horrifically, into Helena's bathroom (p. 10). Helena's patience is tested to the full, but she always manages to be decently restrained and to exhibit stereotypical middle-class feminine qualities of tolerance, stoicism, inoffensiveness and good manners. The plot is designed to test these feminine virtues to the full. The Clureys' humiliation is made more severe by the fact that they themselves are the poor relations of an aristocratic family (Helena went to a Swiss finishing school). Fortunately, this connection provides the means of escape from their downwardly mobile plight. Helena's husband discovers that he is to inherit a baronetcy, and the family is ensconced in its rightful social position in a country house.

It seems that the tensions surrounding Helena's 'proletarianized' postwar status have been resolved by a generic shift to the conventions of romance (the recovery of a fortune through marriage). Now that she is apparently securely installed in her country mansion as a woman of leisure, Helena does not have to confront the contradictions of postwar democracy. But the stability of her new class position and her winsome feminine virtue are immediately shaken. The conventions of romance also engender a new, eroticized villainy in the shape of the reappearance of Helena's first love, the parvenu and adventurer Giles Paraway. The melodramatic details of their involvement twenty years earlier include an elopement to France, a short-lived passion, desertion and dastardly trickery as he later reveals their marriage to be phoney. Having alienated her mother by running off with a social inferior, Helena has to succumb to being married off to her current husband, whom she has never loved. She is horrified when Paraway now reappears as the suitor of her daughter. He is determined to marry into the family fortune and blackmails Helena into silence. With mounting desperation, she watches him ingratiate himself with the dying baronet. Her hatred of Paraway and guilt at concealing her past drive her to distraction. In a crime of passion, she pushes him down the cellar steps.

In order to unravel the moral consequences of this transgression, the novel switches to the conventions of the crime novel: detection and recognition. Muskett gives the reader, who is made only too aware of Helena's guilt, the apparent choice of identifying with either her husband's or Mrs Oliver's response to the murder – both of whom saw her commit the crime. The contrived, class-conscious nature of this choice is made more conspicuous by the use of a far-fetched plot device to get Mrs Oliver to the house at just the right time. While her husband perjures himself in court to protect Helena, Mrs Oliver sows seeds of suspicion in the investigating detective's mind.

Once the detective discovers the facts about Helena and Giles and becomes convinced of her guilt, he faces the same moral dilemma as the reader – whether to place class loyalty above the law. The detective is not convinced by his own ethical teaser, 'Who was worse off through Giles Paraway's death?' (p. 182). In order to redeem Helena's reputation and her feminine virtue in his own mind, he needs the added revelation that Paraway was already married when he eloped with Helena. Knowing that Helena is still legally, if not morally, guilty of a crime, the detective decides to resign – like Blair's gallantry in *The Franchise Affair*, it seems that the age of chivalry is not dead in Welfare State Britain.

But there is one source of tension that remains unresolved. Though unquestionably a cad, Giles reveals to Helena, shortly before she kills him, some telling details of his background. His father was a bricklayer in a small village where tugging the forelock was still common. Giles became a clerk with fierce social aspirations (there is an anticipation here of the 'angry' Joe Lampton), a 'proud, frustrated boy who knew he had it within himself, in his brains, to be the equal of those offshoots of the class he despised and yet longed to join' (p. 100). This confession of a politics of envy does not make him morally any better, but it does revive the theme of social equality previously associated with the disreputable Olivers (Mrs Oliver's presence at the scene of the crime also reinforces this thematic link). Given that Giles's plan to marry into the Clurey money would probably have succeeded had he not been murdered, and given the 'insidious' social triumph of the Olivers (and, by implication, their class), it is difficult not to conclude that Helena's crime is a displaced act of retaliation against the postwar working class and the egalitarian ideals of state policy. To interpret her violence as a socially symbolic act is consistent with her class position but not with dominant notions of femininity – Helena's guilt has the effect of making her feminine identity an unresolved contradiction; beneath her chatelaine exterior she remains a bad girl, paying the price for her 'over-sexed' youthful indiscretion. If only she had taken up a career.

Notes

1. Peter Hennessy, *Never Again. Britain 1945–1951* (London: Vintage, 1993; first published in 1992).
2. Ibid., p. 447.
3. Pearl Jephcott, *Some Young People* (King George's Jubilee Trust; London: George Allen and Unwin, 1954). According to Mark Abrams, *The Teenage Consumer* (London Press Exchange, 1959), teenagers were almost entirely working class and commanded a staggering £1½ billion per annum of disposable income.

4.   Anthony Burgess, *A Clockwork Orange* (Harmondsworth: Penguin, 1972; first published in 1962).

5.   T. R. Fyvel, *The Insecure Offenders. Rebellious Youth in the Welfare State* (Harmondsworth: Penguin, 1966; first published in 1961).

6.   C. A. R. Crosland, *The Future of Socialism* (London: Jonathan Cape, 1957; first published in 1956). See also Daniel Bell, *The End of Ideology* (Illinois: The Free Press of Glencoe, 1960).

7.   See Alan Sinfield, *Literature, Politics and Culture in Postwar Britain* (Oxford: Basil Blackwell, 1989), chapter 11.

8.   Stuart Hall and Tony Jefferson, eds, *Resistance Through Ritual. Youth Subcultures in Postwar Britain* (London: Hutchinson, 1977; first published in 1975).

9.   Dick Hebdidge, *Subculture. The Meaning of Style* (London and New York: Methuen, 1979).

10. Angela McRobbie and Jenny Garber, 'Girls and Subcultures: An Exploration' in Stuart Hall and Tony Jefferson, eds, *Resistance through Ritual*, pp. 209–22.

11. The riot is reported in *Borstal. A Critical Survey* (London: Howard League for Penal Reform, 1950).

12. Information gleaned from *Making Citizens. A Review of the Aims, Methods and Achievements of the Approved Schools in England and Wales* (London: HMSO, 1945); *Prisons and Borstals. Statement of the Policy and Practice in the Administration of Prison and Borstal Institutions in England and Wales* (London: HMSO, 1950); *Prisons and Borstals. Statement of the Policy and Practice in the Administration of Prison and Borstal Institutions in England and Wales* (London: HMSO, 1960).

13. *Borstal. A Critical Survey.*

14. Lionel W. Fox, *The English Prison and Borstal System* (London: Routledge and Kegan Paul, 1952). The book was written for the International Library of Sociology and Social Reconstruction.

15. *Eighty Thousand Adolescents. A Study of Young People in the City of Birmingham* (Edward Cadbury Charitable Trust; London: George Allen and Unwin, 1950), p. 131. See also *Citizens of Tomorrow. A Study of the Influences Affecting the Upbringing of Young People* (London: King George's Jubilee Trust, 1955).

16. See also *Report of the Royal Commission on Marriage and Divorce* (London: HMSO, 1956): 'Women are no longer content to endure the treatment which in past times their inferior position obliged them to suffer. They expect of marriage that it shall be an equal partnership; and rightly so. But the working out of this ideal exposes marriage to new strains' (p. 9).

17. Hermann Mannheim, *Juvenile Delinquency in an English Middletown* (London: Kegan Paul, Trench, Trubner and Co. Ltd., 1948), pp. 95–6.

18. Joan Henry, *Who Lie In Gaol* (London: Four Square Books, 1958; first published in 1952).

19. Josephine Tey, *The Franchise Affair* (Harmondsworth: Penguin, 1951; first published in 1948). This reading of Tey's novel is indebted to Alison Light's essay, 'Writing fictions: femininity and the 1950s' in Jean Radford, ed., *The Progress of Romance* (London: Routledge, 1986), pp. 139–65.

20. Agatha Christie, *Mrs McGinty's Dead* (London: HarperCollins, 1993; first published in 1952).
21. Agatha Christie, *Crooked House* (London: Collins, 1969; first published in 1949).
22. A detailed study of this theme in interwar women's writing can be found in Alison Light, *Forever England. Femininity, Literature, and Conservatism Between the Wars* (London: Routledge, 1991).
23. Netta Muskett, *Give Back Yesterday* (London: Arrow Books, 1976; first published in 1955).

Bibliography

Abrams, Mark, *The Teenage Consumer* (London Press Exchange, 1959).

Allen, Barbara, *Doctor Lucy* (London: Mills & Boon, 1956).

Allen, D. Elliston, *British Tastes: An Enquiry into the Likes and Dislikes of the Regional Consumer* (London: Hutchinson, 1968).

Allsop, Kenneth, *The Angry Decade* (London: Faber and Faber, 1963; first published in 1958).

Anderson, Perry, 'The Left in the Fifties', *New Left Review* 29, Jan–Feb 1965, pp. 1–18.

Arbor, Jane, *Dear Intruder* (London: Mills & Boon, 1955).

Ashton, Helen, *The Half-Crown House* (London: Fontana, 1956).

Baker, Niamh, *Happily Ever After. Women's Fiction in Postwar Britain 1945–1960* (London: Macmillan, 1989).

Banks, Lynne Reid, *The L-Shaped Room* (Harmondsworth: Penguin, 1962; first published in 1960).

Banton, Michael, *The Coloured Quarter. Negro Immigrants in an English City* (London: Jonathan Cape, 1955).

Banton, Michael, *White and Coloured. The Behaviour of British People Towards Coloured Immigrants* (London: Jonathan Cape, 1959).

Barstow, Stan, *The Watchers on the Shore* (Harmondsworth: Penguin, 1968; first published in 1966).

Bean, Philip and Melville, Joy, *Lost Children of the Empire* (London: Unwin Hyman, 1989).

Beech, Jane, *The Way is Long* (London: Mills & Boon, 1950).

Behan, Brendan, *The Quare Fellow* (London: Eyre Methuen, 1974; first published in 1956).

Behan, Brendan, *Borstal Boy* (London: Arrow, 1990; first published in 1958).

Bell, Daniel, *The End of Ideology* (Illinois: The Free Press of Glencoe, 1960).

Bethune, Mary, *Doctor Dear* (London: Michael Joseph, 1954).

Black, Hermina, *The Girl from Van Leyden's* (London: Romance Book Club, 1959).

Blishen, Edward, *Roaring Boys* (London: Panther, 1966; first published in 1955).

Borstal. A Critical Survey (London: Howard League for Penal Reform, 1950).

Bowlby, John, *The Roots of Parenthood* (London: London National Children's Home, 1953).

Bowlby, John, *Child Care and the Growth of Love* (London: Penguin, 1983; first published in 1953).

Braine, John, *Room at the Top* (Harmondsworth: Penguin, 1969; first published in 1957).

Braine, John, *Life at the Top* (Harmondsworth: Penguin, 1966; first published in 1962).

Braybon, Gail and Penny Summerfield, *Out of the Cage. Women's Experiences in Two World Wars* (London: Pandora, 1987).

Bruce-Milne, Marjorie, ed., *The Book for the Home* (London: Caxton Publishing Company, 1956).

Burchell, Mary, *On the Air* (London: Mills & Boon, 1956).

Burgess, Anthony, *A Clockwork Orange* (Harmondsworth: Penguin, 1972; first published in 1962).

Careers. A Memorandum on Openings and Trainings for Girls and Women 18th edition (Women's Employment Federation, 1958).

'Careers for Girls in Engineering' (Women's Engineering Society Conference, Coventry, July 1957).

Cartland, Barbara, *The Dream Within* (London: Hutchinson, 1947).

Chandos, Fay, *Partners are a Problem* (London: Mills & Boon, 1957).

Chandos, Fay, *Model Girl's Farm* (London: Mills & Boon, 1958).

Charles, Moie, *Eve at the Driving Wheel* (London: Chatto and Windus, 1957).

Christie, Agatha, *Crooked House* (London: Collins, 1969; first published in 1949).

Christie, Agatha, *Mrs McGinty's Dead* (London: HarperCollins, 1993; first published in 1952).

Citizens of Tomorrow. A Study of the Influences Affecting the Upbringing of Young People (London: King George's Jubilee Trust, 1955).

Cochrane, Louise, *Marion Turns Teacher* (London: Chatto and Windus, 1955).

Cochrane, Louise, *Anne in Electronics* (London: Chatto and Windus, 1960).

Conway, Celine, *Rustle of Bamboo* (London: Mills & Boon, 1957).

Crosland, C. A. R., *The Future of Socialism* (London: Jonathan Cape, 1957; first published in 1956).

de Beauvoir, Simone, *The Second Sex* (Harmondsworth: Penguin, 1976; first published in French in 1949; first translated into English in 1953).

Delaney, Shelagh, *A Taste of Honey* (London: Methuen, 1987; first published in 1958).

Dickens, Monica, *My Turn to Make the Tea* (Harmondsworth: Penguin, 1972; first published in 1951).

Dickens, Monica, *The Angel in the Corner* (Harmondsworth: Penguin, 1966; first published in 1956).

Dingwall, Robert, Rafferty, Anne Marie and Webster, Charles, *British Nursing: An Introduction to the Social History of Nursing* (London: Routledge, 1988).

Drabble, Margaret, *The Millstone* (Harmondsworth: Penguin, 1971; first published in 1965).

Dyer, Richard, *Stars* (London: BFI Publications, 1979).

Eighty Thousand Adolescents. A Study of Young People in the City of Birmingham (Edward Cadbury Charitable Trust; London: George Allen and Unwin, 1950).

Elder, Josephine, *The Encircled Heart* (London: Lutterworth Press, 1951).

Eugenics Society, *Aims and Objects of the Eugenics Society* (1944).

Evans, Mary, *A Good School. Life in a Girls' Grammar School in the 1950s* (London: Women's Press, 1991).

Fabian Society, *Population and the People. A National Policy* (London: George Allen and Unwin, 1945).

Ferguson, Marjorie, *Forever Feminine. Women's Magazines and the Cult of Femininity* (London: Heinemann, 1983).

Ford, Boris, ed., *The Pelican Guide to Literature. The Modern Age* (Harmondsworth: Penguin, 1991; first published in 1961).

Fowler, Bridget, *The Alienated Reader. Women and Popular Romantic Fiction in the Twentieth Century* (Hemel Hempstead: Harvester Wheatsheaf, 1991).

Fox, Lionel W., *The English Prison and Borstal System* (International Library of Sociology and Social Reconstruction; London: Routledge and Kegan Paul, 1952).

Freeman, Barbara, *Open to View: English Country Houses You Can Visit and How to Find Them* (London: Ernest Benn Limited, 1952).

Friedan, Betty, *The Feminine Mystique* (Harmondsworth: Penguin, 1965; first published in 1963).

Further Education and Training Scheme Progress Reports: Women (London: Ministry of Labour and National Service, 1949–52).

Fyvel, T. R., *The Insecure Offenders. Rebellious Youth in the Welfare State* (Harmondsworth: Penguin, 1966; first published in 1961).

Galton, Lawrence, *New Facts for the Childless* (London: Victor Gollancz, 1954).

Gathorne-Hardy, Jonathan, *Doctors: An Open Look at Doctors' Lives* (London: Weidenfeld and Nicolson, 1984).

Gilzean, Elizabeth, *Next Patient, Doctor Anne* (London: Mills & Boon, 1958).

Glass, Ruth, *Newcomers. The West Indians in London* (London: George Allen and Unwin, 1960).

Golding, William, *The Lord of the Flies* (London: Faber and Faber, 1973; first published in 1954).

Goldman, Louis, *Angry Young Doctor* (London: Hamish Hamilton, 1957).

Gorer, Geoffrey, 'The Perils of Hypergamy', *New Statesman and Nation*, 4 May 1957; reprinted in Gene Feldman and Max Gartenberg, eds, *Protest* (London: Quartet, 1973; first published in 1959).

Gowers Report, 1950, quoted in Roy Strong, Marcus Binney and John Harris, eds, *The Destruction of the Country House* (London: Thames and Hudson, 1974)

Griffiths, Vera Wynn, 'Something to Talk About', first issue of *Woman's Realm*, 22 Feb 1958.

Grimstead, Hettie, *The Twisted Road* (London: Mills & Boon, 1951).

Grimstead, Hettie, *Dream Street* (London: Mills & Boon, 1959).

Hall, Stuart, *New Left Review*, Jan–Feb 1960.

Hall, Stuart and Jefferson, Tony, eds, *Resistance Through Ritual. Youth Subcultures in Postwar Britain* (London: Hutchinson, 1977; first published in 1975).

Hanley, James, *An End and a Beginning* (London: André Deutsch, 1990; first published in 1959).

Haslett, Caroline, *Problems Have No Sex* (London: Hodder and Stoughton, 1949).

Hebdidge, Dick, *Subculture. The Meaning of Style* (London and New York: Methuen, 1979).

Hemmings, James, *Problems of Adolescent Girls* (London: Heinemann, 1960).

Hennessy, Peter, *Never Again. Britain 1945–1951* (London: Vintage, 1993; first published in 1992).

Henry, Joan, *Who Lie In Gaol* (London: Four Square Books, 1958; first published in 1952).

Heron, Liz, ed., *Truth, Dare or Promise. Girls Growing Up in the Fifties* (London: Virago, 1985).

Hewison, Robert, *In Anger. Culture in the Cold War 1945–1960* (London: Methuen, 1988; first published in 1981).

Hobsbawm, Eric, *Age of Extremes – The Short Twentieth Century 1914–1991* (London: Michael Joseph, 1991).

Hodgson, Pat, *Britain in the 1950s* (London: Batsford, 1989).

Hoggart, Richard, *The Uses of Literacy* (Harmondsworth: Penguin, 1958; first published in 1957).

Hood, Roger, *Borstal Re-assessed* (London: Heinemann, 1965).

Hopkins, Harry, *The New Look. A Social History of the Forties and Fifties in Britain* (London: Secker and Warburg, 1963).

Howard, Anthony, 'We are the Masters Now' in Michael Sissons and Peter French, eds, *Age of Austerity 1945–51* (Harmondsworth: Penguin, 1964; first published in 1963).

Hubback, Eva M., *The Population of Britain* (West Drayton, Middlesex: Penguin, 1947).

Hubback, Judith, *Wives Who Went to College* (London: Heinemann, 1957).

Huxley, Aldous, *Brave New World Revisited* (London: Triad Panther, 1983; first published in 1959).

Huxley, Aldous, *Island* (Harmondsworth: Penguin, 1970; first published in 1962).

Ingham, Mary, *Now We Are Thirty. Women of the Breakthrough Generation* (London: Methuen, 1981).

I Want To Be . . . A Girl Book of Careers (London: Hulton Press, 1957).

Jephcott, Pearl, *Some Young People* (King George's Jubilee Trust; London: George Allen and Unwin, 1954).

Jordan, G. W. and Fischer, E. M., *Self-Portrait of Youth, or the Urban Adolescent* (London: Heinemann, 1955).

Karpf, Anne, *Doctoring the Media: The Reporting of Health and Medicine* (London: Routledge, 1988).

Klein, Viola, *The Feminine Character. History of an Ideology* (London: Routledge and Kegan Paul, 1989; first published in 1946).

Klein, Viola, *Working Wives* (London: Institute of Personnel Management, 1960).

Lancaster, Osbert, *Here of All Places. The Pocket Lamp of Architecture* (London: John Murray, 1959).

Lees, Marguerite, *Secret Star* (London: Mills & Boon, 1956).

Lees, Marguerite, *District Nurse* (London: Mills & Boon, 1957).

Lessing, Doris, 'The Small Personal Voice' in Tom Maschler, ed., *Declaration* (London: MacGibbon and Kee, 1957).

Lessing, Doris, *In Pursuit of the English* (London: Grafton, 1989; first published in 1960).

Lessing, Doris, *The Golden Notebook* (London: Granada, 1972; first published in 1962).

Let Us Face the Future (Labour Party election manifesto, 1945).

Lewis, Jane, 'Myrdal, Klein, *Women's Two Roles* and postwar feminism 1945–1960' in Harold S. Smith, ed., *British Feminism in the Twentieth Century* (Aldershot: Edward Elgar, 1990).

Lewis, Peter, *The Fifties* (London: Cupid Press, 1989; first published in 1978).

Lewis, Roy and Maude, Angus, *The English Middle Classes* (Harmondsworth: Penguin, 1953; first published in 1949).

Light, Alison, 'Writing fictions: femininity and the 1950s' in Jean Radford, ed., *The Progress of Romance* (London: Routledge, 1986).

Light, Alison, *Forever England. Femininity, Literature, and Conservatism Between the Wars* (London: Routledge, 1991).

Light, Alison, *Twentieth Century Romance and Historical Writers* (London: St. James Press, 1994).

Little, K. L., *Negroes in Britain. A Study of Racial Relations in English Society* (International Library of Sociology and Social Reconstruction; London: Routledge and Kegan Paul, 1947).

Lorraine, Anne, *Hotel Nurse* (London: Mills & Boon, 1954).

Lorraine, Anne, *Emergency Nurse* (London: Mills & Boon, 1955).

Lorraine, Anne, *White-coated Girl* (London: Mills & Boon, 1955).

Lorraine, Anne, *Hospital on Wheels* (London: Mills & Boon, 1956).

Lorraine, Anne, *My Dear Doctor* (London: Mills & Boon, 1957).

Lorraine, Anne, *First the Doctor* (London: Mills & Boon, 1958).

Lorraine, Anne, *Send for Doctor* (London: Mills & Boon, 1958).

McAleer, Joseph, *Popular Reading and Publishing in Britain 1914–1950* (Oxford: Clarendon Press, 1992).

McBryde, Brenda, *Quiet Heroines: Nurses of the Second World War* (London: Chatto & Windus, 1985).

MacInnes, Colin, *England, Half-English* (London: Hogarth, 1986; first published in 1961).

Macleod, Jean S., *Dear Doctor Everett* (London: Mills & Boon, 1954).

McRobbie, Angela and Garber, Jenny, 'Girls and Subcultures: An Exploration' in Stuart Hall and Tony Jefferson, eds, *Resistance through Ritual* (1977).

Making Citizens. A Review of the Aims, Methods and Achievements of the Approved Schools in England and Wales (London: HMSO, 1945).

Malcolm, Margaret, *Forgive My Foolish Pride* (London: Mills & Boon, 1957).

Mannheim, Hermann, *Juvenile Delinquency in an English Middletown* (London: Kegan Paul, Trench, Trubner and Co. Ltd., 1948).

Manning, Olivia, *The Doves of Venus* (London: Virago, 1984; first published in 1955).

Martin, Nancy, *Jean Behind the Counter* (London: Macmillan, 1960).

Marwick, Arthur, *British Society Since 1945* (Harmondsworth: Penguin, 1982.

Mass Observation, *Britain and Her Birthrate* (London: John Murray, 1945).

Matthewman, Phyllis, *Luck for Lindy* (London: Mills & Boon, 1954).

Matthewman, Phyllis, *Romance Goes Tenting* (London: Mills & Boon, 1957).

Matthewman, Phyllis, *Food of Love* (London, Mills & Boon, 1959).

May, Vera, *A Path There Is* (London: Mills & Boon, 1956).

Mazumdar, Pauline M. H., *Eugenics, Human Genetics and Human Failings. The Eugenics Society, its Sources and its Critics in Britain* (London: Routledge, 1992).

Melosh, Barbara, 'Doctors, Patients and "Big Nurse": Work and Gender in the Post War Hospital' in *Nursing History: New Perspectives, New Possibilities*, ed. Ellen Condliffe Lagemann (New York: Teachers' College Press, Columbia University, 1983).

Mercer, David, *Where the Difference Begins* in *Plays: One* (London: Methuen, 1990; first broadcast 15 December 1961; first published 1961).

Millett, Kate, *Sexual Politics* (London: Virago, 1983; first published in 1971).

Ministry of Labour and National Service, Further Education and Training Scheme, Joint Committee of Award Making Departments. Progress Reports: 1949–1952.

Mitchell, Juliet, ed., *The Selected Melanie Klein* (Harmondsworth: Penguin, 1986).

Modleski, Tania, *Loving with a Vengeance: Mass-produced Fantasies for Women* (London: Methuen, 1984).

Moore, Marjorie, *A Year to Remember* (London: Mills & Boon, 1956).

Moore-Gilbert, Bart, 'The return of the repressed: Gothic and the 1960s novel' in Bart Moore-Gilbert and John Seed, eds, *Cultural Revolution? The Challenge of the Arts in the 1960s* (London: Routledge, 1992).

Morgan, Kenneth O., *The People's Peace. British History 1945–1990* (Milton Keynes: Open University Press, 1992).

Murdoch, Iris, *The Flight from the Enchanter* (St. Albans: Panther, 1976; first published in 1955).

Murdoch, Iris, *The Bell* (Harmondsworth: Penguin, 1985; first published in 1958).

Muskett, Netta, *Give Back Yesterday* (London: Arrow Books, 1976; first published in 1955).

Myrdal, Alva and Klein, Viola, *Women's Two Roles. Home and Work* (London: Routledge and Kegan Paul, 1956).

Neal, Hilary, *Factory Nurse* (London: Mills & Boon, 1961).

Nelson, Valerie K., *The Flower Box* (London: Mills & Boon, 1955).

Nelson, Valerie K., *The Starched Cap* (London: Mills & Boon, 1957).

Norton, Bess, *The Quiet One* (London: Mills & Boon, 1959).

Norton, Bess, *The Summer Break* (London: Mills & Boon, 1960).

Orwell, George, 'The Lion and the Unicorn' (1941) in Sonia Orwell and Ian Angus, eds, *The Collected Essays, Journalism and Letters of George Orwell*, 4 vols (Harmondsworth: Penguin, 1970, vol. 2; first published in 1968).

Osborne, John, *Look Back in Anger* (London: Faber and Faber, 1976; first performed in 1956; first published in 1957).

Owens, Jean Llewellyn, *A Library Life for Deborah* (London: Chatto and Windus, 1957).

Owens, Jean Llewellyn, *Margaret Becomes a Doctor* (London: Bodley Head, 1957).

Owens, Jean Llewellyn, *Sue Takes Up Physiotherapy* (London: Bodley Head, 1958).

Philips, Deborah, 'Mills and Boon. The Marketing of Moonshine' in Alan Tomlinson, ed., *Consumption, Identity and Style. Marketing, Meanings, and the Packaging of Pleasure* (London: Routledge, 1990).

Philips, Deborah and Tomlinson, Alan, 'Homeward Bound: Leisure, popular culture and consumer capitalism' in Dominic Strinati and Stephen Wagg, eds, *Come on Down? Popular Media Culture in Post-war Britain* (London: Routledge, 1992).

Prisons and Borstals. Statement of the Policy and Practice in the Administration of Prison and Borstal Institutions in England and Wales (London: HMSO, 1950).

Prisons and Borstals. Statement of the Policy and Practice in the Administration of Prison and Borstal Institutions in England and Wales (London: HMSO, 1960).

Pugh, Martin, 'Domesticity and the decline of feminism, 1930–1950' in Harold S. Smith, ed., *British Feminism in the Twentieth Century* (Aldershot: Edward Elgar, 1990).

Pugh, Martin, *The Women's Movement in Britain 1914–1959* (Basingstoke: Macmillan Education, 1992).

Pym, Barbara, *Jane and Prudence* (London: Jonathan Cape, 1953).

Radway, Janice, *Reading the Romance* (Chapel Hill: University of North Carolina Press, 1984).

Raybould, S. E., 'University Extra-Mural Education in Great Britain' in *Universities in Adult Education. Problems in Education*, vol. IV (Paris: Unesco, 1952).

Rees, Rosemary and Maguire, Judith, *Living in the 1950s* (London: Heinemann, 1993).

Report of the Royal Commission on Marriage and Divorce (London: HMSO, 1956).

Report of the Royal Commission on Population (London: HMSO, 1949).

Richmond, Anthony H., *Colour Prejudice in Britain. A Study of West Indian Workers in Liverpool, 1941–1951* (International Library of Sociology and Social Reconstruction; London: Routledge and Kegan Paul, 1954).

Richmond, Anthony H., *The Colour Problem. A Study of Racial Relations* (Harmondsworth: Penguin, 1955).

Riley, Denise, *War in the Nursery. Theories of the Child and Mother* (London: Virago, 1983).

Ritchie, Harry, *Success Stories. Literature and the Media in England, 1950–1959* (London: Faber and Faber, 1988).

Robins, Denise, *Something to Love* (London: Hutchinson, 1951).

Robins, Denise, *The Unshaken Loyalty* (London: Arrow Books, 1955).

Rowbotham, Sheila, *Hidden from History* (London: Pluto Press, 1973).

Segal, Lynne, *Slow Motion. Changing Masculinities, Changing Men* (London: Virago, 1990).

Sinfield, Alan, ed., *Society and Literature, 1945–1960* (London: Methuen, 1983).

Sinfield, Alan, *Literature, Politics and Culture in Postwar Britain* (Oxford: Basil Blackwell, 1989).

Snow, C. P., *The New Men* (Harmondsworth: Penguin, 1959; first published in 1954).

Spock, Benjamin, *Baby and Childcare* (London: Bodley Head, 1955).

Stott, D. H., *Delinquency and Human Nature* (Dunfermline, Fife: Carnegie United Kingdom Trust, 1950).

Streatfeild, Noel, *The Years of Grace* (London: Evans Brothers, 1950).

Streatfeild, Noel, *White Boots* (London: Collins, 1951).

Streatfeild, Noel, *Growing Up Gracefully* (London: Arthur Barker, 1955).

Stuart, Alex, *Bachelor of Medicine* (London: Mills & Boon, 1956).

Stuart, Alex, *Master of Surgery* (London: Mills & Boon, 1958).

Tait, Marjorie, 'The Education of Women for Citizenship: some practical suggestions' *Problems in Education*, vol. VIII (Paris: Unesco, 1954).

Tempest, Jan, *House of the Pines* (London: Mills & Boon, 1946).

Tempest, Jan, *Enchanted Valley* (London: Mills & Boon, 1954).

Tey, Josephine, *The Franchise Affair* (Harmondsworth: Penguin, 1951; first published in 1948).

Thane, Pat, 'Towards Equal Opportunities? Women in Britain since 1945' in Tony Gourvish and Alan O'Day, eds, *Britain Since 1945* (London: Macmillan, 1991).

The Woman Engineer, 6(6), spring 1946; 6(9), summer 1947.

Titmuss, Richard, *Essays on the 'Welfare State'* (London: George Allen and Unwin, 1958).

Tranch, Caroline, *Nurse to the Island* (London: Mills & Boon, 1957).

Treacher, Amal, 'What is Life Without My Love: Desire and Romantic Fiction' in Susannah Radstone, ed., *Sweet Dreams. Sexuality, Gender and Popular Fiction* (London: Lawrence and Wishart, 1988).

Trevelyan, G. M., Introduction to *The National Trust: A Record of Fifty Years Achievement*, ed. James Lees-Milne (London: Batsford, 1943).

Vinton, Anne, *Nurse Wayne in the Tropics* (London: Mills & Boon, 1956).

Wandor, Michelene, *Look Back in Gender* (London: Methuen, 1987).

Watkin, Brian, *The National Health Service: The First Phase – 1948–1974 and After* (London: George Allen and Unwin, 1978).

Waugh, Evelyn, *Brideshead Revisited* (London: Penguin, 1988; first published in 1945).

Wauters, Arthur, *British Social Services – Today and Tomorrow* (no date; British Library Catalogue 1946).

Wauters, Arthur, *Eve in Overalls* (no date; reprinted by the Imperial War Museum, London, 1995).

White, Cynthia, *Women's Magazines 1693–1968* (London: Michael Joseph, 1970).

White, Rosemary, *The Effects of the National Health Service on the Nursing Profession 1948–1961* (London: King Edward's Hospital Fund for London, 1985; distributed for the King's Fund by Oxford University Press).

Wilson, Angus, *Such Darling Dodos* (London: Granada Publishing, 1980; first published in 1950).

Wilson, Angus, *A Bit Off the Map* (Harmondsworth: Penguin, 1968; first published in 1957).

Wilson, Elizabeth, *Only Halfway to Paradise. Women in Postwar Britain 1945–1968* (London: Tavistock Publications, 1980).

Winnicott, D. W., *The Child and the Family. First Relationships* (London: Tavistock Publications, 1957).

Winship, Janice, 'Nation before Family: Woman, the National Home Weekly, 1945–53' in *Formations of Nation and People* (London: Routledge, 1984).

Wollstonecraft, Mary, *A Vindication of the Rights of Women* (Harmondsworth: Penguin, 1975; first published in 1792).

Women in Medicine: the Results of an Inquiry Conducted by the Medical Practioners' Union in 1962–63 (London: Office of Health Economics, 1966).

Worpole, Ken, *Reading by Numbers. Contemporary Publishing and Popular Fiction* (London: Commedia, 1984).

Wyndham, John, *The Chrysalids* (Harmondsworth: Penguin, 1985; first published in 1955).

Wyndham, John, *The Midwich Cuckoos* (Harmondsworth: Penguin, 1973; first published in 1957).

Young, Michael, *The Rise of the Meritocracy* (Harmondsworth: Penguin, 1967; first published in 1958).

Zweig, Ferdinand, *Women's Life and Labour* (London: Gollancz, 1952).

Index

166   *Index*